The Gordon Lindsay Story

by Gordon Lindsay

Published by The Voice of Healing Publishing Co.
Dallas, Texas
U. S. A.

TABLE OF CONTENTS

The
Gordon Lindsay Story

Gordon Lindsay

Gordon Lindsay at the age of three with his sister, Gladys.

Mr. and Mrs. Thomas A. Lindsay, parents of Gordon Lindsay.

High school graduating class. Gordon Lindsay is seated at extreme left.

Family photo taken shortly after Gordon Lindsay's graduation from high school. Standing from left: Gordon, Charles, Fern, Gladys. Seated: Helen, Mother, Ruth, Father.

Wedding picture of Gordon Lindsay and wife, Freda, who were married in the Foursquare Church, Portland, Oregon, by Dr. Harold Jefferies, pastor.

Upper: Gordon Lindsay family group — 1950

Lower: Gordon Lindsay family group — 1964

Upper: Photograph of Lindsay family group — 1943. Standing from left: Gladys, Charles, Fern, Gordon, Helen. Seated: Thomas A. (father), Ruth, Effie (mother).

Lower: The Voice of Healing was host to the Full Gospel ministers of the Dallas area in their monthly meeting.

Upper: The Voice of Healing Offices. Center: The Printing Shop.
Lower: The Native Church Crusade Building.

Above: Dr. Walter Parr, Director, standing at pier with World Friendship, loaded with over a million dollars worth of supplies for Korea. Gordon Lindsay served as president of World Friendship for several years.

Right: Gordon Lindsay and Sam Todd conferring with Prime Minister Majoli of Jordan in interests of World Friendship. Prime Minister and ten others were assassinated a few days later in this same office.

Some 300 churches completed during a period of about ten months. In all, over 900 churches have been sponsored and about 600 completed at the time this book went to press.

Upper: Branham Campaign banquet for ministers in Minneapolis, Minnesota, in 1950.

Lower: Voice of Healing banquet at Fair Park, Dallas, in 1955.

The campaign author directed for William Branham in Kansas City, Kansas, in '1948.

The Voice of Healing Convention in Tulsa, Oklahoma, in 1951.

Above: Oral Roberts attended Branham campaign in Kansas City in 1948. The above is a rare photograph showing, from left to right, Young Brown, Jack Moore, William Branham, Oral Roberts and Gordon Lindsay.

Below: Jack Coe hears the acquittal of the charge of "practicing medicine without a license." Gordon Lindsay was a key witness in the trial.

During the 1949 and 1950 campaigns in America, people gave generously to support the first Branham overseas crusades. Upper: The Helsinki, Finland campaign. Lower: The Branham campaign at Durban, South Africa. Both saw a great harvest of souls.

An early campaign with William Branham in Tacoma, Washington, in April, 1948.

Some of the literature sent abroad in the Winning the Nations Literature Crusade.

Lower left: Chapel built by Voice of Healing (lower story) on Mount of Olives in the Holy Land Crusade. Lower right: Mayor of Jerusalem, Gordon Lindsay and S. J. Mattar, warden of Garden Tomb. Mayor attended dedication services.

The San Salvador Center, seating over 1,500, one of about a dozen large evangelistic centers which the Winning the Nations Crusade helped build in the wake of great revivals.

Baptismal service in Manila Bay, Philippines, as a result of joint campaigns with Morris Cerullo, Lester Sumrall, W. V. Grant and Gordon Lindsay in 1959.

FOREWORD

Many persons have, over the years, suggested that I write the story of my experiences. Once or twice I have thought to do this, but upon second thought decided against it. My work has involved that of many persons. It is common knowledge that different individuals recall the details of an event differently. Of course, I must record things as I remember them. However, I do have this advantage. Much of what goes into this story was written down at the time. I have all the records available that have been published month by month in the Voice of Healing, and in other writings.

In recording this story, I have several things in mind. First and foremost, I hope that it will be the means of leading souls to accept Christ as their personal Saviour. And further, that it will encourage them to believe that their God is a God that answers prayer. That they can safely put their lives in the hand of the Great Pilot and that He will see them through.

I have, therefore, tried to prepare this narrative in the way that will make for popular reading. A few chapters have been allotted to the early period of my life. Here I have shown that I lived the normal life of the average boy. But as I grew to manhood, the hour came to me as it comes to all, to make a decision for Christ. As the Scripture declares, Christ is "the true Light, which lighteth every man that cometh into the world." (Jn. 1:9) I relate how that after great strugglings of soul, I finally accepted that light.

In preparing this volume, I have had especially in mind the youth, who hopefully enters the ministry, but finds that everything seems to be against him. The early years of my ministry were during the Great Depression. Preachers in those days often received offerings of only a few dollars for a whole week's services. But because of the flame burning within them, they continued to preach, with or without visible means of support, and God somehow took them through.

I record at some length events of my early ministry, since I believe that those experiences will lend encouragement to other young preachers who are struggling to get a start, and show them that if they remain faithful to God, He will in time bring them into broader fields, and eventually give them a sense of real fulfillment. I verily believe that God has a blueprint for every life, and that if the individual will not become discouraged, but will continue to be faithful and to make prayer a business in his life, he will find that in the end, he will have experienced a rich and satisfying life. His testimony will be that Christ never failed him.

I include in this volume of experiences, God's special words to us in our early ministry regarding the outpouring of the Spirit — things that we were to see fulfilled in our lifetime, and in which we would participate, if we were faithful. It was wonderful to me after many years of toil, to see many of those things come to pass. I record them, however, not for the purpose of dwelling in the past, but that their fulfillment may be considered as an earnest of a still greater manifestation of God's power in the future. Verily, Bible days are on earth again!

In conclusion, I would point out that we are living in the hour of the Church's greatest opportunity. There is an interlude at the present time in which the Church may rise to the great challenge and complete the evangelization of the world. This will require an effort of such intensity as never before contemplated by the Church, but it must be undertaken. Christ said, "And this gospel of the kingdom shall be preached in all the world for a witness to all nations: and then shall the end come." (Matt. 24:14) Two things are required principally. God must raise up men of faith who have the gospel message burning in their souls, and who are willing to carry it to the ends of the earth. Then as the new congregations spring up as the result of these labors, we must help to build shelters and churches for these new converts, so that they may have permanent places of worship.

Finally, we must bury our differences and put forth a supreme effort to seek the unification of all of God's people — not by bringing them all under the same roof, but into a unity of spirit, a oneness of heart, and a singleness of purpose. We believe that this will result in a tremendous stimulus to evangelism, and cause multitudes to believe that God has sent Christ into the world to be their Saviour. This Jesus showed would happen, in the prayer He prayed the Father in Jn. 17:21:

> "That they all may be one; as thou, Father, art in me, and I in thee that they also may be one in us: that the world may believe that thou hast sent me."

May God grant that this may soon come to pass.

CHAPTER I

The Drowning Boy

A little lad of 12 years kissed his mother and after saying good-bye to her descended the steps. He was on his way to a birthday outing.given in honor of one of his classmates from the Beaverton Grade School. The party was actually a picnic which took him and his friends to a small artificial pond that had been made by damming up a country stream just a few miles out of town.

It appeared that there was going to be plenty of fun that day. Large quantities of food had been brought along. Ample supplies of chicken, sandwiches, jams and jellies, with soda pop and ice cream had been included. It looked to the little boy as if he were going to have a very good time.

Of course the main attraction was the swimming. Little time was lost, therefore, before all the young people including the little boy, had changed their clothes and donned swimming suits. By the time he was ready, some of the members of the party were already in the water, swimming lustily around the pond.

The boy remained on the bank for a while. There was a reason for his caution. The water was deep — probably ten or twelve feet. He had told the others that he could swim, although actually he hardly knew whether he could or not. He had learned to paddle "dog fashion" in a shallow creek the previous year, but he had never been in water this deep before. What little he had learned, however, he had pretty well forgotten. But since he had boasted that he could swim, he must now prove it. Foolishly, he chose the moment when the lady who was chaperone of the party was absent, to dive into the water. She was an excellent swimmer and would have known what to do if any member of the party got into trouble.

The boy managed to get out into the middle of the pond, and found he was able by the most vigorous exertions, to remain

afloat, until suddenly he had the mishap to draw a large draught
of water into his lungs. This upset his rather precarious move-
ments, and alarmed, he began to thresh the water in a desperate
attempt to reach the other shore. He now made no progress whatever, and rapidly exhausting himself, went down, taking another
mouthful of water at the same time. Now he was in a real panic.
Somehow, he was able to rise again to the surface, but choking,
went down once more gasping, and drawing still more water into
his lungs.

The youngsters on the shore were at first fascinated, then realizing that their companion was drowning, became terror-stricken.
No adult was near to lend a hand, as they stood on the shore,
paralyzed with fright, and not knowing what to do. Finally, one
of the boys, who could swim some, plunged into the water in an attempt to rescue the struggling lad. But a drowning person does
only one thing, and that is to grab anything he can get his hands
on. Reason is gone and with lungs choking with water, the boy
blindly clutched for the proverbial straw. His arms encircled the
rescuer with a death grip, and down both went.

Fortunately for the latter, the boy had reached the end of his
exertions, and his grip relaxed so that his would-be rescuer was
able to reach safety, and quite cured from further attempts to
help. The drowning lad can still remember vividly the horror of
the realization that he was drowning. With his strength gone and
lungs already full of water, death was closing in. There was no
time to review the events of his brief life, as some say occurs, at
the time one dies. He only knew that death was upon him, and
was overwhelmed by it as he sank into dark unconsciousness. It
was exactly the same experience any drowning person must go
through, and it was not a pleasant one. The lad was not yet a
Christian, though indeed he was old enough to know he was a
sinner, for that boy was I. I experienced a sinner's death. But why
did I not drown, after all?

Back at our humble home was a mother who prayed for her
children. She was a woman who had faith in God. Many were
the nights that I heard her, as she kneeled before her bed, praying earnestly to God for her children, that He would protect them
from harm, and keep them from the consequences of the evil that
surrounded them. I suppose I was not considered a bad boy;
yet, Jeremiah's description of the human heart nevertheless applied to me. "The heart is deceitful above all things, and desper-

ately wicked: who can know it?" (Jer. 17:9) The course of any life without God is toward evil. Mother's earnest prayers, I believe, placed a wall of protection around me. Jesus taught His people to pray, "Lead us not into temptation, but deliver us from evil," before the evil comes.

What happened at the pond? The frightened youngsters watched the tragedy unfold before their eyes. Some screamed for help. But there were no more rescuers nearby, and the one who had made the attempt was hard-put to recover himself from the results of his well-meant but ill-fated efforts to help. The cries of the children at last brought the lady chaperone to the stream. But as far as she was concerned, it was too late. Minutes had now passed, and by all considerations I should have been motionless, down at the bottom of the pond.

But something happened that I have never yet been able to explain. I remember descending into a great darkness. But suddenly the descent was halted. And then as if awakening from a bad dream, I found myself climbing out of the pond on the other side! It was as if some mysterious arm had reached down and lifted me to safety! Nobody could explain it. Nobody was ever able to explain what happened.

Back at home that evening, I gave a report of the activities of the day. I purposely neglected to report the near tragedy that I had experienced. Indeed, it seemed very unflattering to me to have proved such a poor swimmer as to have almost drowned. Moreover, had I explained what happened, it might well have resulted in the curbing of my freedom to go swimming in the future. Mother never knew. But she did not have to know. She realized that her children lived in a world of danger. The best thing she could do was to put them in the hands of God and trust Him to keep them from evil.

Although I was only twelve, I realized that I had not accepted Christ as my Saviour. A thought could not help but come to my mind: what would have happened to me if I had not been mysteriously saved from the watery depths? Death was a grim reality, for I saw it happen to me. The thought made me tremble, but I put it from me. But before going further in my story, let me take the reader back to some of the earlier events in my life.

CHAPTER II
The City of Zion

North of Chicago, at a distance of about forty miles, lies the
city of Zion, having been founded at the turn of the century by
John Alexander Dowie. The ministry of Dowie had struck the
world at the time, like a thunderbolt out of the blue. This strange
figure suddenly appeared in Chicago, denouncing the apostasy of
his day, and tearing the mask off of sin in high places and low.

John Alexander Dowie's career, however, was mainly distinguished by the fact that he as no other man, was responsible
for the return of apostolic ministry to the Church. Miracles took
place in his ministry in such numbers as had not occurred since
the days of the apostles. Noted for his uncompromising preaching
as well as his practice of praying for the sick, he succeeded in so
antagonizing the authorities of the city of Chicago, that in one
year's time they had him arrested no less than 100 times! But
they reckoned, not on the mettle of the man they opposed. For
soon the tide turned and to their great dismay, the whole ad-
ministration, within a year, found itself out of office. A newspaper man who had been particularly bitter in his attacks upon
Dowie, went to prison for two years.

It could be truthfully said that John Alexander Dowie feared
no man. He once challenged the notorious infidel, Robert G.
Ingersol to a debate on religion. That silver-tongue agnostic, upon
learning of the number of miraculous testimonies Dowie planned
to present as evidence of the supernatural, saved his skin by
making a quiet exit out of the city.

Dr. Dowie had literally thousands of documented testimonies
of miracles which included the healing of cripples, the restoration
of sight to the blind, the deliverance of drug addicts, and full recovery from organic diseases of every kind. In a few short years,
he gathered a following of 50,000 people in Chicago alone. All

went well until Dowie conceived the idea of building a dream city on Lake Michigan. The innumerable difficulties and problems involved in building such a city, absorbed so much of his time and strength that eventually his judgment was impaired. Finally, he suffered a stroke and with it complete physical incapacitation. As a result, Zion City went into bankruptcy, causing many families who had invested their life savings there, to suffer severe losses.

Such happened to my own parents who had made their home there. Notwithstanding their financial loss, they never regretted going to Zion, since the faith they gained under Dowie's ministry, more than compensated for all they had lost.

It was while Dowie was still alive that I was born. I saw him once, but of course can remember nothing of the event. The nurse who attended my birth was Mrs. Jeanie Paddock, who herself had been healed of a malignant tumor when she was at the point of death. It was this particular miracle that had caused Dowie to decide to make Chicago his headquarters. The events of Zion were of course before my day. My parents left the city shortly after it went into bankruptcy, and I was too young to remember anything that happened there. But they knew that God was a God of miracles for they had seen them take place!

I will, none-the-less, narrate one event which could have ended my life when it scarcely had begun, the details for which I am indebted to my parents. Electrical storms are not uncommon in the East during the summer. It was only a few weeks after I was born, that a stroke of lightning struck our house. My crib was resting inches from the wall when the bolt hit. Observers saw a ball of fire strike the house in the very area where I was sleeping. Since lightning has the tendency to dissipate its energy in the ground, rather than travel laterally across the interior of a building, I survived unscathed. The side of the house, notwithstanding, was severely damaged. Mother, in a panic of fear came rushing to the room to discover to her infinite relief, that all was well with her child.

Thomas A. Lindsay, my father, had been trained in the teaching profession and decided to go West to the state of Idaho. Having put in his application late in the season, the only openings still available were the least desirable places, all of which were located in the more remote regions. He accepted a teaching appointment in a rural settlement near Council, called Dale. The conditions existing in this sparsely settled community were exceedingly primitive and such as would certainly appall a modern housewife. But mother, who in her youth had enjoyed the advantages of a moderately well-to-do family, adjusted herself to the situation as best she could. It was in this remote area located not far from the Snake River Canyon that I have my first memories. And there my brother Charles was born.

It is always interesting to note the first impressions in life that a person remembers. My first recollection was of an incident in which I got into mischief. There was a small irrigation system in use in the neighborhood. One day, as I was wandering about, I came to a small sluice-gate that held back the water. My curiosity aroused, I found upon experimentation, that by lifting the gate, I could send the water on its way down the ditches where, incidentally, water was not needed. I remember later in the day, that I was sternly warned by the neighbor of the awful things that might happen to me if I repeated the act.

Across the roadway was a little schoolhouse where my father taught. Being conveniently close, mother was able to secure help from two of the larger students, when I got stuck in a snow bank, and was unable to retrieve myself, much to my distress.

After spending two years teaching in Idaho, my father decided to move to Portland, Oregon, where my mother's relatives, the Munns, lived. Annie Munn was an aunt who raised mother after her own mother had died. From thence my father became principal of a school in a small town called Scotts Mills. By now I was six years of age. Many incidents that occurred there I recall clearly, but they would have little interest to the reader.

I remember that once I had on my best clothes, while waiting for my father to take me on a trip, to which I had looked forward with no little anticipation. Unfortunately on my way to the grocery store on a small errand, I slipped and fell into a mudhole, recently replenished by a copious shower. I shrewdly guessed that my carelessness might jeopardize my chances of going on the trip. It occurred to me that my only recourse was to pin the blame on someone else. I thereupon explained that a larger boy had pushed me into the mud. But I was a very inexperienced liar. My parents apparently saw through my deception, for before long they confronted me with the lad whom I had blamed for the deed, and with shame my falsehood was exposed. There was no trip for me that day.

One evening while in Scotts Mills, we heard a cry that rent the night air. Distinctly came the words, "Fire! Fire!" Rushing outside, we saw a neighbor's house ablaze. The instant I saw the flames, I wanted to go at once to the scene. Alas, somebody must take care of the baby. The adults all must go as they might be able to help; on the other hand, my brother and sister were too young to guard the baby. I, it seemed, was the only one who was the right age for that task. Reluctantly, I stayed on the porch and watched the fascinating scene from a distance, with the feeling that I was missing something I would regret all my life. All I got to see were the ashes in the morning. My parents did not miss the opportunity to warn us children never to play with matches, although I am not sure what it was that caused that particular fire.

While in Scotts Mills, I first learned the meaning of death, and its irreversibility. One at a time, all of us children got the whooping cough. Finally, my little baby brother, Harold, caught it. Mother took him at once to Portland where my grandmother could assist her in caring for the child. We received word from day to day that his condition was serious and not improving. Yet we were hardly prepared for the long distance call we received — something quite unusual in those days. My father went to receive the call at a neighbor's phone. When he came back, his head was bowed in grief. "We've lost your little brother," was all he said. It seemed impossible that this could be true, but we knew that it was.

From Scotts Mills we moved to Hubbard where father became principal of both the grade and high schools. He purchased a farm about a mile out in the country, and in the summer we built a house and otherwise developed the farm. Father liked the farm, and I did too — all except the work. But since everybody worked in those days, children and all, I took it as a matter of course. While everyone should be against the sweatshop of yesteryear, where children worked hard and long for a pittance, I believe that the child labor laws as they now exist, often do more harm than good. There is nothing like a certain amount of good, honest toil to discipline a child. I do not mean long hours of it, but enough to take up his idle time. The big cities, where thousands of boys and girls are idle and bored, with nothing to do, have become spawning places for juvenile delinquency.

CHAPTER III
The Horse Traders

We needed a horse on the farm at Hubbard, and father set out to get one. He was no match, however, for the horse traders whom, he found, were well schooled in all the tricks of their trade. Father was by no means naive, but he was unprepared to believe that a man would deliberately misrepresent an animal to him.

So when he explained he wanted a good horse, one that would be gentle with the family, the trader smoothly confided that he had exactly the one that he wanted. I was not present during the bargaining, but can easily imagine the sales pitch that was employed. The man told the truth, but not *all* the truth. The trader had a mare for sale and no more gentle mare was ever known. He guaranteed the horse as absolutely safe with the youngest member of the family. The trader was careful, nonetheless, to omit any reference to the extreme age of the animal — a circumstance that we were to become aware of before many weeks had passed.

The horse proved indeed to be all that the trader claimed for it, as far as gentleness was concerned. And father was congratulating himself upon securing so reliable an animal. But one evening about dusk, as we were nearing home, we noted that the horse was plodding along uncommonly slow. Father tried to hurry up the mare, but failed to get any response from the reins. Deliberately, she wandered to the side of the road, pulling the wagon and its load after her. Having done this, the old mare stood trembling for a moment, and then collapsed in a heap. There were a few fearful gasps and then all was still. The faithful horse somehow realized she was going to die, and made her last contribution to her master by removing herself and the wagon from the roadway so as not to obstruct traffic.

The death of the horse was a serious blow to our household. First of all, father had to pay two dollars to an Indian to perform the no small task of burying the demised animal. Then, because he had to have another horse at once, father was forced to draw on his scanty resources to secure one to take her place. Distrusting the former trader, he went to another dealer. This time he emphasized that he must have a *young* horse. The new trader, like the last one, of course had just what father wanted. Moreover, he took pains to explain to him how to tell a horse's age. He pointed out with pride, that this horse was in the very prime of life, full of energy and vitality.

The trader neglected to add that the horse, though of the age represented, had never been properly broken and would, after performing for a few days, suddenly and unpredictably start out at a pace that would endanger not only the vehicle but the life and limb of the passengers. It was not very long before our family became aware of this unpleasant fact, and experienced several narrow escapes from having the buggy turned over.

The climax came one day as father and I were on the way to the farm. The horse showed no signs that it was about to have one of its fits, for it had been uncommonly docile during the previous few days. As we came to the farm, father got out to open the gate, leaving the reins in my hands. I gave the horse a slight tap on its flank for it to go on and then, suddenly, like a shot out of a gun, it started up and pulled the wagon at racehorse speed after it. I pulled on the lines and shouted for the run-away to stop, but all in vain. My cries only succeeded in exciting the frenzied animal to still greater exertion. The wagon gave a lurch as it struck a deeper rut than usual and the seat, with me on it, took a somersault and together we fell into the bed of the wagon.

On went the horse as if the devil, himself, were after it, for a distance of about a thousand feet. There it encountered a rail fence. It gave a desperate leap, but all it managed to do was straddle the fence, half on one side and half on the other, and there it finally came to a halt, panting and gasping from its exertions.

Father, quite alarmed by the scene that was transpiring, came running up the road, breathless and fearing the worst. He saw me crying, but was much relieved to find me safe and with the exception of a few bruises, with no bones broken. The horse having had its fling, was now quite subdued, and showed the most exemplary conduct for the balance of the day.

Mother became alarmed and demanded that we get rid of the

animal at once. But to whom could we sell it? Everybody in town knew that the horse was not to be trusted. Had they not seen it take the bit in its teeth and suddenly plunge down the road at a pace that made hearts skip a beat, for the safety of those who rode behind it? Moreover, father would never think of selling a horse without honestly describing its qualities to a prospective purchaser.

Father decided to go back to the man who had sold him the horse, to see if he would make an adjustment. Surprisingly enough, the trader acted quite reasonable. He pointed out that the horse was young as he had represented and though fast, was not speed characteristic of youth? He allowed that though the animal was spirited, he knew many people would find it a horse quite to their taste and one they would be proud to own. Howbeit, because he wanted his customers to be satisfied, and since he had promised to stand back of the horse, he would make a trade for another at only a slight sum in addition.

Now that he knew exactly the kind of an animal father wanted, he had just the one that would suit the whole family. The horse was of the right age, and was never known to run away. Moreover, he pointed out that the animal was built as a work horse and possessed unusual strength. Would father be pleased to look at this excellent animal?

So it came about that we had horse number three. The trader was right. The horse was of acceptable age; it never raced; it never ran away. Indeed, we were to learn to our sorrow that on occasion it would not even walk away! We discovered this one afternoon, when old Nig stopped right in the middle of the road, and despite the whip which father used generously, the refractory beast could not be persuaded to move a single inch. Its hide would quiver from the stroke, but as for other movement there was none. The horse remained in a completely stationary position and resisted all attempts to get it to move.

Then suddenly, after a considerable lapse of time, without any apparent reason for a change of mind, Nig would indicate he was ready to go. And for several days or weeks he performed his work willingly and was compliant to all commands, until at some inconvenient moment, whether in the driveway or pulling a plow across the field, the fit came upon him, and then no amount of pleading or threatening could put him into motion until the spirit moved him.

It seemed that this was the best we could do, and we managed by fits and starts to get the farm work done that summer. News of the horse's erratic disposition soon made the rounds of the village, and any prospect of trading him except at a tremendous sacrifice seemed remote. Nevertheless, we were soon to sell him at a public auction, but for other reasons than for his unpredictable temperament.

CHAPTER IV

Utopia In Southern California!

Father, during our two years residence in Hubbard, had with my assistance, considerably improved the farm, for he was a very industrious man and had known only hard labor from his youth. A man by the name of Trout, who lived nearby but was not overly gifted with personal industry, coveted the property and on several occasions had proposed that Dad sell it to him. Father, however, was not particularly interested in his propositions until one day he and mother began to receive information on a new enterprise, that was being founded in Southern California in the Santa Susanna mountains. A minister by the name of Phinias Yoakum proposed to found a Christian community in the communal style of the Early Church, on some property that had been deeded to him. The picture was painted in glowing terms, describing that a truly apostolic community, a heaven on earth, was being set up whereby families could come and find a place free from all the evil influences of the world. It was a tempting prospect. Mother and dad had, as I have said, lived several years in Zion until Dr. Dowie had become physically incapacitated at which time the city had been taken over by the anachronistic, Wilbur Glenn Voliva, whose great ambition was to prove that the world was flat. The rainbow dream of a Christian community had not been realized in Zion, but it might have been, and perhaps in this case of Pisgah Grande, it would be. Dr. Yoakum, by avoiding the mistakes of Dowie, might succeed where he failed. All things would be in common in this community. All would share alike, and all together the people of the community would participate in the dream of a heaven upon earth.

From time to time my parents received further alluring information portraying the great benefits that this proposed utopia in Southern California would provide. The temptation became stronger and stronger, and mother, who possessed an adventurous spirit, convinced father that the thing to do was to go there. Already her children (especially I) were showing signs indicating we were anything but saints. Surely in such a wholesome Christian atmosphere, we would grow up into godly young men and women.

They were to discern too late, however, that there were many things fundamentally wrong with Yoakum's naive utopian scheme. In the first place, the Early Church operated as a communal system for only a short time. The people had experienced a mighty Baptism of divine love. They still were under the impact of witnessing the glorious resurrection of their Lord, and some had seen Him before their very eyes, ascend to Heaven. In addition to this, a severe persecution had been launched against the Church by the Jewish authorities, which had driven the people together, instinctively, in a common defense. Yet, despite all these circumstances in its favor, the communal system functioned effectively for only a short period. Connivers and schemers, such as Ananias and Sapphira, conspired to secure the full benefits of the communal, at the same time privily withholding part of their promised money. Only a summary judgment on them by the Holy Ghost prevented duplicity and hypocrisy from corrupting the Church at its very inception. Not long after, the Grecian widows complained they were not getting their share, and a committee of deacons had to be appointed to settle their grievances. Now under vastly more difficult circumstances, Dr. Yoakum proposed to copy this communal system. It was a proposition doomed to failure before it got started!

But my parents who had become fascinated by the proposal which had been set forth in such alluring terms, decided to cast their lot with it. Father sold the farm, disposing of the household goods and farm accessories at a public auction. Nig, the balker, went for the sum of ten dollars with the purchaser complaining that he was getting the bad end of the bargain. Having disposed of most of our effects, we boarded the train for Southern California, and thus, hopefully, we were on our way to the land of promise. We children, of course, were immensely delighted with the whole idea.

As I have said, the Pisgah Grande scheme was doomed to failure from the beginning. Yoakum, a pious visionary, with none of the genius of John Alexander Dowie, possessed most of his faults. The whole enterprise was a feeble imitation of the Zion City project. There was a complete lack of imagination in the planning. An enormous display of ignorance of the fundamental laws governing human behaviour was evidenced in all the arrangements. The whole project was a perfect set-up for producing discontent and dissatisfaction. Communism succeeds only because a policeman keeps his eye upon those who are under its power. A man will do as he is told as long as a gun is pointed at him. But human nature being what it is, it will not work, it will not produce, nor create, when there is no incentive. Even a bird instinctively wants to call its nest its own.

Pisgah Grande became one of those curious communities which provide copy for newspaper journalists, whose business it is to regale their readers with stories such as that of the strange ways of this new cult which had settled in the mountains.

Our train ride was at last over and an ancient automobile met us at the station in the little town of Santa Susanna. It carried our family with some of our belongings up a long tortuous road, into mountain fastnesses surrounded by towering peaks of imposing grandeur. We children were more and more delighted. What a story-book country in which to play and roam! Life would be just a prolonged picnic. But my parents, with sinking hearts, quickly realized the primitive character of the settlement. They saw that there was a vast difference between the glowing accounts of this utopian project described in Yoakum's paper, and actual reality. The fact was that the good doctor, while not intentionally intending to deceive the people, was a visionary who had been hypnotized by his own enthusiasm. Pisgah Grande had little to offer, and there was no capital available for development of the community.

Although one of the better houses had been reserved for us, most of the dwellings were mere shacks. The place, as a whole, would scarcely have made a fair refugee camp.

Yet my parents, disappointed as they were, could hardly turn around and leave the place at once. We all soon fell into the routine of the community. With the exception of the fact that both men and women lived there, the place resembled and was operated on the order of a medieval monastery. At an early hour each morning the gong rang, summoning some seventy five or a hundred people to the dining hall — the only substantial building on the property — for breakfast.

Here we found consistency, at least. Breakfast invariably consisted of mush and skim milk, the latter having been thinned by the simple expedient of adding water until there was enough "milk" to go around. Bread on occasions was provided — apparently gathered from city bakeries by the sack, which because of its staleness no longer was saleable. Butter was unheard of, nor was sugar in evidence at any time. Occasionally, some fruit was brought up from Los Angeles, the area being a fruit country.

Lunch consisted of one unvarying staple — beans. This dish was served from day to day with absolute regularity. While beans are a substantial food, the monotony of such a diet served continuously, can well be imagined. Minimum vitamin requirements were far from being met. Scurvy or rickets was not beyond the range of possibility on this diet. The evening meal consisted of more of the same, served with the stale bread. Prayers preceded and followed all meals.

By now we had an opportunity to size up our neighbors. There were a few families who had come to the community for the same purpose as my parents — a desire to withdraw from the evil world that they might serve God better. It was the same motive that drew the people to the convents, monasteries and monkeries during medieval times, and the Puritans in 1620 to our shores, a desire that produced a few very great saints but in the main, totally failed in its purpose to inspire wholesome Christianity in the masses. Many people think that if they could only get away from the world, all would be well. But they fail to take into consideration the frailty of human nature, which is just as perverse in an isolated place as it is in the city.

While there were a few solid citizens in the community, the fact was that the majority of the people who had come to Pisgah Grande were misfits, adventurers, reclaimed drunkards, some still taking the cure, people without roots, feeble-minded persons, converted bums, and derelicts of society rescued from the slums and shipped up there, in the hope that they would be less subject to temptation and backsliding. A worthy work indeed, but these people hardly produced a society conducive to advancing the spiritual interests of a family.

Mother and dad, of course, did not discuss much their impressions of the place with us children, as they did not want us repeating what they said. But we could not help but sense that they were deeply disappointed.

As I have mentioned, the conditions in Pisgah Grande were exceedingly primitive and there was no money available for improving or developing the colony. The whole place was run on a shoestring. Father, who was a good carpenter, found little to profitably occupy his time. There were brick and lime kilns which were being worked, but their products by themselves were not sufficient to produce completed dwellings.

The colony was considered an excellent place to send defectives. Mother was somewhat alarmed that one of the morons, who went by the name of Grover might harm the children. He presented a rather grotesque and unprepossessing appearance. He could not talk, but chattered only. The poor fellow suffered a peculiar affliction that caused him to walk backwards wherever he went, and he would suffer no man to turn him around so he could walk normally. Once my father thought to help him. After much persuasion, he walked forward, up a hill. But the moment father let him go, he, after registering his extreme disapproval loudly and indignantly and with vigorous gestures, backed down the hill, and then turned around and backed up again. The poor man seemed to be under a permanent fixation that unless he could see where he had come from there was no use in walking. Funny as it seemed then, I later realized that he represented a tragedy to some mother's heart. Instead of shipping such unfortunates away from society, the Church needs apostolic power to deliver these persons from their chains of affliction.

Grover was strong and muscular, and it was well within his capability, should his twisted mind cause him to go berserk, to seriously injure a child. This and other reasons mentioned, caused my parents to decide to return to Oregon. Dr. Yoakum came out to the colony occasionally. He appeared to live in a dream world, in which he saw great prospects for his Pisgah Grande Utopia. He was a good man, but quite out of touch with reality. His knowledge of human nature was of the most elementary kind. It would be hard to find a man less fitted for the task that he had set for himself. With all the elements of failure inherent in his ill-conceived and ill-planned venture, Phinias Yoakum, nevertheless, was oblivious to all signs of disaster until its flimsy structure crumbled at his feet.

Fortunately, mother and dad had the foresight not to invest all their money in the project — as some alas, had done — until they had decided whether or not they wished to locate there permanently.

The makeshift school in the colony was hardly worthy of the name. Mother and father wished to get us out of there as quickly as possible, and into a public school. So after some six months in Pisgah Grande, our parents pulled stakes and left it, somewhat sadder and wiser. The trip, of course, was exhilerating and exciting to me as well as to my brother and sisters. We thought that the winter had been spent in a most profitable way.

CHAPTER V

Boyhood Days

I shall now pass over events rapidly, many of which I could mention but will select only a few. Our family located in a little community by the name of Huber, some ten miles west of Portland, Oregon. There was a fairly good school in the area, but no church. Consequently, the place was almost completely heathen, a circumstance that was highly trying to mother. We had prayer and Bible reading in the home but that was not enough. Surrounded by ungodly companions, I soon began picking up their ways. It is hard to realize the power of evil that develops in a community, which is completely void of spiritual influences. Christian parents should beware of settling in a place, in which their children, growing up, do not have the privilege of hearing the Gospel preached. The chances are that they will live to regret their decision.

I had read much of the Bible by the age of ten, and found it not uninteresting. Mother would often read long passages to us on Sundays. At times I felt that I wanted to give my heart to God. But most of my schoolmates were as irreligious as heathen and their influence was having a bad effect on my outlook. I became ashamed of the fact that we had family worship. Once when a son of a wealthy family was visiting the neighborhood, I was indignant that mother would call us for prayer while he was there. I made off at the time, and did not return until worship was over. The son of the rich man knelt with the rest of the family during the prayer, without embarrassment. I felt quite abashed.

It was hard work on the farm, and I had many duties which included a full work day on Saturday. On school days I had many chores to do, including milking the cow, feeding the animals, sawing the wood, splitting it by hand and filling the wood box.

It was a marvelous thing later, when I was fifteen, that a neighbor's gasoline woodsaw relieved me of the tedious task of sawing the sticks by hand.

There were not very many events of interest to vary the routine. We all looked forward to the visits of a little soap man who came around occasionally. He was always welcome, because he gathered all the gossip in the community and was not loathe to impart it to willing listeners. He also was somewhat of a philosopher — a self-appointed oracle who had decided opinions on all subjects. He agreed with mother that religion was a good thing. Sometimes he would tarry at our place a half an hour, causing me to wonder how he could afford to give so much time to one customer, if he were to make a living from the soap business. The one thing that endeared him to us, was the fact that he carried with him a liberal supply of store candy. When leaving, he would give each of us a piece of rock candy that would stand a lot of licking. We never forgot the little soap man.

While I was in Huber, I myself, went into the soap business for a short time. A copy of a boy's magazine came into my hands. Inside its pages was an ad showing a soldier's uniform, and a sword sheathed in a scabbard; it informed me, that I could get this ensemble free, or, at least with only a comparatively small effort on my part. To me it seemed to be a natty appearing uniform indeed. The artist depicted "rays" shooting off on all sides indicating its brilliant effect. The most appealing thing to me about the whole thing was the sword held in its scabbard at the soldier's side.

All I had to do according to the ad, was to sell thirty-six bars of soap (I believe that was the number), to my friends and neighbors. This would be easy to do since the soap was a very special kind that did things that other soaps did not do. And so I filled out the coupon, mailed it and in due time there was delivered to our doorstep, a large box of soap. Forthwith, I began my career as a peddler, by selling the first bar to my mother.

From neighbor to neighbor I went with my box of soap, inspired by the alluring picture of the soldier suit that would soon be mine. In my imagination I could see myself promenading up and down the street in an imposing uniform. I would, in fact, to all practical purposes be a soldier!

I discovered it was a bigger task getting rid of the soap than I had anticipated. Nevertheless, at length I had sold all but a few bars. Mother came to my rescue and bought the last ones. I put the money in the mail, and impatiently waited for the suit to come.

Finally, it did arrive. My heart beat fast in anticipation, and my hand trembled as I opened the package. Surely enough, there was a suit inside. I took it out and unfolded it. As I looked it over, I had a hard time to conceal my disappointment. It did not seem to be the same suit at all, that I had seen in the magazine. The color was a greenish drab, and the material was just one grade better than cheese cloth. It was very heavily starched, and once the suit was washed, it practically lost its substance. The greatest disappointment of all was the fact that the sword and scabbard that had been pictured, were missing. I looked at the ad again, but noticed now that nothing was said about including the sword in the offer. I wore the suit a few times, but found it was ill-fitting and that it would rip with the slightest undue exertion. Forthwith, I lost confidence in magazine ads.

One incident happened in Huber that I remember quite well, that is illustrative of father's sterling character. He worked in Portland, but also did some farming by putting in his evenings and Saturday afternoons raising onions. He would contract his crop out to a wholesaler at an agreed price. If the market fell or was glutted he would, nevertheless, get the contract price. One year the price of onions went up fourfold. If father could have sold even part of the crop at the market price, he would have realized what would have been to our family a small fortune. Since the harvest was excellent it would have been easy for him to have held back part of it and sold it at the high prices. Such a thought, however, never tempted him, for he was the soul of honesty.

Excitement did not often come to our little community, but once in a while something happened that kept us in a fever while it lasted.

My friend, Vernon Davies, who lived only a block away and who was a year or two older than I, came bursting into our yard one day crying, "My sister Arlene has been kidnapped. I saw him take her." As great tears rolled down his cheeks, he asked, "Will you go with me to save my sister?"

All alert, I questioned, "Well, who took her?" "It was the peddler," he replied sobbing. "She was on his wagon to look at some of his wares. My back was turned for only a few moments.

Next thing I knew his wagon was dashing down the road and my sister was gone. I yelled after him, but he wouldn't stop." And his tears continued to fall as he pictured the dire fate of his sister!

Well, we couldn't let a terrible thing like this happen without our doing something about it. So we both started running down the road toward Beaverton, two miles away. We ran and ran until we were breathless but of course we couldn't catch the peddler. He was too far ahead of us. Completely out of wind, I suggested that we go to the police station to find someone who would be better able to cope with the situation. The local constable listened to Vernon's story and suggested that we get in his car and go after the peddler. So we got in and I sat expectantly, in anticipation of the moment that we would see the long arm of the law lay hands on the bold, bad man, who had committed this dastardly deed in broad daylight. Surely enough, as we rode out of town we saw the peddler's wagon in the distance, and he was travelling fast. However, he was no match for the constable's car. We soon caught up with him.

The constable ordered the peddler to halt his wagon, which he did, with a very puzzled look upon his face. The officer said, "Where is the girl?" "What girl?" the man asked in bewilderment. "You took my sister," Vernon accused, bursting into tears again. By this time the officer had searched the wagon and saw that there was no one inside. He turned to my young friend and said, "Looks as if there is some mistake; your sister is not here." By now the peddler got the drift. He exclaimed indignantly, "Why should you suspect me of kidnapping your sister? She ran back into the yard, and that's the last I saw of her." And that is exactly what happened. Vernon had missed her, then he saw the peddler racing his team, and had imagined the rest. We walked back to our homes, rather more slowly than we had left. Vernon was crestfallen over his mistake, but quite relieved that his sister was safe.

How we are willing to put ourselves out, when we think our loved ones are in physical danger. Yet, few Christians are alarmed when they see their whole family is going down the broad path of destruction, and are in danger of losing their souls. If we are not alert, we may find that Satan has kidnapped those who are near and dear to us, and we discover too late that they are gone from us, forever.

The time came that my parents felt that they could do better in the larger town of Beaverton, located nearer Portland. In that city we lived until I was converted. We had only been there a short time until something occurred that nearly ended in tragedy. It was the mishap at the birthday party, an event I have already narrated.

There was much more going on in the larger town, and I was happy over the move. One evening we heard a cry, "Fire! Fire! Fire!" Rushing to the door, we saw a tongue of flame leaping out of the upstairs window of the Miller home, a few rods away. I lost no time in jumping fences, and was one of the first at the scene. Since the flames were in the upstairs, some others and I began removing the furniture and goods as fast as possible. Since the fire was just well started, we had time to get most of the important household effects out into the yard. I felt a strange exhilaration as the roaring flames crackled above us, to be engaged in the noble enterprise of saving as much of the neighbor's goods as possible.

We had gotten almost everything out except some of the utensils and canned fruit in the pantry. But since the fire had now reached the lower floor and was burning fiercely and we had already established our claims to heroism, we thought it the better part of valor to retire to the outside. At that moment a young man, a neighbor, just arrived, and as he did not wish to be left out of the excitement, he dashed into the house, and around to the pantry. I stood aghast, for I realized that at any moment the flames would surely break through the door, thus blocking his escape.

Suddenly the panel burned through, and the fire roared into the pantry. Pots and pans ceased coming, and in their place a human form appeared hurtling head first out the high window, his pants scorched and smoking, but otherwise unhurt. Only a man agile as a cat, could have performed this exploit.

At that moment the Beaverton fire department appeared on the scene, its equipment pulled by hand by a crew of volunteers. They finally got the hose connected just as the roof fell in. Forthwith, they began to play a stream of water upon the flames. The fire could not be quenched, however, and had to burn itself out. Within an hour, nothing was left but a pile of steaming ashes, with the exception of the furniture that we had managed to save from the flames.

Although there were plenty of mischievous boys in the community, they were not delinquents and as a rule did not destroy property. Halloween was the most dangerous season. At that time, householders could expect some minor depredations, if they were not on the alert. Occasionally such a thing as a wagon would appear perched on the top of a woodshed. Wood piles would be toppled over and outhouses, not strongly reinforced, might suffer severely on that night.

There was little thievery in the community. Few people locked their doors. Once my brother came home with a hatchet which he had gotten in a trade with another boy. The father, a Mr. Hoover, came hours later to retrieve it. I never saw a man any more angry than he. We gave him back his hatchet, and never saw him again, the reason for which will presently be evident.

Connecting Beaverton with the City of Portland was the interurban electric. Father regularly went to work on the early morning train. My oldest sister, Fern, regularly took the ten o'clock train. A Mr. Ferris, the conductor, of the ten o'clock, was a neighbor who lived down the street a little way from us.

On the morning in question, the train left Beaverton at the scheduled time, and proceeded on its way, stopping at intermediate points until it reached a station called Bertha. Here it was to have stopped to await the Westbound cars. But for some reason it didn't stop, and no one has ever been able to explain why.

Conductor Ferris noted that the train had not waited at Bertha, and should have pulled the emergency brake cord and stopped the cars until he had investigated the cause. He did not, but instead, began to make his way to the front cars to get an explanation. In the meantime, the train was proceeding at full speed toward the Terwilliger bend which would bring passengers into view of the City of Portland. This curve is almost 180 degrees in extent and reduces the front view of the track at this point to a distance of only about 200 feet.

The conductor was still on his way to the front, when the train approached the curve. He never reached the cab and luckily for him, he did not. The Westbound train was approaching the curve at the same time at a high rate of speed. The inevitable happened. Brakes were thrown on but far too late. The two trains hurtled into one another, killing both engineers and, Mr. Hoover, who for some fateful reason was riding in the engineer's cabin that morning. The cars telescoped, taking the lives of at least ten persons and seriously injuring many others. Conductor Ferris was thrown violently forward and was critically injured, but later recovered. He was adjudged partly to blame for the accident because he did not stop the train, when it failed to halt at Bertha. As for my sister Fern, she was not on the train. As I remember it, it was her day off!

CHAPTER VI
How I Finished School

Before I entered public school I was taught certain elementary lessons in reading by my mother. This gave me an advantage over other students. In fact, it was to prove very fortunate for me later on. I shall never forget when the teacher, a Miss Shore, brought me a second reader and told me to study a certain lesson. I did not immediately get the significance of her request, and so instead of studying, I sat there trying to reason out why she had asked me to do this. At length, the second grade was called and I was asked to sit with it. Presently I was called upon to read with the class. Somehow, I got through without trouble, and from that time on I sat with second grade. This was to prove very fortunate for me, for by the time I was fifteen years of age, family finances became so slim I could not have continued my education. As it was, only a very unexpected event made it possible for me to graduate.

Immediately, upon moving to Beaverton I enrolled in the local public school. The teacher was a pedagogue who went by the name of Fisher, and who resembled in many respects the legendary character, Ichabod Crane. Scholastic requirements for teaching elementary grades were not too high at that time, and he possessed only a smattering of academic knowledge. This did not prevent his placing a rather high estimate upon his abilities. He had a number of peculiar idiosyncrasies, one of which I remember, was that he would have the class go to the blackboard and add up a long column of figures. He suggested that we memorize the total. Should we have visitors come to the class, we might amaze them by performing a prodigious mathematical feat. I did not stay long enough, however, to learn much of how he operated.

Mr. Fisher was a rather stern martinet, and he believed in attaining his ends by brute force if necessary. One of the larger boys, Ralph, had committed some infraction of the school law. It is not unlikely that he was at fault and probably deserved some punishment. For some reason, the teacher lost his temper and tossed the lad down the stairs. He was unhurt except for his wounded pride. His parents decided to take him out of school and send him to Huber. It wasn't long until a similar incident occurred and another member of the class took his books and departed. Now it came my turn. One of the boys rolled a marble across the room to another lad, and I, noticing their little game, smiled. The teacher whose back was turned, suddenly looking around and seeing another boy and me smiling, took for granted that we were the culprits and ordered us to get our hats and march for home.

Now there is no doubt that we deserved a rebuke for various petty misdemeanors that he had not caught, but on this occasion the teacher's bad temper was pretty well known. So mother decided that I should finish out the term at my old school, although this necessitated a daily round trip of at least five miles.

Next year it was different. The school board decided that they would do well to make a change, and they secured the appointment of a Mrs. Ada Wilson. I immediately responded to her warm nature, and managed to graduate that year as valedictorian of the class.

The following year I entered high school. Mother had high ambitions for me and wanted me to attend Lincoln High in Portland. Since there was no money in the family til for this costly arrangement, it involved a rather complicated procedure. But mother thought she had everything worked out.

In the morning I would arise at six, get myself ready, walk a mile to the station, spend three quarters of an hour on the suburban. Then, walk another half mile to school. At two-thirty it was arranged that I would get off early, go down to the Evening Telegram, pick up my papers and peddle them to around one hundred customers to pay the tuition and train fare. Then I would take the night train and get home at a rather late hour. After eating supper and studying my school work, it was time for bed. Such an intense routine I fear would be rather burdensome to children today, who want many hours of play, and who are apt to complain over minor inconveniences.

The arrangement did not prove satisfactory. I scarcely got enough sleep and there was so little time for home work, that it was difficult for me to keep up with my class. Moreover, my paper route was in the very section where all the transients lived. These people moved about constantly, not staying long in any one place. When I went to collect the paper bill, it was not unusual to find that the customer had departed to parts unknown. That the little newsboy had to bear the loss did not seem to concern them. In January, much to mother's disappointment I was forced to return to the school at Beaverton.

I do not believe I especially distinguished myself there. Very few in my class were ambitious. The curriculum was not arranged to challenge us to more than average efforts. I enjoyed science and mathematics but abhorred English, a subject which would have been of the greatest value to me later on. I loved to read, however, and made full use of the school library. It was my intense love of books that in time gave me a rather wide knowledge of the world in general.

At the completion of my junior year at Beaverton, the burden of sending all of us five children to school was getting beyond father's ability to bear. There seemed no alternative but for me to drop out of school and go to work. This brought great anguish to my mother's heart, and she prayed that God would work a miracle. But it seemed that no miracle was at hand. To make matters worse, there was a depression on at that time and it was difficult for a youth of fifteen to get any kind of job. After making a number of inquiries for work, I became quite discouraged. I did not want to hang around the house and do nothing. The prospect of hiring out on a farm at the meager salaries they paid was altogether uninviting.

I finally reached a decision. I would pack up my few belongings and start out for the apple country. I knew that I could get a seasonal job there. Then I would travel on like a Horatio Alger character. Somewhere, I imagined a fortune would be awaiting me. Moreover, the thought of seeing the world, held quite an attraction to me.

Someday I would return home, my fortune made, in true Alger fashion. It is needless to say that the chances of any such rosy dreams materializing were weighted strongly against me. An inexperienced youth starting out in that fashion can expect nothing better than joining the army of itinerants, and living a hand-to-mouth existence.

My secret plans which I intended to put into operation were

quickly completed. Naturally, I had not made them known to my parents who would have promptly vetoed them. In the morning, rising early, I would put my meager belongings on my bicycle and start out for the Hood River country, over sixty miles away. I could pedal this distance on my bicycle easily in one day. But one thing I had not taken into consideration were mother's prayers. Although quite unaware of my plans, she daily and fervently put her children into the hands of God. God was therefore looking on the situation and might have something to say about my plans; and may I add here, that with such a wonderful power at our command that God has provided for His people, is it not tragic that thousands of Christian parents fail to have any regular altar of prayer in their home?

On the afternoon before my proposed departure, I was out riding on my bicycle. When I was only three miles from home, a truck passed me on a narrow winding road. Another car suddenly appeared around a curve and the truck pulled in quickly, to avoid it — too quickly, for it caught my handlebars, and violently threw me to the ground, the wheels of which narrowly missed me. The bicycle I was riding was smashed, and my left wrist was broken in two places. In one instant all my plans vanished. I was in fact a rather sorry sight.

At that moment a kindly motorist stopped and picked me up. I explained what had happened. The truck that had struck me, by this time was a mile down the road. Although badly shaken up and in pain, I did have the presence of mind to ask the driver to help me catch the truck and take its license number. Then as I remember, we flagged it down and I told the driver what had happened. He was incredulous but did give me the name of his insurance company. My arm now was numb with pain and I made my way to Doctor Mason, who incidentally was out on a call. There was nothing to do but wait. Eventually the kindly physician came in. I knew Dr. Mason well, for he had lived next door to us for several years. He gave me an anaesthetic and set my wrist.

Naturally, when I arrived home with my arm in a sling, mother was quite startled. And when she heard the details of the accident, she was not a little troubled, reflecting how perilously close I had come to the wheels of the speeding truck. But she gave God thanks for my providential escape from death. It was more providential than she thought, for naturally I omitted informing her of my plans which had been interrupted as a result of the accident. I saw no particular reason now in divulging details of my ill-fated intention of leaving home.

We had the name of the insurance company, and after being turned down by an attorney who didn't think we had a chance to get anything, father and I went to Portland to meet with the insurance adjustors. Of course their chief job is to find ways to avoid paying any claims except what they absolutely have to. And you can't blame them much, human nature being what it is, and with so many fraudulent claims being constantly pressed upon insurance companies.

The adjustors informed father and me that they had made "careful" investigation of the circumstances, and that another truck driver had witnessed the accident and would swear that I had fallen off the bicycle on my own account, and that the story of the truck sideswiping me, was pure fiction. They were sorry, but under the circumstances they could not help me.

I was beginning to learn how the world operated. Father's face fell in deep disappointment.

However, an inspiration came to me. I asked the adjustors how far behind me the other truck had been that they mentioned? They said 100 yards — naming a convenient figure — as they puffed on their cigars. I then said, "Gentlemen, do you know that the exact spot of the accident was established by the man who picked me up, and also by the fact that my bicycle lay on the spot for at least a day before it was stolen?" I took a piece of paper and drew a diagram for them. Now I pointed out, "If your man was a hundred yards behind me when the accident occurred, then by reason of the curve, he was well behind the hill at the moment and quite shut off from view!"

The adjustors had no reply to this. A few days later they settled for $187.50, not much today but a veritable windfall for us then. Not only was I able to return to school, but our entire family blossomed out in new clothes. Thus it was by reason of the accident, that I finished my high school education.

In my senior year I decided to take up debating. There were two debate teams in our school. Our team won the first round and the other dropped out. Next we went to Forest Grove and debated the local team there. We won again. Now we were in the semi-finals, and went to Astoria. If we had won this time, we would have had a chance for state championship. But alas, when the judge's votes were counted it was 2-1 against us!

As a result of our debating, I was invited to be one of the speakers at a special occasion put on by the Masonic Lodge. I was to be a co-speaker with George Baker, mayor of the City of Portland. Just before the meeting I had a light attack of the flu. As I remember it, my efforts were passable, but nothing exceptional.

Mother would have liked very much, if I had been able to go on to college, but I knew that was impossible. The time had come for me to share part of the responsibility of helping take care of the family. I did, however, take a correspondence course in furtherance of my studies. As I have said, I was a voracious reader, supplementing my general knowledge by reading hundreds of books. The right kind of knowledge is a source of power. Nothing is gained by ignorance. Nevertheless, it must be admitted that much of the education given today in our higher schools of learning is tainted with philosophical speculations and theories of evolution which by implication, discredit the Scriptural account of creation, and thereby succeed in over-throwing the faith of some.

CHAPTER VII

My Conversion To Christ

Largely through mother's prayers, the Lord has had His hand upon my life. God mysteriously working behind the scenes, through the exercise of His eternal will and omniscient wisdom, guides unerringly the destinies of those who are responsive to His guidance. Some people hear the still small voice and obey. To others, the Lord must administer severe chastening, to get them to obey His will. Still others stubbornly resist Him to the 'end, to their everlasting shame and loss.

As I have mentioned elsewhere, at an early age I felt the distinct call of God. But as time went on and I entered the period of adolescence, strange forces began stirring within me. I knew I ought to serve the Lord, but something within — which is nothing more nor less than our fallen human nature — made me totally disinclined to acknowledge God. Moreover, religion as I saw it practiced, seemed to me an effeminate thing, quite unable to challenge or stir the imagination of youth. Most of the people who lived in our town were little more than pagans. Few of them attended church, and consequently their children grew up like heathen. I too was developing a singular antipathy and distaste for spiritual things, much to mother's sorrow.

Until I reached the age of sixteen, I felt constrained to attend the local Methodist Church, but I found within me a growing opposition to religion as I saw it practiced. The pastor of the church where I attended was a good man, and sincerely desired the salvation of my soul, but he seemed powerless to reach me, so strong were my carnal inclinations and so weak was the church's influence. In fact, I was becoming ashamed to be seen attending church at all. I recall one instance when I neared the church, some of my school companions were passing by. I hid from view lest they should see me attending church.

The fact was, the whole community was ungodly and did not

take religion seriously. The church was looked upon as a harmless and ineffectual institution. Some of the parents sent their children to Sunday School, but most of the people went their several ways and to church was not one of them. It exercised little or no influence in their lives. Only when there was a funeral did religion take on significance. Then the good pastor was supposed to give suitable words of consolation and to leave the general impression that the deceased, regardless of the ungodly life he may have led, had by some mysterious magic, suddenly become a saint and was even then being welcomed inside the pearly gates I do not mean to wound the feelings of the bereaved, but I have always felt that it is the sheerest hypocrisy to preach people into heaven at death, when they have steadfastly spent their lifetime living only for themselves and this world.

Like most sinners, I had my stock answer to give when anyone questioned me about my soul. I had read enough to know a little about the doctrine of predestination as it was preached by Calvinists, and which, in its extreme form is actually Mohammedan fatalism in disguise. I would ask the person if he believed that God had foreknowledge of all things. The reply was of course in the affirmative. When I continued, "What God knows cannot be changed. That is, God cannot make a mistake in His foreknowledge. Is not that right?" Again the answer was, "Yes". "Then God knew before I was born, whether I would be saved or not?" Once more the answer was in the affirmative. I would then point out triumphantly, "Well, if the fact has already been established before I was born, indeed before the foundation of the world, then nothing I can do, will change the issue."

In my foolish pride, I made myself believe that I had an invincible argument. And the sad thing was that no one seemed to know how to challenge it. Surely, the defective theologies of men are handy tools in the devil's workshop. The answer to all my sophistry was of course as simple as could be. There is indeed a predestination spoken of in the Scriptures. *But any interpretation of this doctrine must be consistent with the Scriptural teaching of man's free will.* That man has a free will is taught far more explicitly than the doctrine of predestination. Yet men brush aside all that is said of this and make predestination to be fatalism, an irresistible force determining our destiny. This, I hold is a gross perversion of the Scriptures, and a favorite tool in the hands of the enemy to make men think that they are not God's elect, and therefore lost forever, or, if God's elect, they can live like the devil and all is well; they are infallibly assured entrance into the pearly gates.

The compatibility of the free will of a human being with Divine predestination whatever it includes, must be accepted if one is going to believe the Bible at all. Eternal mysteries are involved in the creation of the universe, human life, and Divine predestination. Just as the human mind cannot conceive how God created the worlds out of nothing, so the finite mind is unable to comprehend the mysteries of predestination. The facts simply are that all men may be saved who are willing to repent of their sins. Anyone who challenges this truth strikes at the very heart of evangelical Christianity.

> "For God so loved the world, that he gave his only begotten Son, that whosoever believeth in him should not perish, but have everlasting life." (Jn. 3:16)

When I was about fourteen years of age, an old time holiness evangelist came to town. His name was Dave Hill. He was a bold preacher and a good man, who feared neither man nor devils. He preached as a veritable John the Baptist, giving forth the truth as he saw it. The meeting made a considerable stir in the community, and the evangelist's preaching powerfully affected me, as well as many others. My silly excuses melted like snow in the summer sun before his straight preaching of repentance. For the first time in my life I was near the point of being converted. However, at that very time, our whole family went to the fields to work for a couple of weeks, to get money to outfit us for school, and I accompanied them. In the course of time, most of my feelings left me. Yet not altogether. Faith had been imparted to my heart, that continued its silent work for several years to come.

In reading the Bible, my imagination was stirred by some of the great characters of the Bible. When they prayed, things happened. I was fascinated by the story of Elijah, who called down fire from heaven in his challenge of the false prophets of Baal. I never tired of reading the dramatic story of Daniel, who when cast into the lions' den because of his faith, yet emerged unscathed because God sent His angel to protect him. The life of Jesus, His miracles, His ministry, and His claims, was a thrilling story that could not be duplicated in the annals of history.

Christ's disciples, inspired by the glory of His resurrection, went forth in a ministry of power that compelled my respect and admiration.

None-the-less, one thing genuinely troubled me. Why did not these miracles of Bible days take place today? Had God lost His power? Certainly there was nothing in the Bible that indicated that the days of miracles were to cease. Again, it occurred to me that if miracles were necessary to prove that Jesus was the Son of God in days of old, certainly they were needed today, for obviously there were more unbelievers living now than ever before. A weak, defeated church, able to interest only children and the aged, was a poor attraction to a young man who was full of life and energy. It seemed to me that ministers, if they were anything, should be men of faith and of action rather than mere ecclesiastical functionaries whose main duties were to perform marriage ceremonies, conduct funerals, and preach pious sermons which lull people asleep in their sins.

Mother's faith in God always exercised a strong effect upon me, and which I found impossible to shake off. I well remember an incident which took place in our home town, while I was attending high school, that well illustrated her faith for divine healing. In the local church, there was a deacon whose wife had become seriously ill. The pastor of the church, completely ignorant of the Bible truth of healing, could give her no encouragement, outside the resources of the medical profession. The physicians had advised that an operation would be the only hope of saving the woman's life. The family had no ready cash but being desperate to save the mother, negotiated a loan of five hundred dollars at the local bank.

My mother learned of all this and felt it was a shame that the family, which could ill-afford that outlay of money, did not receive healing for their mother. Consequently, without consulting the local pastor, who no doubt would have counselled against such a course as dangerous, she went to the woman and told her that she could be healed, and did she desire that a man of faith be called to pray for her?

Ordinarily, the family would have argued against divine healing but now they were desperate. The woman said she would be glad to have someone come and pray for her healing.

Mother called Dr. Lake's divine healing rooms, to see if he could come to pray for this lady. Dr. Lake did not happen to be there at the time but another minister, Bill Wright, was present — a man who was noted both for his strong faith for healing, and also for his rough methods in dealing with those for whom he prayed. He was quite willing to go with mother.

Entering the house of the stricken woman, he gave the lady a few instructions and then anointed her with oil. Wright had a powerful voice and his prayer could be heard by people a block away. After rebuking the devil of sickness, he commanded the woman to arise from her bed. Doctor's orders, of course, had forbade her to move. But with fear and trembling, yet believing that God had indeed touched her, she arose from her bed, healed by the power of God!

The next day the whole family was rejoicing in the deliverance of their mother. She continued to recover her strength rapidly, and became a wonderful testimony in the church to the power of God to heal. The pastor was amazed and though he said little, he did considerable thinking. In later years, he completely accepted the truth of divine healing. He, himself, was healed and later identified himself with a Full Gospel church. I saw him before his death, and rejoiced with him in his new faith in God's power.

A few days after the healing, the husband went down to the bank and returned the five hundred dollars to the amazed teller, who was informed of what had happened.

This event made a considerable impression upon me, but despite it, I found myself attending church less and less until I dropped out altogether. I was becoming interested in too many things — science, invention, astronomy, in new developments such as radio, which had just begun to come into popular use. Beside these fascinating things, the church seemed a dull place indeed. I was little aware, however, that an event was about to occur that would completely change the entire course of my life for time and for eternity.

Mother came to me one Sunday and said, "Son, there is an evangelist at the Portland Church who is an unusually interesting speaker. I know you would enjoy hearing him. Would you go with us to services today?" I replied, "Mother, you know I have gone to church for years, but the services are dull and uninteresting to me. Please do not insist on my going." Her face seemed sad, but she said nothing more. A few minutes later, I heard the footsteps of the family die away as she and my brother and sisters departed without me. A pang of conscience stung me. I had not treated my mother right, in refusing her when she had been such a good mother to me. I made up my mind, that if she asked me again that week, I would go.

What if she had thought that it was no use to ask me again, and had said nothing further? But she was not discouraged, and the very next night she gave me another invitation to go with the rest of the family. Affecting a reluctance, I replied that I might as well go, just to please her.

When I arrived at the church, I found the atmosphere was electric with revival — a complete contrast to the dull services I had been used to. As my eyes wandered over the building, they rested upon a curious collection of crutches, casts, moulds, braces, and what not. Upon inquiry I was informed that these had been discarded by people who had been miraculously healed. I said to myself, now either a base deception is being practiced here in this church, or else something is going on that would be worth my while to look into. My interest was increased when I heard people testify that they had been healed miraculously of diseases of the most desperate nature.

The speaker, whom I had been invited to hear, was none other than the noted Charles F. Parham, the man who had conducted the historic Apostolic Bible School at Topeka, Kansas, where on the first hours of the Twentieth Century, the Holy Ghost fell according to the Pentecostal pattern of the Early Church. Parham was at the very zenith of his effectiveness when he was in Portland. Not only did he possess a powerful anointing but the keenness of his mind and his incomparable eloquence and wit, held the congregation spellbound in his hand. Never at loss for the right word, he at one moment had his audience rocking with laughter and the next moment weeping. His preaching and logic were irresistible. I soon realized that all my excuses and reasons for not accepting Christ were being swept out from underneath me.

I found myself for the first time since the Dave Hill meetings, strangely wanting to go to church. The following night I hoped mother would ask me to attend again, since to go on my own initiative might make it appear that I was getting interested in religion, something I wished to avoid by all means. On that score however, I need have had no fear. The following night, I was invited to attend again and after that it was taken for granted I would go.

Night after night the powerful preaching of this man of God was having a devastating effect upon my philosophy of life, and everything I had planned for the future. I knew beyond a doubt that this was my hour to accept Christ. Yet at the same time the carnal nature within me revolted against surrendering my will to the will of God. The war that raged inside was painful and excrutiating. I determined to hold off as long as possible, but my convictions were becoming so deep that it was impossible for me to shake them off any more than I could lose my shadow. Fortunately, my family had enough wisdom to wait until I was fully ready to surrender. Conviction had to really lay me low before I was willing to give up.

Then one day I realized I could resist no longer, as the conflict within was becoming intolerable. I must make the decision. I thought, nevertheless, it would be easier if my family were not present on the night I went to the altar. I, therefore, made the excuse that I had some extra work to do at the office, and would not go home with father that night. (He and I both worked for the same company.) It had occurred to me if I were not available to drive the car, that the family would be content to remain home this one night.

So strong were my feelings, however, that I could do no work at the office. I left shortly, walking all the way to the church, a distance of several miles. My little stratagem, nevertheless, proved of no avail. Just before the service started, I looked around and lo!, my whole family and their friends were coming through the door! Not one was missing, and they took seats just behind me.

That night, another powerful message came straight to me. I knew it was my time to act. But my feet were frozen to the floor. At that moment, however, my mother for the first time, during the meetings, said, "Come on, son, let us go forward tonight." Strangely enough I, who a short time before, would have scorned the thought of any such act on my part, now found myself going to the altar and kneeling down — a thoroughly broken and subdued young man. A fountain of tears gushed forth and flowed copiously down my cheeks and upon the altar, as I made a broken confession of my sins before God. I was at the altar for possibly an hour, not because it takes that long for God to save a person, but because repentance is something one need not hurry through. I saw that my sinful life had offended God. But I also realized that He was merciful, and mighty to save.

At length I arose with the assurance that God had saved me, a peace had come into my troubled heart, and a realization that I was beginning a new life. Strangely enough, my first thought was that God had called me to preach the Gospel. Many other things ran through my mind. One was that I must at once break away from the old crowd. I did not feel that I was strong enough, nor had enough of the qualities of a hero to buck the worldly, godless crowd with whom I had run. Now that I was saved, I did not want to take any chance of losing the precious thing I had found, and which had torn my whole nature apart, before I could accept it.

That was one of the happiest days in my mother's life. Many times at night, I had heard her earnestly praying for me and the other children. I was not overly pleased by her prayers at that time, as I feared that in some way they would interfere with my plans. But now at last her prayers had been answered.

Immediately upon my conversion, I promptly put away all my worldly interests. I ceased attending the theaters and motion picture houses. I am even today, surprised to find Christians who can reconcile theater attendance with a Christian profession. As for me, I wanted to give myself completely to the new life and calling I had received. The church where I was converted, held services of some kind every day of the week, and I began attending nightly. Each day upon coming home from work, and after eating supper, I drove back into the city of Portland to attend the evening services. The thrill of my conversion to Christ was something so wonderful, that I could never forget it.

Not long after I was converted, I was invited to receive the baptism of the Holy Ghost. I therefore joined the seekers, and every night after the preaching, I would be at the altar waiting upon God for this experience, which I had been informed was for me. I did not realize then that God had been waiting a long time to give it to me.

One night, only a week or two after the campaign had ended, I was at the altar again seeking for the baptism of the Holy Ghost. Suddenly, while I was praying, a mighty wave of power began to settle upon me. As I prayed on, a vibrating, surging force began to permeate every part of my body. Each moment it went deeper and deeper, until this mighty power, like pulsating electricity — only something wonderfully pleasant — had taken control of every part of my being. How long this continued, I cannot say, but I knew that I had received something out of this world, something very real. It was a heavenly experience beyond human ability to describe, which brought me into such a close relation with God that I could think of nothing else at the moment than to devote my whole life to His service. Several other times the power of the Spirit of God would come upon me, and each time this occurred, I was more convinced that God had something special in store for my life. I had a very long way to go before I was of much value to God, but at least I was on my way.

There was one thing that disappointed me. I had received a powerful anointing of the Spirit, but I had not spoken in tongues as others did. I noticed also that Jesus had said, "These signs shall follow them that believe . . . they shall speak with new tongues." Paul had said, "I would that ye all spake with tongues," so why should I not speak in tongues also? Yet though I sought God earnestly each night, I did not seem to receive the experience in the same way that the apostles had, or my friends did.

There was something else that disturbed me. During my youthful days, I had not been above occasionally taking things that did not belong to me. I would have resented greatly any one calling me a thief, but the fact was, I had several times taken things that had belonged to others. How perverse is the human heart?

The thief crowds God out of his thoughts and is not ashamed of his sins, if only he can keep the knowledge of them from others. My stealing included taking some equipment from the public school a few years before. There were other small things I had taken now and then, and these I had made right as far as I could. Zacchaeus had said, "Behold, Lord, the half of my goods I give to the poor; and if I have taken any thing from any man by false accusation, I restore to him fourfold." I realized that restitution went along with conversion. Not that we are saved by doing these things, but our faith is confirmed by our deeds. We are more likely to continue to live a godly life if we have righted the wrongs we have committed, as far as it is within our power to do so. We should certainly not be like Farmer Green who prayed, "Lord, I sin every day with an outstretched hand. It is impossible to live without sin. Forgive me for stealing forty-seven loads of hay from Farmer Brown. Lord make it fifty, as I am going after the other three tomorrow!"

This matter rested heavily upon my conscience. The thought had occurred to me that I could return what I had taken anonymously. But that did not seem to fully satisfy my conscience. The superintendent of the school was known to be a stern man and not given to leniency. Should I go to him and report my petty depredations? Might he not turn me in and expose me, and if he did, did not I deserve it? I tried to pray through on the matter but found that I got nowhere. Finally, in desperation, I gathered up the things I had stolen and took them to the superintendent's home. In the best way I could, I explained what I had done, but that my life had now been changed and I wanted to make things right. The principal was visibly moved by my confession. Then recovering himself, he warmly commended me for my action and told me that no one but he and I would know anything about it. I believe that my testimony, brief as it was, had an effect upon him.

I might add that just a couple of days after this incident took place, while I was kneeling at the altar, I suddenly began to speak in tongues! We do not earn salvation, nor the baptism of the Holy Ghost by performing good works, nor by doing penance, but we should make restitution as far as possible, so that we have a conscience that is void of offence toward God. A guilty conscience can affect our faith. I am also convinced that if new converts would make redress and restitution as far as possible for the wrongs they have committed and ask forgiveness of those they have slandered, there would be far less backsliding. Repentance should include more than a superficial profession of religion.

Having upon my conversion immediately felt the call to preach, I gladly would have attended a Bible College, but there were few Full Gospel colleges at that time, and I had no money to pay for such schooling. My parents, having just recently moved to Portland, needed what help I could give them to take care of payments on their new home. However, I took advantage of such opportunities as were available to me. A group of young people met on the street each night to preach at a nearby corner located in the very heart of the city. I joined this group and thus began my first preaching of the Gospel. I do not know just how great the results of our efforts were. But we succeeded in drawing a large crowd from night to night, and not a few followed us upstairs to the hall where the after meetings were held. One man who is now a highly successful businessman came up to the service, accepted Christ, and later married one of the church's young ladies.

Occasionally, some of my old friends would stop by when I was testifying on the street. Since what they witnessed was the most unlikely thing that they could imagine happening, it took them some time to recover from the shock.

One lady, who learned about my conversion, held a position with the same company I did. She was one of the socialites of our community, and being a very high-toned person, she seemed far above my humble status as a poor sinner that naturally needed salvation. I was rather surprised a few years later to learn that she had gone to a large department store and charged goods from time to time on the account of a prominent family. The local detectives finally caught up with her, and she was forced to resign her job in disgrace. She was a sinner just the same as I was, and everyone else for that matter. The only difference was that I knew I was a sinner and she didn't. As the Scripture says, "For all have sinned, and come short of the glory of God." (Rom. 3:23) "Therefore if any man be in Christ, he is a new creature: old things are passed away; behold, all things are become new." (II Cor. 5:17)

CHAPTER VIII

Dr. John G. Lake and the Church at Portland

Thus far I have not mentioned the pastor of the church where I was converted. Dr. John G. Lake was a most remarkable person and I must take a moment to describe his extraordinary and unusual ministry that was to have such an effect upon my life. Years before, Dr. Lake had been a missionary to Africa, and his experiences there were not only of the most remarkable nature but made history on that continent.

John G. Lake had been one of those who had lived in Zion during its halcyon days. After its decline and fall, Dr. Lake, who was in the insurance business, continued preaching along with his work.

For a long time he had been eagerly seeking the experience of the Holy Ghost baptism — something quite new to the Church at that time. One afternoon as he went to minister to a lady seriously crippled with arthritis, he received a powerful baptism of the Spirit. When he touched the woman who had the arthritis, the power of God struck her and she was instantly healed. Soon afterward, he was called by the Spirit to go to Africa. Impelled to follow the Apostolic custom of the Early Church, he disposed of a large estate of considerable value. Then without a penny, he made plans to go to Africa.

By various supernatural providences, the way was opened for Dr. Lake to take along a party of some seventeen, including his own wife and family. As the boat neared South Africa, he realized that he would be required to show possession of a certain sum of money, before he would be allowed to disembark. Just before the time came for him to make his presentation to the immigration authorities, a man came over to him and asked him to step out of line. The stranger informed him that he had been peculiarly impressed to give him a certain sum of money. It was gratefully received, and thereupon Dr. Lake was permitted to land with his party in South Africa. Immediately upon disembarking from the ship, he was met by a lady to whom God had spoken, informing her that a missionary with a certain number of children was coming to Africa, and for her to go to meet them. She immediately offered the party her home.

Then began five years of apostolic ministry in South Africa, that must forever rank as an epic in the history of missionary work. Dr. Lake and members of the party knew nothing of the languages of the region, and most of his preaching had to be interpreted. Yet this ministry was manifested by such unusual power, that within a few months the fame thereof spread throughout the land. Signs, wonders, and miracles flowed in such profusion as to utterly confound the skeptic and the unbeliever. Many of the interesting incidents occurring at that time, I was later to have the privilege of hearing as they were related from Dr. Lake's own lips. These remarkable events were corroborated by other witnesses. A detailed account of them would rival the record of the Acts of the apostles. (Some of the Lake story is told in the book, "The John G. Lake Sermons.")

Once a hypnotist attended the meetings. One of his patients, a girl possessed of an evil spirit, came forward for deliverance. She was instantly healed. This resulted in the hypnotist's becoming belligerent, and he began to disturb the services. Dr. Lake, under a mighty anointing, stepped forward and laid his hands upon him, telling him that from that hour he would never be able to hypnotize any one again, but that he would now have to earn an honest living. The man soon found that this was so, and was compelled, shortly after, to go to work in the mines.

The revival spread the length and breadth of South Africa. Hundreds of churches and missions sprang up as a result of this work. There is no record up till that time in modern missionary history, of any work spreading with the force and power of this South African revival. Due to various circumstances, after a period of five years, Dr. Lake decided to return to America, leaving behind him a monument of accomplishment that stands unique in the annals of missionary history.

Upon returning to America, Dr. Lake founded a Divine healing mission in Spokane. Within five years, some 100,000 healings were recorded, and an investigation of Divine healing, which had been instigated by hostile groups, was stopped dead in its tracks, by the overwhelming evidence revealed in the testimonies given at a public hearing. Coming to Portland in 1920, Dr. Lake founded a similar healing mission there. In a short time, he had a work established which included a membership of some 500. His ministry in Portland attracted attention throughout the state, and miracles occurred of such a nature as to draw wide attention. It was at this particular time that I was converted to Christ. Unfortunately for me, one month later, Dr. Lake decided to conduct a healing campaign in San Diego. And so the opportunity to sit under his ministry at that time was gone. However, it was my privilege to hear him preach many times in the years to come.

I have alluded to the fact that when I began attending the Portland Church, I was immediately struck by the fact that a veritable apostolic ministry was being carried on there. I was familiar with the healing of the Methodist lady, who had been prayed for by one of Dr. Lake's preachers. But I was hardly prepared for such an evidence of miracles as was provided by the array of crutches and braces that had been discarded, and had accumulated in one corner of the auditorium. From night to night, I heard the ringing testimonies of those who declared that they had come there as invalids, but had been healed by the power of God. I have also previously mentioned that I was convinced that either something wonderful was taking place here, or else one of the most clever hoaxes of all time was being foisted upon the people.

I soon saw, however, that beyond all shadow of doubt, the miracles were real. Indeed, I saw some of them happen before my own eyes. I believe, however, that the healing of George West, one of the deacons, and the one who baptized me in water, was the miracle that impressed me the most at that time. Brother West, a large man weighing over 250 pounds, was a stevedore who worked on the docks. One day, a heavy object accidentally fell on one of his feet, crushing the bone.

Brother West had the foot X-rayed and the bone set. Hobbling on one foot, with crutches, to church, he displayed the X-ray and then said that he expected to be healed. I thought at the time that this showed a remarkable boldness of faith. But having given such a testimony, I also thought that he had better come back healed! Surely enough, two or three days later he returned to church without his crutches, and with a ringing testimony of how God had perfectly healed him!

CHAPTER IX

The Call to the Ministry

As I have said, upon my conversion I immediately felt the call to preach the gospel. So strong was the feeling, I could scarcely have done anything else. My soul began to pray for a ministry that would reach the multitudes. How it could be done, I did not know. As for myself, I realized that there must be a period of preparation before I could be useful to God. I eagerly read every book that I could lay my hands on, which dealt with the subject of apostolic ministry. I had the privilege of taking the Straight-Way Bible Course conducted in the church, by a Mrs. Salinger. It proved to be of the greatest value to me, in laying a foundation for my future studies.

I realized the importance of prayer, and sometimes I waited all night before the Lord, asking that He might send a visitation of His mighty power. I was to learn, however, that these things for which my soul was praying, were not to come easily. I soon discovered that powerful forces of evil ruled the earth and blinded the hearts of men and women. I was to see how helpless man was, by himself, to combat these powers of darkness. The more I prayed, the more helpless I felt. Yet, as I waited on God, something seemed to give me a feeling that some day, if I were faithful, I would see the things for which my heart longed, come to pass. But first of all, God would show me something of the nature of the powers of evil with which I would have to reckon. It was an exceedingly, distressing experience at the time, but as a result of it, I found myself able to discern between the work of the Holy Spirit and that of false spirits (I Jn. 4:1-3), a knowledge that would prove of inestimable value to me in years to come.

My heart was hungry for a deeper revelation of God's wisdom and power. Sometimes I would give hours, even nights waiting upon the Lord. During this period I was joined by another brother, who often spent considerable time with me in prayer. He was almost a full-blooded Indian and we called him "Indian Bill." Indian Bill seemed quite sincere and it was not until some time later that I learned that he indulged periodically, in heavy potations of strong liquor, at which time he became quite another man. Actually, I believe that he desired to be a real Christian, but when temptation pressed him he would yield to it, thus opening the way for the operation of demon powers.

Being a new convert, I was rather naive in my understanding of spiritual things. At the time, I supposed that most Christians who had the baptism were only a little less than perfect, and altogether I possessed a very inadequate knowledge of the cunning and subtility of Satan.

One night while we were praying, Indian Bill began to hear a voice. The voice claimed to be of God. It then informed him that he had been specially favored of God to receive certain "revelations." Bill was far from an educated person, and the "revelations" certainly indicated that another intelligence than he, was doing the speaking. In fact, most of the subjects discussed were well beyond the ken of my companion's knowledge. Such subjects as heaven and hell were minutely discussed, and the conditions of those places described in detail. I had a novice's fascination for all this and at the time had no doubt but that the communications were of God. Having reached the place at which we had unreserved confidence in the "messages," the voice then began to play on our human ego. Foolish dupes that we were, we were elated over the thought of being the recipients of what seemed to us to be revelations as great as those in the Bible.

After a time, the voice began to speak to us against certain ones in the church who, it warned, would not accept these revelations. We were told that these people were jealous, and that under no circumstances should we give them heed.

Then came the climaxing "revelation." Indian Bill was told that he was "Elijah" returned to earth! (Poor Elijah! How many people in the course of history have supposed that they were Elijah, and have gone to extreme efforts to prove the alleged identity!) Indian Bill was soon convinced that he was Elijah and the voice warned me that I must accept him as God's special prophet. Naive as I was, now for the first time I began to entertain suspicions. When the young man began to publicly declare his office as that prophet, I at last saw that something was decidedly wrong. It might appear to the reader that I should have become suspicious sooner, but it must be remembered that I was just a young convert, and was fair game for the enemy. Nor did I at that time, know about my companion's addiction to alcoholic beverages and his periodic relapses — which made possible the operation of seducing spirits.

Nevertheless, inexperienced as I was, I became convinced that the voice must be a seducing or familiar spirit, and I was shocked to realize that I had been so easily taken in. I then earnestly plead with my companion to seek God for deliverance from the deceiving spirit. In justice to him, I must say that he was willing to listen. We knelt together to pray. But the voice with great urgency warned us that we must not doubt, that all was well, if we did not doubt. Finally it said, "I will prove to you that I am of God." At that very moment a guitar standing in the corner made a sound as if a hand had been drawn over the strings, producing a set of chords! This was repeated several times . . .

However, I was no longer deceived. I realized that actually we were having a demonstration of spiritualism, and that the spirit speaking through Indian Bill was evidently a seducing spirit. I then challenged the voice, declaring it was not God but was in fact a familiar spirit. Immediately there was a surprising result. The devil unmasked, plainly confessed, "Yes, I am the devil. God has permitted me to deceive you because you have committed the unpardonable sin! You are forever lost!"

For several days I was almost ready to believe this, and I went through great anguish of soul. I thought perhaps I had committed the unpardonable sin. However, God came to me with the following Scripture: "Let not your heart be troubled. Believe in God, believe also in me." The Lord then made me to know that He had permitted me to go through this experience for a purpose. That I must not trust every spirit, but I must try the spirits and learn the difference between the true and the false. It was a valuable lesson to me in the years to come, and one that I never forgot.

While this experience was very painful, I look back on it as a salutary one. It is important for us to understand that demons are very real and that they are deceiving many people. Jesus said, "If it were possible, they shall deceive the very elect." (Matt. 24:24)

During the years which were to follow, God actually did speak to us and gave us certain revelations as to the future, that were very precious to me. Many do not realize that God can and does speak to His people, in the same way that He did in Bible days. But it is true. Bible days are here again! The Lord showed us that we were nearing the ending of the age. That in the years to come there would be an outstanding moving of the Spirit, in which all the gifts of the Spirit would come into operation. That signs, wonders, and miracles would be manifest. That there would be large campaigns in which thousands would be healed and delivered by the power of God.

We were also told that Satan would arise and deceive many. That we must therefore be prepared and be able to discern between the power of evil and the power of God, for the enemy's manifestations would become increasingly evident as the age drew to a close. But, nevertheless, when the enemy would come in like a flood, the Spirit of the Lord would raise up a standard against him.

I rejoice to say that during the past fifteen years, we have seen many of these things that the Lord declared would happen, come to pass. We have seen the great outpourings of the Spirit. We have witnessed the mass revival. There has also been the moving of Satan, even as chaff among the wheat. All these things have happened even as they were told to us.

Nevertheless, if I may be pardoned for anticipating, we have not yet seen all that the Lord has said would come to pass. The Church, right now, is going through the purifying. God's people must learn that with the gifts of the Spirit there must also be manifest, the fruits of the Spirit.

I shall not speak further on these matters at this time, but they will be related in due course. Suffice it to say that God did show us these things. He did speak to us and tell us in actual words concerning what would come to pass, and they have happened as He said. Now to return to our story.

During the year following my conversion, two remarkable evangelistic campaigns were held in the City of Portland. One of these was the Billy Sunday meetings. There is no doubt but that this man did a great deal of good. He was an orator with a down-to-earth manner of dealing with the common man. His language was full of Americanisms which at times assumed a rugged and almost flippant style, and no doubt offended some. Nevertheless, he preached the gospel message, fearlessly, as he saw it. To such institutions as the vested liquor interests, he showed no quarter, and asked for none. He perhaps represented the ultimate in influencing the masses through sheer oratory, and the use of pungent and expressive language delivered in a rapid-fire manner. Thousands of people responded to his invitations to accept Christ. I feel it safe to say that multitudes date their conversion to his ministry.

Shortly after this campaign, while the large tabernacle in which Billy Sunday held his campaign, was still standing, arrangements were made to bring the noted evangelist, Charles S. Price, to town.

Saved from rank modernism, Dr. Price was converted and received the baptism of the Holy Spirit, as a result of Aimee Semple McPherson's ministry. He had held a series of healing revivals in Canada, and had filled vast auditoriums seating up to ten and twelve thousand people.

We looked forward, eagerly, to his coming to the City of Portland. Violent opposition, however, was being stirred up against him, in the denominational circles. Because of the strong opposition, the municipal fire department that had considered the structure quite safe for the Billy Sunday meetings, now said it was a fire-trap and condemned it for use in public meetings. The pressure became so intense that Dr. Price, after holding a couple of weeks' meetings, was forced to terminate his campaign in the city. This was a great disappointment to us, but it gave us an example of the power of ecclesiasticism to obstruct the preaching of the gospel.

The time was drawing near when I felt that God would have me to begin my active ministry. I was far from having the proper training for this work, but the fire burned within me as it did in the bones of Jeremiah. My biggest problem at the moment was the fact that my parents needed my help in making payments on their new property in Portland. I keenly felt this responsibility, for the Scriptures clearly teach that children should assume some financial responsibility to their parents.

So I made it a matter of daily prayer, that in leaving my job to preach the gospel, this problem involving my parents would be taken care of. After praying much, one day I felt that the way had become clear. I did not know how God was going to work it out, but I was sure that He would. So it was that same week that I served notice on my employer that I would be terminating my employment, the news came to my parents that the people who were buying our old property in Beaverton, had received money from an unexpected source, and therefore were paying off the mortgage at once! Thus did God solve the problem.

But who would go with me? Suddenly, God spoke to not one, but two young men. One was Leon Hall, who was to be my future brother-in-law. The other was Tom Welch, who had been converted shortly before me. The story of his conversion is one of the strangest I have ever known.

Tom had been an orphan. He was brought up under infidel influences. The works of Tom Paine and Bob Ingersol were made available to him, and more or less became his philosophy of life.

But I shall let him tell his own story, of his strange experience and marvelous conversion:

* * * *

When I was 18 years old, I left Canada and came down to this country. I went to work out from Portland at the Bridal Veil Timber Company. I had been to a number of gospel services in Portland before I went out there, but it seemed as if I just couldn't believe, though I enjoyed hearing the man's message. And on the first day of this particular job, I was working on a trestle that was 55 feet above the ground. I missed my footing someway, and fell over backward. The trestle was a structure that had never been trimmed up, and beams were sticking out of it four or six feet long all the way down the side of it. As I tumbled off one to another, it just smashed my body to pieces. The first place to strike was on my head. It broke my skull wide open. The scar from that wound can still be felt by the hand. All of these ribs on one side were broken. The marks are still there. One of the ribs was torn loose in my back and punctured my lung. My jawbone was broken. So was my right shoulder blade. It was a bad shape to be in.

I am sticking to the details because what I am telling you is just the way that it happened back there in 1924. They all stand out vividly in my memory as well as in the minds of many others who witnessed the accident. Down under the bridge, there was a pool of dirty water about four feet deep. This pool had been damned up.

I lay in that water from twenty to thirty minutes. Some men were able finally, to fish me out of it. There was no water in my lungs, which proved, the doctors said, that I had not breathed during the period of time that I lay in that water. I had departed from this world!

The first thing that I observed when I departed from this scene of action was a great burning lake, a rolling turbulent, flaming mass. It appeared to be what the Bible says it is — a lake of fire and brimstone. There was nobody in it yet. I wasn't in it. I saw people whom I had known years before when I was a little fellow — people who had died, and died in sin.

They were looking at the same place, although they were not in it yet. Then I prayed — it was the first prayer that ever went up from my heart. I said, "Oh, if I had only known about this, I would have made preparation."

I looked around for some way to get out. But there was no way. I was about to give up in terrible despair, when I saw Something. It was Christ standing in the distance! Away on the horizon

I saw Him. Hope sprang up in my heart. Somehow, I knew that if I could get His attention for a moment, then everything would be different. But it appeared at first that He wasn't going to look. He went on by. And then just before He went out of sight, He turned around and looked. And when He did, that is when I came back into this body. His look was enough! There are those today who are doing everything they can to discredit the Word of God and its solemn warnings. But I am here today to tell you that they are true.

Before I was able to open my eyes at all, I could recognize the voices of people about me. I recognized the voice of a lady, Mrs. Brocke, whom I had known much of my life. She was like a mother to me. She was praying, I could hear her calling upon God, to not let me go out of this world in the condition I was in. Thank God for people who know how to pray! They told me afterward that she had her hand upon my head, while the blood was oozing out between her fingers. She refused to believe that I was going to die unsaved.

GOD DEALS WITH ME

They took me to the Good Samaritan Hospital in Portland. It was about 1:30 when I fell, and they got me into the hospital just before six o'clock. An ambulance took me into town; the doctor did what he could. They put me on a cot. A nurse was left with me while they waited for me to die. But I had already been dead. I knew that I wasn't going to die. They brought me in on Monday evening and I lay there till Friday morning. In those four days I talked with God. He helped me by sending the Spirit of God which led me out of the darkness that I was in. As I lay there and meditated, I remembered the things that I had heard that precious man of God preach. Among other things, I remember a great text he used, "Whatever ye ask in my name, ye shall receive." Faith came into my heart. At about eleven o'clock that morning, I had reached a conclusion. God had talked with me. He asked me if I would preach. This was a hard thing. The thought of preaching before a large crowd frightened me. I hardly realized what I was promising God, but I said, "Yes." And I meant what I said. I have kept my promise.

But I added, "Lord, I can't do it lying here." By this time I was almost completely stiff, wrapped up in all sorts of bandages. The nurse was there, reading to me trying to cheer me up. I said to the nurse, "Will you put a screen in front of the door and leave me alone for a little while?" She very graciously did, having no inkling of what was about to take place. When I was alone, the Presence of the Lord came down, and I talked to God just like I'm talking to you this day. I reached up and threw the blankets off, knowing that if God didn't do something, I couldn't put them back, but I did it anyway.

When I did, the mighty lightnings of God hit that place where I lay. Brother, it went down through me like a flash from on High, and right down to my feet. And before that nurse could get back, I was up and had my clothes on — and was out of the room and down three flights of stairs and out of the hospital. This thing wasn't done in a corner. There are hundreds of people that know the facts of what had happened — and know it to be the truth.

That was on Friday when God healed me. On Saturday, I went back to the mill and was on the job again. The next day I went to the schoolhouse where they had services, and told the story of what God had done for me.

*   *   *   *

This is the true story of one of the two young men who went with me when I started to preach. The other was Leon Hall, who I said, was to be my future brother-in-law, and who would marry my sister, Gladys. We shall hear more about him as we proceed further in the story.

CHAPTER X
We Go to El Cajon

The decision had been made that we go to California. Dr. Lake was in San Diego, establishing a mission there. Perhaps he could help us to get started.

Our only means of transportation was an old, dilapidated Chevrolet. The lowliest Bible School student today, would have disdained to be seen riding in it. It needed a lot of repair, but Tom was a mechanic by trade. In a few days, under his supervision, we had put the car in fair running condition, although the truth was that most every part of it was about worn out.

We attended to final preparations, gathered together our meager possessions, loaded them on the ancient vehicle, and then one crisp, January night, we prepared to set forth on our odyssey. Grandfather Munn came over that evening to bid us goodbye. He was a good man and loved God. Years before, he had been led to give his heart to Christ in the D. L. Moody meetings. We did not know it at the time, but he had only months to live. I never saw him again after that night.

Mother had a light meal prepared for us. After it was over, we all knelt down, and father prayed that God's blessing would be upon us on our journey, and give us good success. We got into the car which was loaded to the hilt, said our final goodbyes, and prepared to leave. As we turned the corner, I got a final glimpse of the family's waving at us.

At last, we were on our own — three teen-age boys, not out to seek our fortune in the world, as did the legendary heroes of Horatio Alger, but to find an open door somewhere, where we could begin preaching the gospel. We knew there was no one waiting for us nor expecting us. We were just three boys, all as green and inexperienced as could be. It would be difficult to find any aspirants to the ministry, more unprepared from the natural standpoint, than we were. There was only one thing in our favor. A flaming fire burned within us to win others to Christ, and to proclaim the message of the gospel to a dying world. Somehow, we were sure God would open doors to us. A feeling of exaltation and rapture swept over us that night. How little we knew at the moment the number of trials and tribulations we would go through, before we could feel that we were really reaching our goal.

On through the night we drove, ever southward toward California. Morning found us in Central Oregon but still we drove on, stopping only for gas and to make minor repairs on the car. The lengthening shadows of early twilight found us in the extreme southern part of Oregon. Here we were to meet our first adventure, the nature of which we had not anticipated. Six miles out of Medford, we developed motor trouble. The distributor gear had sheared off, and there was no possibility that we could travel further, without going into town and procuring a replacement.

It was arranged that I was to stay with the car and guard its contents, while Leon and Tom would go into Medford and secure the needed part. This necessitated their hitching a ride into the city. A passing car slowed down to pick them up, then apparently as an afterthought, the driver changed his mind and instead speeded up. The boys thought nothing of it. They flagged down another car and went on into town.

A couple of hours later they were back, and were in the midst of repairing the distributor, when suddenly we found ourselves surrounded by police officers. I was still in the back seat trying to get some sleep, as I had done much of the driving and we had driven steadily for almost 24 hours. I was startled to hear the officers exchanging words. "Yes, these fellows answer the description." And that is how we found ourselves under arrest as armed highwaymen! One of the officers began to interrogate us while others started searching the car. There seemed no doubt in their minds that they had picked up some criminals.

My heart sank! Here we were only one day out and already under arrest! We soon gathered that Leon's and Tom's signal to hitch a ride into town had been mistaken for an attempt of highway robbery. In their fright, the people imagined the metal parts the boys held in their hands were guns and they fled to notify the Medford police department, doubtlessly embellishing their story with such additions that terror usually conjures. The officers had conjectured that this attempted "holdup" might be the work of scoundrels, who had been operating recently in that vicinity. The area had been marked by some very daring robberies. Some time before, one of the most notorious train robberies in history had taken place at the nearby Siskiyou Tunnel. Three men, the De Autremant brothers, had been responsible for that terrible crime which involved dynamiting a train, and the death of several of the crew members. And there were three of us!

For the moment it looked as if we would tarry in the public jail, until we could prove our identity and clear ourselves. How unflattering this would be to us when the news got back to Portland, that we had been detained as suspects in an attempted armed robbery. The police had a lot of questions for us to answer. I will relate them as nearly as I can remember.

"Where are you from?" an officer demanded suspiciously.

"We are from Portland."

"Are you not that criminal gang that has been operating in this vicinity?"

"No sir. Indeed we are not sir."

"Do you know that you have been charged by certain people that you attempted to hold them up just a little over an hour ago?"

"Well, they are quite mistaken. We were trying to get a ride into town to buy a part for the car," one of the boys explained.

"Hmpp. What is your business?" the officer asked quite unconvinced.

"Well sir, we are preachers."

The officers' eyes widened as they looked at each other significantly. A likely story, indeed! Three teen-age boys accused of a hold-up, claiming to be preachers. Well now they had heard everything!

"All right," he said, "where have you been preaching? Remember anything you say can be held against you."

"Oh we haven't preached anywhere yet. We are just starting out."

The utter incredulity of the officers was apparent. It looked more and more as if we were going to spend the night in the lock-up. But deliverance was nearer at hand than we thought. Other officers had been searching the car and now they came upon boxes of song books, religious literature, and Bibles, instead of guns and weapons they had expected to find. It seemed that our fantastic and incredible story was true after all.

Suddenly, it occurred to the officers that they might be the ones to look foolish, arresting a trio of young preachers. For though we might seem a rather poor representation of the ministry, they suspected that they would add nothing to their credit, by taking us into custody and locking us up. After mumbling something to watch ourselves in the future and keep out of trouble, they unceremoniously made their departure. In a few moments we had the car running, and we passed through Medford without stopping, not having any particular desire to tarry in the vicinity, lest the police change their minds. Within an hour or so our crestfallen spirits rose, and soon we fancied we had handled the situation in a creditable manner. We did not immediately report the details in our letters home, however, lest the situation might be misunderstood and it be supposed that we did not know how to keep out of trouble.

Since we were anxious to reach our destination as soon as possible, and also as a not unimportant consideration that we did not have money to spare for hotels, we travelled day and night except for such occasions as necessity compelled us to halt to make repairs on the car. For the ancient automobile strained under the wear and tear of our cross-country tour and was constantly breaking down. The radiator boiled, the clutch slipped, tires went flat, but all these minor troubles were mere harbingers of what lay ahead.

As we approached Sacramento, a connecting rod bearing went out, a trouble unmistakably identified by a banging in the engine which could be heard most of a mile away. By all rules, a motor should be stopped at once when this happens. But alas, we knew we could not repair such a serious trouble on the highway. Leon's relatives, where we planned to stop, were still two hundred miles away. In a desperate gamble, we decided to keep on moving, in hope that we could reach the home of the relatives.

As we entered Sacramento, it was just getting dark. The vibrations caused by the pounding on the crankshaft loosened the other bearings, one by one. The din set up by a motor taking such terrific punishment, heralded our approach far in advance. Consequently, people came out of the shops and stores, and lined both sides of of the streets to view this strange vehicle that sounded like a battery of threshing machines, all going at the same time!

A few jeered us, but for the most part people were frozen into silence as they viewed this one-car parade as it made its slow but steady progress down the main street of their community. We knew we were breaking every anti-noise ordinance the city had, yet no man laid a hand upon us. Probably, they were thankful to see us moving on. Our sidewalk audience watched us as long as it could see us, and no doubt was able to follow us by ear for some time after that.

Leaving Sacramento, we thundered on through the night. Whenever we reached the smallest habitation, we never lacked an audience. However, we had no time to be embarrassed. Our only thought was how could the motor continue running without breaking a crankshaft, or throwing a piston loose in the block?

We marked off the miles one by one, till at last as the first streaks of dawn crossed the eastern sky, we rolled into the front yard of Leon's relatives. Needless to say, we didn't have to ring the bell to announce our arrival. I can only wonder what thoughts these people must have had as they heard that awful clattering coming nearer and nearer until at last it stopped in their own front yard!

But the Hayes family, for that was their name, were wonderful people. They treated us royally, affording us every facility they had for repairing the car, feeding us and taking care of us in general.

About five days later, after replacing parts from the bottom up, we finally had the car running again.

We stopped a day at my sister, Fern's, at Terra Bella who gave us the kindest reception. However, we must have been a puzzle to my brother-in-law, Lawrence Purnel. That three young teen-agers would start out preaching, had never been heard of before in that country.

Nevertheless, he extended us every courtesy, and even filled up our gas tank as we got ready to leave. Years later, I had the great joy of leading him to Christ.

Another day brought us to San Diego, California. As we drew near the city, the car suffered numerous breakdowns. We did makeshift repairs and barely made it into the town. It was late at night, and we rented a room and soon fell into deep sleep. The following day we visited our only friend in that part of the world, Dr. John G. Lake. He was very kind to us. We heard him preach in several services and our faith rose to great heights.

It is fortunate that we went to Dr. Lake. He was probably the only minister in the world at that time who was willing to put confidence in a trio of utterly untried, young preachers. He had a tent that he had been using in the mild, San Diego winter — it happened to be February. Now he was going into an auditorium. Would we like to use the tent? Would we? Well, that was one time we didn't have to think about the answer. We gave our assent in a united chorus. And so it was that we made plans to begin meetings in a little nearby city called El Cajon.

CHAPTER XI

Three Young Preachers Try Their Wings

With great industry, we set to work to pitch the tent and get things in order for our meetings. We announced the date of our first service and had handbills printed which we scattered over the community. Evening time found us waiting hopefully for the crowd to come. By eight o'clock we had a modest attendance. One of us led the song service, another made announcements and a third preached the sermon. We did passably well, so at least the people told us. Alternating thus from night to night, our campaign got under way.

Our first adult convert was a man by the name of Keaton. He was proprietor of a garage and did mechanical work. The night he got saved was a service of great rejoicing. After a while we had our man get up and testify. He announced with boldness that he intended to become a great Christian. He little realized the problems that his own unstable nature would occasion. Keaton lived only a few years after that. But I believe that he professed the faith until the end, although not without going through some great, emotional crises.

I said that Keaton was our first adult convert. This did not take into account a number of teen-agers who came forward before many days had passed. By a curious coincidence, most of these were girls. One night just before services began, the whole side of the tent suddenly began to shake as if an earthquake had struck. We rushed outside to see what had happened. A man driving up in a Ford, had lost control of it. In his excitement he had slammed his foot down on the low gear pedal. Consequently, he kept on going until he was stopped by the tent stakes. The car had knocked down one of our young converts. By some amazing miracle, she had been thrown to the side, her arm falling into a rut, so when the car passed over, the depth of the rut protected her arm from injury!

This girl, the daughter of the local postmaster, had an older sister. Some months later, one of the boys started going with her.

This so roused the ire of the postmaster that he threatened him with a shotgun, if he went out with her again. For a time, I noticed that he left the getting of his mail to the other two members of the party.

This brings up a problem. Evangelists have a right, like anyone else, to choose a companion and get married. Experience shows that in many cases they are better off if they have a good wife, than if they continue single. Yet a young man must exercise the greatest of caution in this matter. An unmarried evangelist is considered especially eligible. But because of the number of his opportunities, he is a poor risk during courtship, and likely as not, is apt to break the heart of some young maiden because of his fickleness. In so doing, he vexes the pastor who hopefully assumes that his evangelist will benefit his church and not add to his problems. An evangelist wisely postpones his courting to periods between campaigns. If he is prudent, he will refrain from promising his hand in marriage until he is reasonably sure he has made the right choice, and better yet, until he has had opportunity to establish his ministry.

During our stay in El Cajon, we soon learned that the preaching of the gospel, especially by young preachers just starting out, is not the most profitable occupation as far as finances are concerned. People brought us in groceries, and enough money came in by the collection plate to provide for our meals and pay rent, but there was not much, if anything, over.

Our automobile, as we have previously noted, was in a complete state of immobilization. It was useless to think of buying parts and repairing it further. There was just too much that had gone wrong. However, we learned that a neighbor had an engine of the same make, in fairly good condition. We thought that between the two, we could possibly assemble one. But, since we did not have the cash necessary to pay the sum being asked, we agreed to dig a well for the man, as payment.

We did not realize what we were getting in for. After we had dug soft earth for about four feet, we reached hard-pan. It was like rock, and we soon found that our pick and shovel made little progress. Fortunately, Tom was acquainted with the use of dynamite, and by means of a few dollars' worth of the explosive, we made rapid progress.

To bring the loosened earth up, we borrowed a windlass, by which we could haul up seventy or eighty pounds of earth at a time. We alternated at the task. One of us would go below and shovel the earth into a bucket, while the other would haul it up by winding the wildlass, dumping the contents, and then returning the bucket.

All went well for a while. But just before we had completed the digging, we came very nearly having a tragedy. It was my turn at the top of the well and Tom's at the bottom. I was bringing up a load and had gotten it nearly to the top.Just as I went to reach for the bucket, it happened! The windlass suddenly gave way on its shaft, and the great weight of the earth caused it to revolve rapidly, carrying the load of earth straight for Tom's head. There was no time nor way to escape. But then the unbelievable happened! Suddenly, that bucket of earth stopped in mid-air, a matter of inches from my friend's head!

We were never able to explain what really took place, except that each day we had asked God to be with us and to protect us from harm. The Psalmist says of the believer, "There shall no evil befall thee, neither shall any plague come nigh thy dwelling. For he shall give his angels charge over thee, to keep thee in all thy ways. They shall bear thee up in their hands, lest thou dash thy foot against a stone." (Psa. 91:10-12)

We were to have many more such experiences in the course of the years. I have found that God's promises of divine protection are to be relied upon, if only we put our complete trust in Him.

We repaired the windlass, and had no further trouble with it. We soon finished our digging activities and were free to give our time to rebuilding the car. One afternoon a man, whom we knew slightly and not favorably, stopped by to watch us work. He was a man given to arguing religion, and in fact, took the opposite view of everything for which we stood. I remember that he especially resented the doctrine of hell, something he did not believe in at all. It was all a delusion he said. His religion consisted more or less of a parcel of notions. As far as we knew, he did not go to church anywhere. Yet, he had much to say. He especially loved to disprove the Bible, bringing up old arguments about the Scriptures being full of mistakes, etc. We wearied of him, but every so often he would drop around and argue some more.

On this particular occasion, the story of Jonah was mentioned. Did we believe such a ridiculous yarn? Yes, we allowed we did. Well, then what he wanted to know was how Jonah could have lived three days in the belly of the fish and come out alive?

I told him that I didn't know exactly how it all happened. I knew that God could perform any miracle that was necessary to accomplish His purpose. I said that when I got to heaven, I would ask Jonah to explain the mysteries about it. The skeptic fell into the trap. "But," he protested, "suppose Jonah didn't go to heaven?" I now saw that the Lord had delivered him into our hands. "Then you can ask him," I said, and pointed down! There was a baffled look on his face. He muttered something, turned on his heel, and strode away. I do not recall that he ever bothered us again.

Our days in El Cajon were drawing to a close. Soon, we would have to give up the property, on which we had pitched the tent. The people had been very kind to permit us to use it all those months. But then something happened that almost terminated my ministry before it was well started. I was stricken down with an almost fatal case of ptomaine poisoning.

We were never quite certain what brought about the attack, but it undoubtedly resulted from something that I had eaten. My friends had gone somewhere for the day. It was about noon when severe pains began to seize me, and I lay down, thinking that presently I would be better.

This I shouldn't have done. For, had I taken dominion over the thing at once in the Name of the Lord, no doubt I would have secured relief. Instead, in a very short time, agonizing cramps began to strike me at brief intervals, which left me without breath or strength to pray. I believe right there I made a mistake that many Christians make. Instead of rebuking the enemy when he appears with the first symptom, people yield to the thing, and before they realize it, Satan has secured a foothold.

When my brethren returned, they saw that I was in a bad way. They prayed for me and others prayed, but at that time I received no visible deliverance, and rather, the cramps apparently increased. I have no desire to exaggerate, but the suffering seemed as intense as it is possible for a human being to experience. Everyone knows how painful a brief cramp can be, but these attacks were not for a moment, nor an hour, nor a day, but were to continue at intervals of a few moments, over a period of two weeks.

Naturally, my brethren became somewhat disturbed over the fact that my condition did not improve. Some kind neighbors who attended our meeting, volunteered to take me into their home. But in spite of the best possible care, I showed no improvement and steadily grew worse. Of course I could eat nothing; the very thought of food increased my nausea. After a few days when they saw no sign of improvement, these good folk became alarmed and insisted that a physician be called. I thank the Lord for physician friends, but I must testify that as God has revealed Himself as my Great Physician, I have always felt that I must lean upon Him alone. Besides, had we not been preaching to the people that Christ could heal, and now if I could not show these folk that I trusted the Lord for myself, would not that part of our preaching have been in vain?

The family with whom I stayed, was in a dilemma. They knew little of Divine healing except what we had preached. All evidence seemed to show that I was getting worse rapidly, and that unless something were done, I would die on their hands. In such event, they reasoned, perhaps correctly, that they would be in trouble with the health authorities. To them, there seemed no alternative. Either a physician must be called, or they dare not keep me in their home.

Fortunately, Dr. John G. Lake, who at that time was in San Diego, sent word for me to be brought to his home. I shall ever be grateful for his kindness and hospitality. The ride of sixteen miles, to San Diego was agonizing, although the driver was as careful as possible. Dr. Lake, who had prayed for tens of thousands, and had seen multitudes delivered, prayed for me each evening. Nevertheless, it seemed that nothing could stay the progress of the affliction, which now had reduced me to a condition of extreme helplessness. In my mind, though I hated to think of it, came the recurring thought that death was approaching.

Gradually, weakening in body and wracked with constant pain, I resigned myself to death. Yet, I pondered the reason for all that had happened to me. Why should I be cut off at the very beginning of my ministry? Why, in a few hours of time, must a telegram be sent to my mother with the words, "Your son passed away at such and such an hour"? I thought of the grief that would come to her. I had wanted to preach the gospel of good tidings more than anything else in the world. Now it appeared that my ministry would end with abruptness. Was this the Will of God?

But God was to show Himself. First, through His Word. Sister Lake had been kind enough to give me some typed sermons by her husband, on the subject of healing. As I read those messages, my attention was taken from my suffering to the power of the Risen Christ. Even as I read, I began to feel the moving of faith in my soul. Certain Scriptures came to me with force and vividness. The words quoted by Peter in Acts 10:38, concerning Jesus, "Who went about doing good, and healing all that were oppressed of the devil," left a deep impression upon me. Again in Luke 13, Jesus, in healing the woman bowed over, showed that the infirmity was caused directly by the binding power of Satan. It dawned upon me that it was not the Will of God that I should die, but rather the will of the devil. It was he who would be pleased if he could end my ministry before my time.

Another Scripture came especially to my attention. It was Mark 11:22-24, and is yet today my favorite passage. The words, "What things soever ye desire, when ye pray, believe that ye receive them, and ye shall have them,".fascinated me. A light was dawning, and I began to understand the difference between passive and active faith. Here was a direct warrant for my immediate healing if I would dare to accept it.

I could wait no longer. An emergency bell was beside my bed and I gave it a ring. A nurse in the household came, and inquired of me what I wanted. I replied rather unceremoniously that I wanted my clothes, so that I could get up. I do not remember her answer except that she hesitated, perhaps not knowing whether I was in my right mind. But faith had fired my soul and I was insistent. "Come," I said, "you have been praying for my healing. Believe your own prayers and bring my clothes." Not knowing what further to answer, the lady decided to humor me and my clothes were brought. How I got into them I do not know, for I was very weak, and though the cramps had lessened, they had not ceased. But my thoughts now were not on my pains, but upon the living reality of the promise of God. I knew I was healed!

There were some things God showed me in my healing that I have never forgotten. If God could heal me after I was so close to death, how much more could He deliver me and protect me from sickness? It was plain to me that God desired to fulfill His promise by keeping me free from sickness. And so, during the past many years, I and my family have proven that the Lord is not only Healer of our diseases, but that He can keep the plague from our dwelling. He has not failed us, and we can fully recommend Christ as the Healer to every home.

I had lost twenty-five pounds, and my clothes hung upon me grotesquely, but I gave no heed to this. As my feet touched the floor, I began to praise the Lord for healing. At that instant my cramps vanished. And for the first time in many days, I felt the sensation of hunger. I sat down to a hearty meal to the astonishment of everybody except the Lake family, who was used to seeing miracles take place.

Summing up, I had learned two great lessons:

1. Faith is an act. After prayer is made for healing, there is a time to act upon the Word of God. Deliverance came to me at the moment that I acted upon the Word of God.

2. Though it is wonderful to be healed, it is better to be delivered from sickness before it overtakes us. The Word of God clearly teaches that Divine health rather than Divine healing is God's plan for the believer. (Exodus 15:26)

CHAPTER XII

Frank Burns the Broom Man

After my sickness and recovery, our lease on the property ran out and we had to take the tent down. By a strange coincidence just at that time, the evangelist who had so impressed me years before, Dave Hill, came to town and set up his tent at the very time we were taking ours down. We were glad to turn our converts over to him, and when we left El Cajon, he carried on.

On the whole, we felt we had achieved some success from our labors. We had won a number of souls although we realized how inexperienced we were. I decided with the others to return to Portland. I wanted to give myself to more prayer and study of the Word. I read every book on which I could get my hands, that told the story of the great soul-winners of the past. I realized from reading about their lives, how much prayer played a part in their ministry. Many a night I spent in prayer and waiting before God. At the same time, I took such opportunities as were open to me to preach the gospel.

To young men who are looking for an opportunity and who complain there is no opening for them, permit me to say this: Go where the poor and the under-privileged are. They will be glad to hear you. When you have learned to bless them, others will be calling for your services. Don't wait for opportunity to come walking up to you. Go to meet it.

I received an opportunity to preach in an old schoolhouse, in Portland. The invitation was given by Rev. Clara Brooks who later became the famous "Cousin Clara," that wrote many years for Sunday School literature.

During the meetings, a lady was saved and healed of cancer. She was a great one to testify of her healing. Her testimony to others opened the way for me to hold a campaign in her city. Among the converts resulting from my ministry in that town, was a family that included several children. One of the boys later married my sister, Ruth. I am very proud of my four sisters, who are all good Christians. I have already mentioned Gladys and Fern. Helen Lahodny and Ruth Eckhardt, with their families, have lived many years in the vicinity of San Jose, California.

Perhaps everyone in his lifetime can recall some mystery that can't be completely explained. This lady who was healed of cancer, was as sincere a woman as I ever met. As long as I knew her, she was busy witnessing and winning souls to Christ.

One day she asked me to come and see her. She had something important that she wanted to tell me. Her husband was also present at the time. He too had been greatly impressed by the miracle of her healing, and wherever he went, he testified to what God had done for his wife. Now this is what the woman told me. She said that her father owned a large number of valuable mines in Pennsylvania. In fact, he was fabulously wealthy, a multi-millionaire who owned millions of dollars of property in addition. But he was a miser. The greed of gold so controlled him that he would spend little on himself or anyone else. She had been rather independent and had not asked him for much. As the lady told her story, her husband who was an intelligent man, fully agreed with all that she was saying, indicating that he was familiar with all the facts about his wife's father and his great wealth.

The woman continued by saying that now that she knew Christ as her Saviour and Healer she was interested in really doing something for the cause that had saved her life, when she was in the last stages of cancer. Her father was now very old, and soon she, the only child, would fall heir to all his wealth. How could we use this money for the promotion of God's work?

Could this all be true? Or were both the man and wife under hallucinations? They wanted to know if I would make a trip with them back East, to visit her father and see the great properties he owned. I decided against making the trip, figuring that there would be ample time for consideration of the matter, after she actually had come into the inheritance. Four or five years went by and I saw her and her husband from time to time. They still talked about the matter. Then suddenly the woman died. And that brings this story to an end. The question I have always wondered about is this: Were two intelligent people who claimed to know as fact that the woman's father was worth many millions of dollars, and who also owned a great system of coal mines, under a complete delusion? There was no reason for a planned deception. It is one of those mysteries which has always made me wonder.

Going back to my story, with the coming of Spring, I determined to go out into the evangelistic work again.

I was still quite young and mother felt that because of my extreme youth and inexperience, I should work with an older man. This is generally sound advice. A young man will profit much if he can work for a time with a seasoned minister, whether in a pastorate or the evangelistic field. He may learn to avoid some of the pitfalls that lurk before the unwary and the novice.

In those days, however, there were comparatively few Pentecostal churches. In fact, such as there were, existed in the main cities and larger towns and many of these churches were small and weak. Itinerant evangelists came and went. Some of these pioneer preachers pursued their calling at great sacrifice. Not a few lived from hand-to-mouth, but they were the men responsible for the building of this movement. They often preached in vacant store buildings, schoolhouses, and even on the street. These faithful ministers will surely reap a great reward for their valiant and sacrificial efforts.

Unfortunately, some of these roving evangelists were unstable and erratic in their conduct. No doubt they meant well, but their roots were not deep enough. They had a call to preach, and felt that they must obey it. Financial difficulties continually beset them, and as a result when the pressure became strong enough, they sometimes would leave debts or engage in unethical practices. Worse yet, a few of them had a weak moral fiber, and sometimes succumbed to temptation that brought reproach upon the ministry. Nevertheless, this is not something to be unexpected. Human nature being what it is, there have always been those who started the race, ran well for awhile, and then faltered under temptation.

Perhaps the above will serve as an introduction to the man, whom I shall call Frank Burns. For obvious reasons I have not used his real name. He was an evangelist and at the same time a travelling salesman. Coming into the City of Portland about the time that I had planned to set out on my second evangelistic tour, he impressed my mother with his personableness. He was of a buoyant nature, an extrovert, and a fairly good speaker. Because of the precariousness of his evangelistic earnings, he added to his income by following the role of a broom salesman. This might seem to be a rather doubtful way to make a living, but actually he did quite well at it. Besides, he could get the supply of brooms without advancing money.

My mother, in talking with him, happened to mention that I was planning on leaving soon for the South. When he heard that I owned a car, he immediately became interested. Why could we not go together? He assured mother he was a man of much experience as an evangelist, and would take me under his wing and show me how to avoid the pitfalls. He was smooth, suave, and convincing. He had a hearty laugh and an easy manner, but I was later to learn that he had a very serious weakness. Yet, I can say he proved to be at least a very cheerful companion.

Upon being introduced to Frank, I learned why he was anxious to join up with me. He led me to the garage where his car had been impounded. The first thing that I observed was that it was loaded to the hilt — with a supply of brooms.

As I surveyed the car, I saw that there was good reason for which he needed to change means of transportation. That his car had reached the end of the line, there was no doubt. For one thing, its whole body listed like a sinking ship. Several of the springs were broken, indicating that the driver was a man not given to undue caution. In those days, roads were poor compared to the magnificent highways that now cross the nation. Burns was always in a hurry. It was plain to see that his encounters with the rough roads had produced some rather unfortunate results. I had seen cars before, on which one spring was broken, but never had I seen any in the shape that this one was in. Beside that, three of the tires were flat. They were worn through to the carcass, and the wonder was that they had held up this long to all go out together. I learned also that as poor as the exterior appeared, the engine was in even a worse condition, having reached the place where further repairs would be useless. Altogether, it appeared to me something like the traditional one-horse shay that went to pieces "all at once."

Burns seemed to take for granted that I would accept his offer to travel with him. I was not sure that it was the Lord speaking, but like many a young minister who is not certain where to go, or how to get a start, I looked upon any opportunity as a door the Lord had opened. I will not say that in going with Burns I got out of the will of God — perhaps I should say that I was in His permissive will. Certainly, I learned some things that were of great value to me later on. Sometimes, God overrules even our faulty judgment. Moreover, the only way to get experience is to do something. I possessed almost no training for the ministry and had little to offer a congregation. Nevertheless, I did have a burden for souls, and thank God that He rewarded my efforts, amateurish as they were, with not a few precious souls.

So it was settled that Burns and I, together left for Houston, Texas. He had a call from that city, to get there as soon as he could. My former pastor, Dr. John G. Lake, had left San Diego and had gone to Texas to establish a new church in Houston. He was, however, at that moment in California, having been called away because of a serious accident that his son had. He needed someone to take his place in Houston.

So on a fine May morning, we started on our way. We travelled for an hour or so, until we were well out of the city. I was now to receive a practical course in salesmanship. Burns had a special system of his own, and it was an education to watch him put his special talents into operation. He had an unerring instinct to know just what place to stop and display his wares. And make sales he must, because while I had a rather modest sum of cash with me, I learned that he was flat broke. I was soon to discover that no matter how many brooms he sold, he never seemed to have any money in his pocket. As I look back on it now, I can understand that as a result of his free and easy ways, Burns probably had a small army of creditors breathing down his neck.

His practical eye would size up the places of business as we passed them along. They must not be too classy in appearance. Proprietors of such places were apt to be sophisticated and would look upon peddlers as a nuisance. Nor must the business appear too shabby, lest it be an institution approaching bankruptcy, in which case the owner would not likely be interested in purchasing one of his brooms.

Burns cautioned me to let him do the talking, which I was quite willing to do. I understood nothing about the art of salesmanship, and would not have known how to begin. Nonetheless, I carefully observed the technique of my companion. It rarely varied from a formula that he had perfected.

Having chosen a likely place to stop, perhaps a filling station, or a restaurant, he would walk briskly into the establishment with a confident air and an ingratiating smile. He would not immediately address the proprietor, preferring to wait for a brief moment. Instead he would take the broom, screw the handle into the socket and precede to sweep up a portion of the floor. As soon as he had gotten the man's full attention, he would look up and turning on all his charm, begin to engage him in conversation.

"Mister, this surely is a fine broom. Nothing like it being offered on the regular market. The quality of this product is nowhere equalled. And the price? Well, here is the chance to get the finest, at less than the cost of inferior brands. And for wear it will practically last indefinitely. No one really knows how long this broom will last. And look at the job it does. Doesn't leave a trace of dust behind. And does the work several times as fast as an old out-of-date straw broom, yet with only half the effort."

And so he would continue his sales pitch in a smooth, effortless way. Suddenly, he would hand the broom over to the proprietor and tell him to try it. "Just take a hold of it mister, and see how it handles. See how easily it glides along; no effort at all. Just try it yourself, and see if what I am saying isn't right." In many, if not in most cases, the proprietor would take the broom, try it, and be persuaded to make a purchase. Once Burns had the cash in his pocket, he would follow his second rule, that of getting himself off the premises as quickly as possible.

Nevertheless, if the proprietor showed an unusual readiness to succumb to his sales appeal, he would then try to sell him another broom, remarking that the little woman at home would probably need one, and here was a chance for a bargain.

Not all prospects, however, would be easily persuaded. But sales resistance only challenged Burns to his best efforts. He would then bring forth his reasons for which the purchase should be made. He would watch closely for a sign of wavering, and then if he thought he had the customer close to decision but not quite, he would bring out his clincher that usually did the trick. He would look at me and say, "By the way Gordon, don't we need to fill up the tank?" I thought so. "Look mister, we'll take it out in trade. This will make you a real, real bargain." Usually the wavering proprietor by this time would give way, and the sale was made.

That we needed gas was almost always true. Burns made it almost a rule never to buy gasoline unless he could trade it out. Sometimes he was so successful in making direct sales, that our gas level would get lower and lower, and this on a few occasions led to some very unfortunate results, as we shall presently see. We would obtain our meals in the same manner — trading them out. As the reader may imagine, our meals did not follow a very definite schedule. Moreover, since many of the restaurants were in connection with a garage, the food we ate was not always up to standard. However, I was not used to fancy meals at sophisticated restaurants, and I did not complain.

If we didn't have car trouble, we could travel quite a distance in a day, even though Burns would make at least a dozen stops, if not more, to ply his broom trade.

Eventually on the third day, after leaving Portland, we arrived in Sacramento where we met our friend, Dr. John G. Lake.

Dr. Lake had left Houston and was in Sacramento, because his son had been involved in an almost fatal accident. Dr. Lake's faith had pulled him through, but it would be sometime before the young man would be recovered and released from the hospital. Lake wanted to be near his son and for a number of other reasons, it seemed prudent for him to remain on the coast. Because the work in Houston was comparatively new, and he had to leave so suddenly without being able to put anyone in charge, he was much burdened over it. He told us that there seemed to be no prospect that he could return. Upon learning that Frank and I had confirmed our plans to go to Houston, he seemed considerably relieved.

Before I realized it, Frank, upon learning that Dr. Lake intended to leave immediately for Los Angeles, to keep a speaking engagement, impetuously invited him to ride along in our car! Those who recall how small the old 490 Chevrolet was — and it was already loaded with our own baggage and Burn's big supply of brooms — will understand how puzzled I was about how it all could be arranged. Nevertheless, I looked forward with great interest to the fellowship we would have with Dr. Lake, who was probably one of the most remarkable conversationalists that it has ever been my privilege to hear. He was also a good listener and a most agreeable companion, but naturally, we preferred to listen to him and the amazing stories that he would relate of the great miracles and remarkable events that had taken place under his ministry. The fund of stories was almost inexhaustible, and would leave the listener in a state of rapture and exaltation. Indeed, after listening to him tell of the astounding episodes of Divine intervention he had experienced in South Africa, one soon had the feeling that all things were indeed possible.

In anticipation of the enjoyment I would experience listening to Dr. Lake, I was willing to sit on the top of our baggage in a rather cramped position, during the entire drive to Los Angeles.

There was, however, an incident or two, that took place on the journey that proved not to be so enjoyable.

As I have explained, Burns would only buy gasoline when he could trade it out. Consequently, the gas level at times would become perilously low. I would remind him of the situation from time to time, but he was always sure that there would be enough until we got to the next place. Once we actually ran out of gas, but were not far from a station and were able to get out of our difficulty without too much trouble. But Frank would not take the warning, and finally when we were deep in the mountains where there were no filling stations within many miles, the engine sputtered and stopped. There was no mistake; we were out of gas again!

I had one little trick in reserve. Cars in those days employed a gravity feed from the gas tank. By the simple expedient of turning the car around and backing up the hill, the slope permitted the small amount of gasoline left in the tank to flow to the engine. Thus we were able to reach the crest of the hill. For several miles the road then went down hill, and we were able to coast along using the power supplied by gravity. When we came to level road again, there was still enough gas to continue a few more miles. But finally the engine coughed and stopped. The region was the wildest on the entire highway, and no filling stations were available for many miles.

While we were debating on what to do, we noticed a cabin set back from the highway and Dr. Lake suggested that he and I go there and see if we could secure some gas. We were fortunate in that the tenant had both a can and a few gallons of gasoline. We went back to the highway, confident that we would soon be on our way. It had now become dark and we noticed nothing unusual until we reached the highway. We looked and to our surprise there was no car, no Burns, no nothing. We looked both ways on the highway, but couldn't see a single light. Our car had had the lights on and they should be discernible for a distance of several miles. We waited a few minutes more but could see nothing. Burns and the car had completely vanished. Dr. Lake was an even-tempered man, but his patience was not inexhaustible. He began to wonder how in the world he had ever listened to Burn's invitation to accompany us on this trip. Where had the man disappeared to? Had the earth swallowed him up? Had he gotten another car to push him and was he on his way to a station? If so, maybe it would be an hour before he would be back. That he had gotten someone to tow him seemed the only reasonable conclusion. So we took the can of gasoline back, and then began to walk slowly down the highway.

About a half mile down the road, we saw the gleam of a tail light. Surely it couldn't be . . . but it was! Burns had pushed the car down the gentle slope a half mile by himself. Then thinking it easier to push it backwards, he had turned it around. That is why we didn't see the tail light. Lake rarely took a man to task but this time he did. Of what could the man be thinking? Did he realize that Lake had a meeting in Los Angeles tomorrow? Here we were marooned out in the wilderness. It seemed as if Burns wanted him to miss his meeting.

But fortune was with us; Burns, seeing he was in a tight place and anxious to restore himself to favor, managed to flag down an obliging motorist who towed us to the next station, many miles down the road. Dr. Lake quickly forgave and all was well when we arrived in Los Angeles late that night. We retired at once to a hotel, and quickly fell into slumber.

Dr. Lake had a speaking engagement at the church, pastored by Dr. E. W. Kenyon, the famous writer and author. I had the privilege of hearing this brilliant teacher. His writings place a peculiar emphasis on faith, which many people have found to be greatly helpful. Like all geniuses he was apt to over-emphasize, to get a forgotten truth across. In his effort to get the faith message over, he almost left out repentance. Notwithstanding, his writings have great merit.

After a day or two, we were ready to begin our long trip to Houston. I shall never forget it. All was well until we got into Arizona. The roads in that state at that time were terrifically bad. Heavy rains chewed up the roads, leaving them full of ruts and chuck holes. Sharp rocks cut into our tires, and the unevenness of the road seemed almost to shake the car to pieces.

Twenty miles out of Tucson, the rear end went out. I had to go to town to get a new differential gear. It was dark by the time I was ready to return. I walked for many miles, then hitched a ride. Somehow I got the car into running condition the next day, and picking up Burns at Tucson, we proceeded on our way. By the number of brooms that had diminished, I saw he had had a good day. However, he was broke as usual, and it was all we could do to keep gas in the car.

I shall not relate the vicissitudes of our travel, as we drove into West Texas. Burns was anxious to get into Houston by Sunday, and he pressed the car for all he could get out of it. Again and again the Chevrolet broke down, unable to stand the punishment it was receiving. I made a number of minor repairs, but finally saw that we would never make it to Houston. The end came within five miles of Pecos. The engine had been steaming for some time, until there was no water left in the radiator. I brought the car to a stop, but the motor was so hot it acted like a diesel and ran with the key turned off! Finally we got it stopped, but there was no way of getting it running again. A kindly Texan towed us into Pecos, where Burns sold it for the sum of fifteen dollars.

Our plan was to ship our belongings to Houston and travel lightly. Burns prepared his brooms for shipment, and we sat down and waited for the express agent to pick them up. He never came, and finally fretful over the delay, Burns got another individual to come and get us. To our amazement, we learned that the express agent, in his hurry to pick us up, failed to see a passing train. They had taken him to the hospital . . .

That, and the next day were spent in hitch-hiking to Houston. This was the only time I used this method of travel since I entered the ministry, regarding it as an inconvenient method of transportation. Burns, however, seemed to know just how it was done. In no time at all we were picked up, and were speeding on our way. By night time, we had covered quite a distance. But the circumstances for travelling after dark were unfavorable for hitch-hiking. It was Saturday night. How could we possibly get to Houston by the following evening, to meet our speaking engagement? Looking at a railroad schedule, we noted that a night train struck straight across the prairie for Waco. The train would get us there by morning and then we would be within striking distance of Houston. We had just enough cash realized from the sale of the Chevrolet, to pay our fare. The train was soon due and when it came we hopped aboard.

Morning found us in Waco. Soon we were on our way, hoping to get to Houston before dark. But it was Sunday, and almost no cars were on the road. Finally a Ford stopped. "Are you going south?" Burns shouted. No, the farmer was going to Mart. To my surprise, Burns accepted the offer of a ride, although it took us in a general south-easterly direction instead of south. I whispered to Burns his mistake, but he said nothing. We got out at Mart, and looked for a car to take us back on the main highway. We waited a half hour and nothing showed up. My patience was rather exhausted and I finally complained about Burn's way of doing things. He chided me reproachfully, and said that I got discouraged too easily. We would get to Houston that day. Just wait and see!

At that very moment a railroad locomotive came pulling by with several gondolas behind it. Burns shouted at the engineer, as to whether we could get aboard. The trainman looked at us and seeing we were wearing Sunday-go-to-meeting clothes and did not look like ordinary hoboes, told us to jump aboard. This we did as the cars headed cross-country for the city of Marlin.

That was the first time I had ever hitched a ride on a freight train, but Burns seemed to know the ropes. "Come, let us get into the last car," he said. "Now crouch down." I soon saw the reason for his advice for the engine was belching out cinders and black smoke that blew directly upon us. Before long we had cinders in every part of our clothes, and our faces gradually darkened from the falling soot. In Marlin, we jumped off the gondola and retired to a filling station where we made an attempt to clean up.

Somehow, we got to Houston by sundown just as Burns had promised. By meeting time, we had changed clothes and my companion was in high spirits. In the pulpit that night he was at his best. I marvelled at the aplomb he showed. One would have supposed we had travelled in a pullman reserved for a business tycoon, instead of a gondola with dense smoke blowing in our faces.

Now comes the sad part of the story. Burns had many excellent qualities, and could have been of great service in the cause of Christ. But he was unstable. I shall not describe the cause of his downfall. One morning I went to visit Sister Lake and I saw at once that she was greatly agitated — news had just come to her of his misdeeds. I soon discovered my erstwhile companion had fallen into evil ways, and had even fled from the city. It was a terrible blow. It left me in a state of utter confusion. How could a man of God betray the cause of Christ as he did?

There was a woman of prayer in the congregation, who had the ministry of a prophetess. I went out to visit her, to have her pray with me. She knew nothing of what had just transpired, and I didn't have the heart to tell her. But she saw by my countenance that something had gone wrong. The Spirit of God suddenly came upon her and she began to speak, "My servant Burns has gone backward. He has gone backward. I must deal with him with My arm of chastening."

Then I realized that God was on the throne. That He knew all things and that there was nothing hidden from Him. God had me to understand there were men who would fail in the ministry, but that I must not stumble over it, but keep my eye single before God.

I only heard of Burns once or twice afterwards. The chastening hand of God was indeed upon him, and he confessed to someone whom I knew, that He had tasted the cup of bitterness to the full. As the Scripture says, "Be not deceived; God is not mocked: for whatsoever a man soweth, that shall he also reap." (Gal. 6:7)

For several months I stayed in Houston and pastored the small flock. I made a number of friends there, and learned several things about the work of the ministry. The Burns incident, however, was quite a blow and caused most of the people to lose confidence in the work. As Fall came on, I decided to return to the West. In the meantime, I had purchased another car. Dr. Lake was writing for his family, and arrangements were made that I should take them back with me, in the car. It took me a week of steady travelling to do this, but we got the whole family back safely.

Dr. Lake invited me to spend a couple of weeks with him in a meeting in Fresno. There I met the Myers family. Bob Myers did some singing during the meeting. Actually, he was not really converted at that time. But, a few years later, after striking the bottom, he was wonderfully converted, and created the well-loved program on the radio called "The Haven of Rest", with "First Mate Bob and the Crew of the Good Ship Grace."

CHAPTER XIII

Experiences on the Evangelistic Field

From this time on, I labored steadily on the evangelistic field. For a season, a brother from Oregon, Chet Hoffman, and I worked together in meetings. He and I, and my brother-in-law, Leon Hall and my sister, Gladys, joined together in a team to hold a tent meeting in the mining town of Grass Valley, California.

We were offered a piece of land, rent free, on the edge of town, and accordingly set up our tent there. We soon learned that the cheapest place is not always the best place. The first night we had only one person in attendance! There was nothing to do but to take the tent down and put it up in a better location. This time we decided to erect it in the very heart of the city, and soon we had a fair if not a large attendance. God gave us a number of converts, and one officer of the local Salvation Army who attended, received the baptism of the Holy Ghost. In the joy of his experience he did considerable shouting, enough to be heard by the neighbors in the area. Of course, we were not going to stop him.

Across the street there lived the company doctor, a self-important man who exercised considerable influence in the community, and who in a previous generation, would have been called a squire. When he heard the Salvation Army brother shouting, his indignation was aroused and he promptly called the local constable. Fortified by the long arm of the law, the pair marched down to the tent and ordered us to shut down operations, immediately.

This, however, we were not ready to do. We were having a very successful altar service at the moment. There was not a lot of noise, but there was some loud praying and it could be heard through the thin walls of the tent. The constable, whose hand was shaking like a leaf, goaded on by the arrogant doctor, pulled out his watch and said that we had just five minutes to comply with the order to close down, or we could consider ourselves under arrest. We answered by telling the constable and the doctor to go in and stop the meeting themselves, if they wanted it closed down. But before they did so, to remember that the constitution of the United States gave us the free right of worship, and to consider the consequences before they took such unlawful action to disturb a public service. We reminded the officer that he should be the defender of public worship, rather than be in league with its enemies. The poor constable hardly knew what to do.

The doctor, who was a large, overbearing individual, and had expected to end the matter in a brief moment, severely rebuked the unhappy constable for his hesitancy, telling him to do his duty, and that he was no friend of his if he didn't go into action at once. Upon this outburst, my brother-in-law walked up to the doctor and began to point out to him the seriousness of his act of disturbing a place of worship. It was quite dark on the street, and the doctor, mistaking Hall's tone of voice, thought he was about to use physical violence on him. He began backing up, retreating across the street, until he got to the fence. Hall, who wouldn't have thought of touching him, saw that the man was now on the defensive and followed up his advantage, rebuking him in a stern tone of voice. The doctor, alarmed, thought it the better part of valor to crawl through the fence while he had opportunity, and make good his escape. After putting, what he thought was a safe distance between him and us, the doctor turned around, shook his fist angrily and vowed that he would "see us run out of town, even if it took five hundred dollars." The disturbance by this time had caused the praying in the tent to cease, and the constable, considering that this was a good opportunity for him to make his departure, did so without delay. We felt sorry for him. He was probably a family man and apparently had little taste for the thing he was forced into. He acted like a badly frightened man.

In the morning, we looked for the doctor to attempt to make good his threats and in this, our anticipations proved correct. We were soon served with a summons to appear before the justice of peace that day, to answer a charge of disturbing the peace.

Our first act was to enter into prayer to ask God to protect us, and to give us guidance in the situation in which we found ourselves. We reminded the Lord that He had promised to give special wisdom to His followers when they were called before magistrates. Following prayer, we decided to go to the district attorney who was at Nevada City, a few miles distant.

We soon found that he intended to give us little encouragement, saying that he, as district attorney, might be called upon to prosecute us.

We returned to Grass Valley to answer our summons. On the

way, we decided upon our course, that a good offense was the best defense. We would be courteous, but would stand firm on our rights. Upon meeting the justice and hearing the charge, we explained that the constitution of the United States provided us with full rights to preach the gospel where we would. That we were astonished that in this country of America, there were still men who objected to the gospel's being preached, to the extent that they would try to close up a meeting and drive the preachers out of town. We explained that our services were not unnecessarily loud, and as far as our disturbing the peace was concerned, it was not nine o'clock when the constable appeared. Dance halls in that town stayed open indefinitely. We let him know that we regarded the entire matter very seriously; that a gross violation of our rights had occurred. We were, however, willing to overlook this break of the law by the constable and the doctor, providing there was no repetition. Our words perhaps may have had a little bravado in them, and we would have been in a hard way to employ legal talent, seeing the modest state of our finances.

The justice of peace, nevertheless, apparently decided that he had a weak case and was anxious to get it off of his hands. But to save some semblance of face for the doctor he said, "Now, I am sorry but I am going to have to ask you to close your meetings at such and such a time." It was the very time that we regularly closed down! We recognized that the justice was taking the easy way out, and we promised to comply with his order.

We never saw the doctor again. But we noticed that each evening, he set his radio in the window and turned up the speaker as loud as possible. He apparently suddenly lost his interest in preserving the quiet of the community, and showed that he was not at all concerned about our disturbing the peace, but that we were disturbing his peace!

The meetings continued on for several weeks in that city, after which time Leon and I took the tent to Lincoln where we held some services. He and my sister remained in the city to establish a work there. Hoffman and I then became supply pastors in Marysville, California, for a couple of months.

Among the converts in that city was a young lady of a family from Sierraville. At the end of my time in Marysville, her family invited me to come up to hold some services in their little village in the Sierra Valley.

I looked forward to the meeting, and when the time came to make the trip, I was eager to be on my way. It was late in November — the day before Thanksgiving — and bad weather was setting in. On the day I was to leave the valley, a steady rain began falling. An old-timer warned me not to attempt the trip. "I have lived in this country many years," he said, "and I know that a heavy rain here this time of the year, means snow up in the mountains."

This information caused me to pause. However, I had no other meetings arranged and in my youthful enthusiasm to be on my way, I disregarded his warning and started on the trip. When I was about halfway up to the pass, the rain turned into snow and slush, which gradually got deeper the farther I went. By the time I had gotten to a mountain village, the going was getting pretty rough, and my car had no chains. But I was still determined to continue my journey. I stopped at the general store and bought a quantity of rope. The wheels of my car, being of the type that had spokes, enabled me to wind the rope around the tires, thus giving them extra traction.

The snowfall, however, had almost become a blizzard and it was now long after dark. I asked the storekeeper what the outlook was concerning the weather, and he told me that storms like this often lasted for days. When he saw that I was going to attempt to cross the divide that night, he looked at me as if he were seeing a madman. "Young fellow," he said, "no one can get over that pass tonight. The snow is already a foot deep up there, and you can be stranded there for days. At the best you will suffer from the cold and exposure, and there will be no one to rescue you. If you go, it's your own funeral."

Looking back, I realize that my actions were rather rash, and I am not recommending that any one else do what I did. Paul the Apostle advised the captain not to sail his ship against the impending storm. Yet, here in the midst of a blinding snowstorm that might continue for days, I was planning to do the impossible. But something kept urging me to get over the mountan, so I could preach the following night. And like a person with a fixed idea, nothing could stop me.

Notwithstanding my youthful zeal, I believe God put a supernatural faith in my heart. I seemed to see myself preaching the following night, in Sierraville. So I pushed on. I discovered at once that the ropes I had put on the tires were of material assistance in driving through the snow, and for a while I was able to make very good time. But it was a false omen. The snow got deeper and deeper, and finally it piled up so high in front of the car's bumper,

cept in performing his duties, he never went into a billiard hall nor a movie house, nor any worldly place of amusement.

Some of the testimonies of converts in these cities of the West, might seem rather peculiar to people of a city church but they were usually sincere. One man who was converted, not in the Wilcox meeting but in another Arizona town, had rather vigorously opposed his wife's attending church. At last she got him to go, and the Lord got a hold of him in the first meeting. After he had prayed for a long time, he arose to his feet, and when invited to testify he solemnly declared, "Any man who says there ain't no God, is a liar."

I remember that my brother-in-law, L. D. Hall, was having a fellowship meeting in his church on one occasion, when a preacher happened in that advocated snake-handling. He said that it was commanded in the Bible, and if we were going to leave that out of the Scriptures, we might as well leave it all out. He referred to Mark 16, where Jesus said, ". . . They shall take up serpents and if they drink any deadly thing it shall not hurt them." Of course any Bible student knows that this was a promise of protection against danger, not an excuse for tempting God. As nearly as I can remember the details, Hall slipped out and got a bottle with a poison label. Returning he said, "Mister, we don't have any serpents here but you can demonstrate your doctrine by drinking this. It may kill a man in a few seconds, or it may not. However, I am sure that it will be perfectly safe for you to drink it." The mountebank turned pale, and after excusing himself, slunk off the premises and was not seen again. Hall was right, in that the liquid was perfectly safe to drink, since the bottle contained only water. But, of course, the pseudo snake-handler did not know that.

After conducting several campaigns in Arizona, I left to join my brother-in-law in Northern California, who was then preaching up in the mountains. I had driven all day, and in my desire to reach my destination, continued driving most of the night. I had reached a treacherous part of the Sierras, with deep canyons yawning first on one side and then on the other. Notwithstanding, there had gradually come an irresistible urge to yield to sleep, and I found myself nodding time and again, for a brief instant, but each time roused myself immediately. There was no place there to park, and so not knowing what else to do, I drove on. Suddenly, I nodded again and when I came to my senses, to my horror the wheels of the car were skirting the very edge of the precipice! By the merest fraction of a second, I recovered in time to keep from going to instant death. The shock of my narrow escape so affected me, that I had no trouble staying awake for the rest of the night. The thought came to me often, afterward, that many people who are on the very edge of eternity are in the same state of stupor, and need a shock to awaken them to their terrible peril.

During the summer, my brother-in-law and I decided to hold a campaign in the state of Washington in the little town of Cheney, a few miles south of Spokane. A tent had been loaned to us, and we prepared to set it up. Cheney was a college town, and one of its professors lived not far away. We had just gotten the benches finished, when the professor walked into the tent and coolly ordered us to take it down. He had decided that it was a public nuisance and since according to him, he wielded considerable influence in the community, he could have the authorities remove it, but he preferred to give us a chance to take it down before proceeding with legal action. My brother-in-law, exasperated that, after all the work we had been put to, the man would have the audacity to expect us to take the tent down, flatly refused to consider his suggestion.

We knew, however, that the professor would not rest until he had exhausted all means in attaining his objective. It was not long before a man who drove a milk truck showed up. He identified himself as the son of the old lady who had given us the use of the lot, rent free. He told Hall to move at once, and that if we didn't, when he got through with his milk route, he would take the necessary action. Hall lost no time. Quickly, he went to the old lady who had given us permission to use the lot and explained to her that while we greatly appreciated her generosity, just to make everything legal, we were giving her a dollar to make it a contract and would she sign a receipt showing that we had the lot rented? She was quite willing to oblige us. We never saw the milkman again, and we could imagine his discomfiture when his mother told him we had legal possession of the lot. Or perhaps he didn't care, but had to satisfy the professor, who was one of his customers, that he had done his best.

We decided to take no chances, so went down to see the mayor of the city, Mayor Martin, who incidentally later became governor of the state of Washington. We related the details, got a vague promise from him of his protection, and began our meetings. The mayor dropped in one night for a service, and apparently decided there was not sufficient reason to put us out of town. At any rate, we were never molested by the authorities. The professor for some reason, never passed by the tent again, but always walked around the block.

One night during the Cheney meetings, a gang of ruffians gathered around the tent and during the altar service, began to pelt the seekers with green apples, hurling them through an opening in the sidewalls which had been made for ventilation. Hall went one direction and I went another. One of the young hoodlums, in his flight, ran into a dead-end alley of an adjacent school from which he could not escape. I shouted at him to halt in the name of the law. (Not everyone knows that a private citizen is empowered to make an arrest, if he sees someone breaking the law.) When I came upon him, he was shaking like a leaf. I told him that he and his friends had broken the law, that we were glad for young people to come to the meetings, but I was astonished that any would come to disturb the work of God. That I could have him arrested for violation of the law, but if he would promise never to disturb the meeting again, I would let him off. We experienced no further trouble with the gang.

We had a number of very fine converts out of this meeting, several of whom actually went out into the ministry. One young woman became a successful evangelist, and held meetings in various cities with scores of people receiving the Holy Ghost.

The tent season is short in Washington, and when it came time to take the canvas down, the only place that could be found to carry on the work was in an abandoned funeral parlor. This was not the most felicitous place to conduct services, but it served the purpose. One room of the mortuary housed a large number of empty coffins. There were also living quarters in other rooms. My sister, while not particularly appreciating the arrangement, nevertheless, accommodated herself to this situation, as she did to many other things. After the Cheney meeting, I decided to return to Arizona to hold campaigns again in that state.

It was about this time that I was licensed in the Assemblies of God movement. The following year, I received full ordination. To me it was a solemn moment to receive ordination. Yet, I realized that the hands of man in ordination are of value only as God has first laid His hand on the individual. Man can only recognize what God has already done.

It was the custom for the ordination committee to call the candidates in one by one, and ask them some straight questions. This is probably a good practice, for though it is necessary to make certain that a man has properly equipped himself for the ministry, it is even more important to those entrusted with the responsibility of granting credentials, to see that those they ordain show the proper Christian spirit.

So it was, that my time came to be called in. One or two routine questions were asked. Then, an elderly brother by the name of Jamieson looked me squarely in the eye and said, "Do you put in twenty-four hours of study each time, before you preach a sermon?" I paused a moment. I did not want to say anything improper, nor did I want to tell an untruth.

I looked at A. G. Osterberg, the superintendent, who was sitting with the committee, saying nothing. He had the reputation of being a stern man, but was always kind to me. I then answered, "No sir, not every time." "Why not?" the old gentleman asked severely. "Well," I replied, "for one reason, Brother Osterberg has asked me to preach several times at five minutes' notice!"

Brother Osterberg took it good-naturedly, and when they had gotten through, someone remarked that they had better be getting on to the next candidate. So that ended the interview, as far as I was concerned. I have always loved the Assemblies of God movement. It has been greatly used of God. Although our work today has extended to many groups all over the world, I am proud that in my early years I was able to help found a number of Assemblies' works that have become strong churches today.

CHAPTER XIV

We Go to the Deep South

While I was in Arizona, I met two young men in Phoenix who were anxious to get into the Lord's work. One was named Harold Francis and the other was Jewel Linam. Harold had French blood, was exceedingly emotional, and seemed to have a natural bent for getting himself into awkward situations.

Our plan was to travel to the deep South, holding a campaign or two on the way. Our adventures began not long after we got into Texas. Stopping at Abilene to do some repair work on the car, I had just climbed out from under the motor when I noticed Harold's face was white as a sheet. When I asked what the matter was, he pointed in the distance to some whirling clouds. I said, "What is that?" He replied, as if groping for words, that it was a tornado! I asked, "Are you sure?" He said, "I was in St. Louis when a cyclone struck, killing hundreds. But come, let us get out of here!"

We were galvanized into action. As we pulled out into the highway, signboards blown from their foundations, were sailing by. We soon were going top speed in the opposite direction of the storm. The wind was behind us and corresponded with the speed of the car. Consequently, with no air passing through the radiator, the engine became over-heated, blowing out a geyser of steam and water. A snapshot of our flight would have made an interesting picture. We felt like Lot did when he was fleeing from Sodom.

About midnight, we decided to drive off the road and get some sleep. Our funds were low and instead of going to a tourist court, we generally slept by the roadside. We had a large folding spring bed that we would set up. Finding a place that we thought was suitable in the middle of a field, we set up our bed and, weary from the excitement of a long day, dropped into sleep. Early in the morning, I thought I dreamed that a car was coming straight for us. In the morning when we arose, I saw it was no dream! What we thought in the night was a field, proved to be a side road! A car had actually driven down this road early in the morning, but the driver, seeing that we had camped on it, thoughtfully drove around us.

At Farmerville, Texas, we were invited to hold a service for a night. The pastor, whose name was James Hart, then asked us to remain for the balance of the week. We stayed nearly three weeks, with a goodly number of souls saved and baptized in the Spirit. Years later, we learned that several of the pastor's sons became evangelists, who were especially noted for their musical ability.

We had intended going further East, possibly into Mississippi and Alabama. However, the unusually heavy rains had swollen the Red River and travel was unsafe in that direction. So we drove to Southern Louisiana. Just before we reached De Ridder, Harold who was driving, had a slight accident. He got too near a truck that had stopped on an incline. The driver, in getting started, allowed the truck to roll back a few feet, smashing our radiator in, thus causing it to spring a leak. That meant that we would have to stop at the town for repairs. Just before leaving the city we met the pastor, Charles Smith. We talked with him a few minutes, and then started to leave. We had made it our policy never to ask outright for a meeting. We believed that if God wanted us at a place, He would make it known. But before we could get out of the driveway, Brother Smith came running after us, to ask us if we would preach at his church that night. As a result of that service, we preached in De Ridder and De Quincy all summer, with scores of souls saved and many receiving the baptism of the Holy Spirit.

The three of us occupied quarters in the church building. Outside was a large arbor, where the night services were held. As the number of converts increased from day to day, it was decided to have a baptismal service. This was held Sunday afternoon, and attendance equal to half the town's population attended the service. At the last moment, Harold took sick and decided to remain behind. He lay down on a cot in the corner and was nearly asleep when he heard a strange noise, as if someone were trying to open a window. Then he heard voices and somebody was saying, "The coast is clear. We'll see what they have." One of them was nearly through the window, when he happened to spy Harold lying on the cot. The thief almost fell on his head getting out. Young Francis heard a tattoo of footsteps beating a hasty retreat. It was providential that Francis remained, for all the personal possessions we owned were in the room and with money being as scarce as it was in the South during depression days, it would have been a severe loss to us. Harold was scarcely over his fright when we returned.

As I have mentioned earlier, young Francis attracted trouble like honeysuckle attracts bees. As the revival gathered momentum, individuals would go off into the nearby woods to pray through. It seemed that the Spirit of God was moving on the community in a most unusual way. Young folk would gather, then retire to some isolated place where they could pray, get saved, and receive the baptism. To me it was a thrilling thing to see the Spirit working so wonderfully in a community.

But the enemy was not idle. One day, a group of young people dropped by and asked if Harold could accompany them to the nearby woods to pray. There was a young lady with them who seemed at times to fall into a peculiar trance. Despite these unusual manifestations, she showed no victory nor Christian joy, as a normal convert should.

While everyone was praying, this girl fell into one of these trances. Soon she started speaking. The spirit in her began to recite some of the things that Harold had done before he was converted. Poor Harold was so humiliated by these exposures before the others that he blacked out and fell into a dead faint. It all seemed strange to the group, but surely they thought, it must be the Spirit of God speaking, to be able to reveal these things which nobody else knew about but Harold. The young people came back to the church where I was, and related what had happened. When I heard their story, instantly I realized that the girl was possessed with a familiar spirit. The past being under the blood, the Spirit of God never makes exposures under such circumstances. It was the devil trying to confuse and hinder the revival. We laid hands upon the girl and cast out the evil spirit. I heard no more of the girl's having trances.

Thus the summer sped by with services being held every night and altar services lasting for hours, while people prayed through to victory, or, received the Holy Spirit. With the campaign coming to a close, we decided that we would leave out immediately after the last service, and head for Phoenix where Jewel Linam's parents lived. It was a terrible stormy night, the rain fell in sheets while lightning crackled and thunder crashed, as nature put on one of its most dazzling exhibitions. The lightning gradually diminished but the rain continued to pour unabated. We could see only a few feet ahead. It certainly was no night to be traveling. I was in the back seat trying to sleep, but after awhile I was aware that the car had stopped and one of the boys was saying, "I wonder if we should go on. It certainly is very steep here, and I can't understand why it should be like this on the main highway." The other lad said, "Let's get out and see just what's ahead." So they got out. In a moment they were back with fear and horror written across their faces. They explained that at the bottom of the incline, with nothing barring the way, was the roaring Sabine River, now a veritable torrent of raging water. Somehow, they had gotten on the wrong road and somebody had left the ferry dock completely open to traffic. It was a close brush, for had the car toppled into the swirling waters, the chances of escape would have been practically nil. Our guardian angel apparently had not forgotten us.

For three days and nights we traveled across the continent, until at last we reached Phoenix, where we enjoyed the hospitality of the Linams. Harold was to be with me only a short time more, as someone offered to send him to Bible school. However, he was to have one more adventure while we were in Phoenix.

Harold had a girl friend in this city, and of course he must see her while we stayed over. Something had gone wrong with the generator of our car, and the battery was down. I warned him to be careful — words which meant little to him. Somehow, he must have forgotten to turn the lights off and as he tarried very late at his girl friend's home, when the time came for him to leave, the battery would not start the car. Nevertheless, by cranking it by hand he did manage to get the engine going. Bidding goodbye to his lady friend, he started for the house. However, as the battery was already low, the lights quickly drained it, and soon there was not enough current to keep the motor running. So as chance would have it, the car stopped dead in the loneliest part of town.

While Harold was collecting his wits wondering what on earth to do, another car drew up beside him and the occupants asked if they could help. Young Francis quickly accepted their offer of assistance as he got in their car, and started, supposedly, for the house. But soon to Harold's dismay, he observed that they turned off in another direction toward the city dump, where not a soul could be found this time of night. Harold protested that they were on the wrong road, but he received the alarming reply that they knew where they were going and for him to keep quiet if he understood what was good for him.

Harold knew full well that a number of murders and robberies had occurred in this lonely part of town, and a sickening fear swept over him. There was only one thing to do. He began to cry to the

Lord with all his heart, to protect him from the danger in which he found himself.

His loud praying had a most remarkable effect. The companion of the driver was a negro, and suddenly he cried out, "Boss, I can't go through with this. I can't, I can't!" So the driver turned around and after letting out a volley of imprecations against his accomplice whom he accused of being chicken-hearted, took young Francis back to the main road and dumped him off. He needed no encouragement once he was out of the car; as soon as his heels hit the pavement, he lit out at a faster pace than he had traveled for many a day. Dashing into the house, pale as a ghost, he woke us up and poured out his story between gasps. The sickly hue on his face left no doubt that the story of his nocturnal adventures was true, and realizing that the rogues no doubt at that moment were dismantling everything removable on the car, we got into Mr. Linam's automobile and made for the scene as rapidly as possible. Just as we expected, the thieves had already drained the gas out of the tank and had taken the spare tire. As we drew up, they dashed off down a side street and disappeared into the night.

With a rope we had brought along, we towed the car home, thankful we had lost no more than we did. As for Francis, he had saved his skin by having the sense to call on the Lord. In many ways, he was a likeable lad. He loved the Lord but lived in a perpetual state of excitement. He was accident prone, and it seemed dangerous to have him around. When someone offered to send him to Bible school, I viewed it with mixed emotions. I was sorry to see him go, and yet it was a relief.

Experience has led me to believe that every one who launches out in apostolic ministry, must build up spiritual bulwarks against the attacks of the enemy. Harold had the enthusiasm, the love for souls, but had not taken time to lay the proper foundations nor prepared the necessary spiritual defenses against the powers of darkness. Consequently, he was uncommonly vulnerable to them. Within a year, a report came that he was in serious difficulties. Later, we heard that he died from causes which we were not able to certainly determine.

CHAPTER XV
I Start a Church in Ajo

During the following winter, I held meetings in Taft, California, and several other cities. Seeing that preaching in a new community and leaving the converts to shift for themselves was not good, it thus became my desire to establish churches in the new fields where I would labor. I knew that I was now able to preach and secure results, and I felt led to establish a church somewhere in Arizona. I little realized the problems and difficulties I was to encounter in the process.

One of my very fine friends, Earl Lombard had given me sufficient funds to purchase a tent. After holding a few meetings in California, I set the tent up in Douglas, Arizona, where I let a friend of mine hold services while I was away on business. Imagine my dismay, when I returned to Douglas and passing the site where the tent had been pitched, found it gone and the lot absolutely vacant! Astonished, I drove up to the parsonage and there learned for the first time that several days before, a small tornado had struck it and had absolutely destroyed it. My friends felt badly but not as badly as I did. If ever I was discouraged, it was then.

I returned to Phoenix for a few days. The pastor, S. S. Scull, in talking the situation over with me, recommended that I go to investigate a desert city called Ajo. It was one of those copper towns. He thought there was an opportunity to do something there for God. I prayed about it and decided to go, although it would take the last dollar I had, to buy gas to get there. I had so many reverses that it seemed as if the enemy were going to defeat everything I attempted to do. Many a young preacher goes through similar, discouraging experiences and what I would say to him is this: "Brother, don't panic, don't give up. God is still on the throne." The devil is a strategist, nonetheless; he will strike a succession of blows as he did in the case of Job, until he will get a person to think there is no use and he might as well give up. But to yield to this temptation, would be the greatest mistake that one could ever make.

I reached Ajo late one afternoon and met a man by the name of Dunn who was the self-appointed leader of a group of saints that included three members, plus a Sunday School of sixteen children. The community was a moral waste as far as spiritual things were concerned. Dunn was an Irishman, who with his limitations as a preacher, had a sense of humor. He had invited me to stay at his home. Upon visiting his place, I was astonished when I learned that the sixteen children that attended the Sunday School were all his! After all, he had a strong case that he had done more to build up the Sunday School than anyone else!

That night I shared the outside of the house, under the stars, with their pet billy goat. Wondering what another day would bring forth, I dropped off to sleep on my pallet. The morning sun awoke me bright and early, and a good thing it was, too. The goat had arisen still earlier and was ready to make a meal of some of my possessions. A few days later, I might add that the billy goat offended again by eating what he had no right to eat, and for that he was put into a pot.

I knew that God had to move on my part, for I had exactly one dime left in my pocket. There were car payments to be met and by missing one payment, the car could be repossessd. That night I held my first service in Ajo. It was by no means reassuring. I took up the offering. It amounted to the sum total of ten cents.

Two weeks went by. The crowds slowly increased. A kind neighbor gave me my meals. At night I slept in the church. But after two weeks, there was still no sign of a break. Never in my life had my fortunes seemed so low. Then one day I went out into the desert. In sheer desperation, I called upon God to break the powers of darkness, to let me see a little light. And lo, the miracle took place! As I went back to the church, the burden had lifted! That night, as I preached seemingly without any undue effort, four adults came to the altar and prayed through. The next night the same thing happened. And then night after night souls were at the altar, seeking God and praying into a clear-cut experience of salvation.

The revival swept through the entire community of Gibson, a suburb in the northern part of the city. Hardened miners came forward and wept their way to God. As the publican of old, they beat their breasts and asked God to have mercy on their souls.

I cannot describe the many wonderful conversions that took place, of people who are still standing true to God today. There was one family who lived a block down the street. They had fallen under deep conviction, but had held out against the Spirit's call.

About eleven o'clock the lady could stand it no longer and began to cry out to God for mercy. Another sinner, in a nearby home, heard her cries and began praying.

Others began to join the chorus. This went on for quite a time. After awhile, I could hear shouts of victory. I never stirred nor went near them. I had done my praying during the time they had been indifferent. Now, while they sweat it out, I decided to lie in bed and take it easy. At midnight, they came under my window and told me how they had prayed through. I told them I had heard about it already!

After the revival got into full swing, I decided not to have a service on Monday night, but rest, for I was weary in body. However, one of the persons attending, insisted I drive out seven miles into the country where lived seven families, who maintained the wells — the water supply of Ajo. I obliged, a little reluctantly. We held a service under a tree. After preaching briefly, I asked for decisions for Christ. Three of the families responded, and became pillars in the church.

For six weeks the revival continued with unabated power, and a strong group of Christians was established. My old friend, John Eiting, who has now gone to be with the Lord, came and took the pastorate.

There are many memories wrapped around my meetings in Ajo; many are pleasant, some poignant, and some humorous.

Near where we stayed was a house in which a little boy lived, who was about eight years of age. He was an adventurous type of child, and wanted nothing more than a chance to drive his father's Model T Ford. Of course, this privilege was not permitted him. But one day, the father unwittingly left the key in the car and the boy saw that the chance that he had long been awaiting, was at hand. Somehow, he managed to get the motor started. As every one knows, the Model T had three foot pedals, one of which was low gear, and which was located next to the brake. A person in a state of excitement might, in trying to stop the car accidentally get his foot upon the low gear pedal instead of the brake. Of course, the harder he stepped on the pedal, the more certain he was that nothing would stop him until he hit something solid.

So it happened with the little lad. When he wanted to stop, he got his foot upon the low band, while at the same time the gas lever apparently was fairly well advanced. The steering wheel had been turned at an angle, and so the Ford and the little boy began describing a great circle that was to carry him a distance of several hundred feet. The first things to go were some flower bushes; these were promptly laid flat. As it continued on, the car took more bushes and flowers in its path. The car then came within range of a neighbor's small building. This frail structure got the full impact of the Ford, with its motor running at full speed, in low gear. It was flattened level to the ground! Still the Ford did not stop. The way was now clear for it to jump the main highway, which fortunately for all concerned, especially for the lad, was empty of traffic at the precise moment. Having crossed the highway successfully, a more formidable obstacle loomed before its path. It was a house set on large concrete blocks, and inhabited by an Indian and his family. The Ford struck the corner of the house a solid blow, moving it around on its foundations. The Indian woman could not, of course, imagine what terrible thing had happened, so she took to her heels out the back door as fast as she could go.

The husband, nevertheless, had more presence of mind so he came out the front door; when he saw what had happened, all he could do was to shake his head. A crowd gathered as the little boy still sat at the controls, quite unhurt, saying nothing, but looking quite solemn. Finally, however, he got out of the car and mumbled something about that he guessed he ought to be going and disappeared from view.

While in Ajo, I received an invitation to hold a meeting in Wickenburg, Arizona, a city in which I had held a campaign a few years before. I remembered the kind hospitality I had received from the Davis family, with whom I had stayed. I answered the letter, stating that I would return there at a later date, but did not feel led to come at that particular time. Ten days later, I picked up the Arizona Republican and noticed the blazing headlines, TRUCK-TRAILER BECOMES FUNERAL PYRE IN WICKENBURG! I read the story and was horrified.

Coming into Wickenburg, from the west is a highway that slopes into the heart of the town. The driver of a big truck and trailer, filled with 7,000 gallons of gasoline, picked up a hitchhiker on this road. For some incredible reason, he turned the driving over to the hitchhiker and went to sleep. As the truck rolled toward town, the hitchhiker lost control of the brakes. Gathering speed each moment, this fearful catapult of destruction came hurtling into the city. At the edge of the business section, there was at that time a right angle curve, which could not be negotiated at much more than ten miles an hour. The truck must have been going forty or fifty by the time it reached the curve. It was utterly unable to make the turn, so plowed into the Davis home at the end of the road. The gasoline exploded and the house became an inferno. The family was wiped out. It was the home in which I had stayed when I held the meeting in Wickenburg before, and where I might have been that fatal night, when disaster struck, had I accepted the invitation!

CHAPTER XVI

Experiences in Dixie

While in Arizona, I received an invitation to hold a meeting for a pastor in Dallas, Texas. After driving all that distance, I was informed that the pastor was not ready after all to begin the meeting. We often hear complaints that an evangelist has not kept his word regarding a meeting that has been promised, after the advertising is out, etc. But pastors also have a responsibility, and can seriously disrupt an evangelist's plans by a last minute cancellation. Both parties need to be very careful in keeping their word, in matters of this nature, and only a most urgent reason should give cause for a last minute change.

The pastor, nonetheless, directed us to an official in the southern part of the state, who, he said would help us get a meeting. This also proved to be a false lead. We then crossed over into Louisiana, and there in Shreveport, I was invited to hold a campaign by Rev. Lout. This meeting, while marked with rather inconspicuous results as far as the number of converts was concerned, nevertheless, led to my becoming acquainted with his son-in-law, Jack Moore, a very remarkable man of whom we shall hear more later.

I shall not recount the many campaigns I held in different cities during these years. Some were rewarding, others had indifferent results. In one meeting held in Portland, Oregon, during a visit home, there was as I recall it, only one convert. This lone convert, however, happened to be a young lady who later became my wife. Freda came of an industrious and God-fearing family, but like all of us, had to have a personal experience with God. Her mother, of German stock, had lived in her youth on the plains of Russia. A most fortunate decision led her to immigrate to America. Had she not moved when she did, she would have been caught in the disastrous Communist revolution, and perhaps suffered the fate of millions who starved to death, rather than bow to Communist tyranny. If she had survived, then she would have been in the path of Adolph Hitler's savage invasion. Freda's mother at 82, is still active, at the time of writing, a faithful and devoted follower of the

Lord. Her father was also an excellent Christian. He died, suddenly, not long after her conversion.

In preparing this account, I have especially had in mind young men who launch out in the ministry, and meeting with many discouragements, are tempted to give up their calling. It is my desire to encourage these youths to take new faith and to keep their eyes on the goal. In time, faith, prayer, and perseverance will win out. God has a special purpose for each of us to fulfill in life, that no one else can, and the only truly happy people are those in whom God's purpose for them is achieved. This applies not only to ministers, specially called into the service of the Lord, but also to all Christians. God's perfect will for us is not always immediately apparent. We have to pray into that will. But if we are faithful, if we make prayer a business, if we keep our ears tuned to the still small voice, in time we shall be led out into broader fields and shall eventually experience the satisfying knowledge that our intended destiny on this earth has been fulfilled. That we have not lived in vain but have done our part toward fulfilling our responsibility to our generation.

During these years, I was holding an average of one campaign a month, and it would take a large book indeed to describe even the most interesting events that happened in each one of them. I have intended only to recall typical incidents as will give the reader an idea of how evangelistic work was accomplished in those days; how we managed to carry on God's work with a very minimum of finance; how God supplied our needs, took us through fire and trial, but eventually brought us safely through all our mishaps and temptations.

I found it convenient to have at least one other young man with me in my evangelistic ministry, for companionship and to lead the song service. In time, several of them who worked with me, went to preaching on their own.

Ivie Parker and Bill Coxe joined my party for a couple of years, during our labors in the South. Few of these campaigns were large. Nevertheless we usually filled the churches on our best nights. The depression was still on, and we lived on a very minimum budget. (Our budget was always the amount of money we received.) This resulted in some circumstances that rather sharply contrast with those a young preacher faces today. It is not always easy for a young man to get started in the ministry, and from a financial angle, it was far harder to get started then than now. An evangelist who had been on the field for years, might receive anywhere from five to fifteen dollars a week, beside his room and meals. An offering as large as twenty-five dollars was a veritable windfall. The pastors did not fare much better. The depression did one good service in showing us how many things we can get along without. And that a happy life does not consist in the number of material things that we possess.

During these years, there were practically no large campaigns on the field, as we have seen in recent years. It was almost impossible to finance them, and the ministry of healing that had been given a great impetus by Dr. Charles S. Price, Raymond T. Richey, F. F. Bosworth, Aimee Semple McPherson, and others, gradually tapered off. Evangelism was kept alive by ministers, who went from church to church, preaching the gospel simply because the message burned in their souls and they could not desist if they would.. They preached with or without financial remuneration, sometimes in an attractive place of worship, but often in a simple structure with tin roof, located on the wrong side of the railroad tracks.

A typical campaign when we were in the Texas Panhandle, was held in the town of Snyder. Since the time we were there, a rich oil field has been discovered and black gold now flows from hundreds of oil wells. But at that time the depression was at its very worst. I clearly recall that our first offering amounted to twenty-one cents! With an income in that bracket, it required a certain amount of wizardry in the handling of finances. For one thing, the boys decided that they would do their own dry-cleaning. This decision led to some humorous results, while we were in Snyder.

Despite the depression, the boys had by one means or another, accumulated a rather extensive collection of trousers. Gathering them all together, they went outside and set up for business. The sum total of their cost would be for a few gallons of gasoline. So picking up an oil can that was handy, they went to the nearest station and returned with a sufficient supply to do the job. They did, however, fail to observe that still left in the can, was *a pint or two of kerosene.*

After a few hours, they had the line full of trousers, flapping in the breeze. Now they would go into their rooms and practice on their trumpets. I strolled outside for a few minutes and happened to look over at the line. There were dark rings around every pant-leg, not unlike the stripes on the clothes of prisoners of a chain gang. Returning to the house, I informed the boys that I did not think much of their skill in the dry-cleaning business. They thought

I was joking with them, but they did go out to take a look. When they reached the line, I noticed that a silence fell. They did not come back to discuss the matter, but slunk down the alley, each carrying a pair of trousers. They had to have at least one pair cleaned, or else they could not attend the services the following day.

The next night after church, we returned to the house. It was bitterly cold at night, for it was in the dead of winter. The pastor would bank up the stove before leaving for church. Upon returning, we would take some kindling and place it on the bed of coals. To help matters along, Bill would throw on some kerosene to make the fire roar, and to warm the room up as fast as possible. That was what the can of kerosene had been used for, from which they got the gasoline and had absent-mindedly forgotten to empty it of kerosene. Now there were a few pints left in the can, not kerosene this time, *but gasoline*.

It slipped Bill's mind that there was a change of fuel in the can. Since he was freezing cold, he rushed into the house, threw a few sticks on the coals, then poured a liberal supply of the contents of the can upon the whole. The gasoline steamed a moment until a real, combustible mixture had been obtained and then it exploded. I was still outside at the moment, when looking up, I saw a tongue of flame shoot out of the chimney. Fearing something terrible had happened, I rushed in and discovered that Bill was comparatively unharmed except for the loss of his dignity. His face had taken on a black smudge. He was also minus eyebrows, and the front part of his hair was singed.

I advised him that after such a run of hard luck, it might be well to call it a day, before anything else could happen. The boys decided to take my advice and retired for the night.

We met and made many friends in Texas. After a service, it was customary to gather around the pastor's table for a snack and for fellowship. At one household, a particular young lady felt constrained to make a cake for the evangelistic party. She informed us proudly that she had made it all by herself and added, as if thinking that this entitled her to additional merit, that she had not even used a recipe. I took one bite and had plenty of evidence that what she said was true. No recipe could be that bad! To have told her I could not eat it would have been cruel, yet, I felt that if I ate the cake, I would become ill. There was not else to do but to say nothing and hold it in my hand. When I left the house, I quietly dropped it in a nearby irrigation canal.

This is no reflection on southern cooking, which is among the best in the world. But during the height of the depression, southern housewives were sometimes sorely taxed to provide a well-balanced meal. Sweet potatoes were one of the great staples. In some areas especially hard hit, we would have sweet potatoes for breakfast, dinner, and supper. Hot and cold sweet potatoes, sweet potato pie. In most places, however, the diet was varied by servings of corn pone, sow belly, black-eyed peas, grits, hominy, and sorghum syrup.

Yet, it was unusual to leave the table hungry. I cannot truthfully say that I ever really suffered from hunger except in one home, which was located in a mill village. Here the wretched inhabitants suffered from every misery that ignorance, malnutrition, and ill-fortune could visit upon them.

Breakfast consisted of strips of sow belly which were thick slices of salt pork, mostly fat. Added to this, were some pale, white biscuits cooked on a stove which, from long usage, sagged visibly in the center. Trying to get enough wood in the stove to make a hot fire often resulted in filling the room with smoke. A can of sorghum syrup completed the repast. It is not surprising that I left the table with hunger pangs quite unsatisfied. Mill village women, typical slatterns, were raised, lived and died in the most squalid poverty. The children, fed constantly on such an inadequate diet, naturally were ill-favored and showed signs of rickets, and other dietary disorders.

At night, sleep was broken with bed bugs which came out of their retreats and advanced on their victims. Apparently, the family had gotten used to these nocturnal visitors, but I found it impossible to sleep at all when they were in the vicinity.

It was the only time I ever stayed in a mill village. But the experience was wholesome. It showed me with what poor people had to put up, and from which many had no hope of escape. I am certainly in favor of the social laws that were put in effect a little later, and which were designed to alleviate such conditions.

The situation of the colored people was even worse. They lived under the most primitive conditions. The shacks that they inhabited had been built in the most part, during or shortly after Civil War days. The squalid structures generally leaned in one direction or other, and a strong pole was set on the leeward side to support it from collapsing altogether. Since the days of the depression, the whole South has made phenomenal advances. And many of the colored as well as the white, now live in brick homes and draw salaries that are princely in comparison with the income of those days.

As I have said, southern evangelists lived in a most precarious manner — usually from hand-to-mouth. They rarely had as much as twenty dollars in their pocket. They moved from city to city, accepting such opportunities as opened to them. A few of these ministers now are pastors of the largest churches of the nation. For the most part, they are not ashamed of the poverty they shared with the people, and the lowly circumstances they experienced in those days. As Paul says, a minister of the gospel should know how to be empty and how to abound, as the times may require.

There were also shiftless and ignorant preachers who were no credit at all to their profession. They came to town expecting to be put up and fed, but were so ill-prepared in the work of the ministry, that it could result in disaster to give them a free run of the pulpit. A few were little more than tramps, who seemed to be proud of their escapades as they roamed the country. One young fellow I recall, a sort of a lay-preacher, loved to recount his experiences in wandering through the South. He was married to a quiet girl. I wondered how she found it possible to put up with his purposeless peregrinations. One incident he recounted, I still recall. In one of his aimless journeys through the country, he came upon a farm-house. Being hungry, he went to the door to inquire if the lady would be so kind as to serve him a meal. The woman, after giving a searching glance at her perspiring visitor, did not look upon him with the favor that he would have liked for her to show. She led him to the back porch, lecturing him at the same time that only those who worked should eat. She showed him a sizeable wood-pile and a large barrel standing by. "Now," said she, "split this wood, fill the barrel, and then come to get your meal."

Had it not been for the increasing pangs of hunger, he would have been tempted to walk off. The barrel was large, the wood tough and full of knots, and the axe bore great nicks in it. While he was pondering his dilemma, a thought occurred to him. Making as much noise as possible to give the effect of great industry, he cut up a small pile of wood, then turned the barrel over and *piled the wood on its bottom!* When the good lady returned and saw what seemed to her a most astounding effort, she became much more cordial, invited him into the house, and sat him down to a good meal. He proceeded to keep her engaged in conversation, lest by any chance she should go out and divine his deception. He anticipated that the encounter under such circumstances would be very unpleasant for him. Having finished his repast, he betook himself off the premises as rapidly as possible. It is of course, not difficult to imagine the feelings of the lady when she afterward discovered the trick that had been played upon her.

I am glad to say that such men were not typical representatives of the gospel, but indicate in a way, what the ministry in the South suffered.

CHAPTER XVII

My Last Year in the South

Having held a number of meetings in the South with moderate success, I felt a burden to establish churches in some of the cities. After considerable prayer, the Lord opened the way for Bill Coxe, Bradley Chitwood, and me to go to Huntsville, Alabama. Today, Huntsville is a great city of nearly 100,000 population. It has for years been the space center of America and the home of the famous Wernher Von Braun, the man who put the first American satellite in the sky; but at that time it was a humble cotton town of 10,000 souls.

Bradley had a tent for which we agreed to pay him rent, and we pitched it in a convenient location in the town. Immediately, we drew considerable attention, and the tent was packed night after night, through the entire summer. Services continued every night, and there was scarcely a meeting in which someone did not find the Lord. Among those reclaimed was a backslidden Baptist preacher by the name of Harris. He had quite a testimony, and usually cried, while he testified. The remarkable healing of his wife, which took place in the meeting, had a most powerful effect upon him and many others. His erratic conduct greatly diminshed the effect of his testimony, however.

Mrs. Harris was a godly woman, who had professed faith in Christ for many years. She had a paralyzed arm that she had not been able to use for a long time. Once a week, we had a special divine healing service, and during one of these services she was prayed for. Suddenly, she discovered to her extreme delight, that she could use the arm that had been paralyzed for so long a time — a circumstance that everyone in the tent knew to be true. This miracle of healing broke the meeting wide open, and all summer we had capacity audiences with scores being won to Christ.

We had adopted a rather free and easy way in our meetings, inviting those who could sing to come to the platform to join our improvised choir. One of the boys, noting that a finely dressed lady had an excellent voice, invited her to the choir. When she hesitated, he pressed the invitation. The next day, to his great embarrassment, he learned that she was a local madame who kept a well-known house. After that he was more careful whom he invited to the platform.

By the time summer was over, we had a very substantial congregation. The meeting was carried on for several weeks longer with considerable success, by two lady evangelists. Afterwards, Bill Coxe rented a hall and carried on the work. Not alone, however. He married one of the lady evangelists, a Miss Lois Leonard, and together they pastored the new church.

While we were in the South, I joined in an effort to establish a church in a little country community just across the Tombigbee River. The services met with a good response, but there was no money to buy lumber for the church. We resorted. therefore, to the expedient of cutting down logs, getting some lumberjacks to haul them for us, and persuading a sawmill to cut the lumber. We soon had a building up, although as I remember it, we were unable to secure a responsible minister to carry on the work.

While we were holding meetings in that community, we rented a house which, like most of the houses in the area, was open underneath to permit air to circulate around the timbers. Razor-back hogs circulated the village at will. Because our house was located at a convenient place, these pigs had a great habit of coming under the house at about two o'clock in the morning and rooting around. They, of course, made so much noise that they woke us up and often kept us awake the rest of the night. The situation became so intolerable that one morning the boys decided to teach the hogs a lesson. One of them posted himself at the open gate with an armload of brickbats, and as the pigs were chased out, he landed a brickbat on the flank of each one as it passed through the gate. Each pig emitted a deep grunt, as if he had been seriously hurt. But the next night they were all back again without exception.

Not far from this community was the town of Waynesboro, where a little later I conducted a campaign. One of the members of this congregation had enjoyed the unusual distinction of being the man they tried to hang but couldn't. So famous did the incident become, that it was carried some years ago in the Reader's Digest. This is the story:

In the year 1893, in Columbia, Mississippi, an ambush party killed a man by the name of Will Buckley, because he had declared that he would testify to a grand jury about the identity of certain persons involved in a horsewhipping. The brother of Will

Buckley escaped the ambush and testified that the one responsible for the shooting was a young man by the name of Will Purvis.

Five neighbors and relatives testified that Will Purvis was at home when the murder was committed. Furthermore his own shotgun had not been fired for months. Nevertheless, the jury doubted their testimony and gave a verdict of guilty.

A Rev. W. S. Sibley was then pastor of the Colombia Methodist Church. He visited Purvis in jail and became convinced of his innocence. During the conversation the earnest pastor succeeded in persuading the young man to accept Christ as his Saviour. Rev. Sibley then called a weekly prayer meeting to pray that God would spare what he believed was an innocent man, from death on the gallows.

It did not appear, however, that their prayers would avail. The courts sustained the conviction. On the day of the scheduled hanging, 3,000 people gathered at the Marion County Court house Square to witness the execution. The sheriff and deputies, experienced in their duties, had seen to it that the rope and the trap door were carefully tested. Both the hands and feet of Purvis were tied together and the black hood made ready. Rev. W. S. Sibley standing near prayed, "Almighty God, if it be thy will, stay the hand of the executioner."

The crowd cried out as the body shot through the opened trap door. But lo! as they looked the hangman's noose swung up, empty of its victim! Will Purvis was still very much alive. The deputies dragged him toward the top of the platform to hang him again. The miracle had changed the minds of the people, and they would, no doubt, have rescued the man had the executioners tried to go on with their work.

Several appeals were made to the governor and the Supreme Court but the pleas were turned down. But then a number of the local inhabitants now convinced of Will's innocence rescued him from the jail. Despite a reward offered by the governor, the law was unable to apprehend him. Then a new governor was elected who had promised during his campaign to commute the sentence. Will Purvis then gave himself up and his sentence was commuted to life imprisonment. Later he received a full pardon, and married the daughter of a Baptist minister. Every Sunday, Will and his wife attended Church and gave thanks to God for saving his life.

Then when Will was 47 years of age, an old planter by the name of Joe Beard, confessed on his deathbed that he and another man had committed the crime. The state legislature paid Purvis $5,000 to atone for the mistake that was made. Will Purvis died a respected member of his community. His testimony was, "God heard our prayers. He saved my life because I was an innocent man."

While in Waynesboro, I had an experience which I never forgot. It involved a man who once had been wealthy, but who died in extreme poverty in the county poorhouse.

It was after midnight, when the call came from the county farm. Traditionally, the poorhouse of yesteryear was a most unprepossessing structure. The good citizens of a community were rarely in a frame of mind to be unduly generous or disposed to allocate any more funds than were required, for the barest necessities in maintaining that drab yet necessary institution. In those forlorn buildings men and women, individuals who once enjoyed happier days with never a thought that they would cke out their declining years as inmates within the poorhouse walls, nevertheless, because of changes of fortune, found that they had nowhere else to go. At best, the food provided was of the cheapest kind; the persons who were then selected to be custodians of the town's indigents, were often of a coarse and insensitive nature. In recent years, the increase of national wealth has wrought considerable changes in the better care of the aged; but the time of which I speak was during the Great Depression. And in the deep South, depression was experienced in its acutest form.

The man who died was at one time comparatively well-to-do. During the Twenties, he was considered one of the most substantial and respected citizens of the community. As was the case of others, however, the market decline, bank failures, and other circumstances resulting from it, wiped out his holdings. Money laid aside for old age had been swept away. Now in his seventies and unable to work, there was no other place for him and his wife to go but to the Waynesboro poor farm, the house of last resort.

He had some relatives. While they were unable to support him, they felt it was their duty to see that he was given a burial. This responsibility they did not evade. These kinsmen attended the church where I was preaching and that was the reason for which I had been called. The deceased was an agnostic, although his poor wife was a professing Christian. I had been asked to accompany some of the relatives to the poorhouse, for the purpose that shall soon become apparent. As we came near the dilapidated building, never have I witnessed a more depressing scene. An eerie moon shed its feeble glow over the dismal landscape. A dog took notice of our arrival by howling dolefully. His mournful baying alerted the master of the ancient institution, who came up to open the gate, to permit our car to enter. There were a few words of greeting and an exchange of conversation as befitted the circumstances, and then we walked up to the door.

It was a long, monotonous building constructed after the plainest fashion. Rough boards were erected vertically to a frame structure, in the manner commonly used in building hen coops and woodsheds, with cleats to cover the cracks. It had never seen a coat of paint. Such an unnecessary expenditure had never occurred to the good men who served in the capacity of trustees.

Upon entering the building, one could see at a glance that only the barest and most essential furniture had been installed in the place. As it was late at night, all the inmates had retired, but they were very much awake. Our entrance resulted in a long row of beady eyes peering out from under covers at us. As I recollect it, there was no reception room and the dead man lay in one of the beds nearest the door. With death impending, it was an obvious advantage to have the dying near the door where he could be more easily removed, since the beds occupied a large part of the space.

I have neglected thus far, to explain the reason for which the inmates, at this late hour, were all awake. The wife of the deceased, an aged woman, sat by the bed and wept out her grief. Sobbing, she cried out again and again, "John's gone! He's gone! I'll never see him again." Over and over she repeated these words, and was inconsolable. How I pitied her. The last thing she had in the world had been taken from her. Her husband was an agnostic, and therefore with no hope in this nor the world to come. And the poor woman knew it only too well.

There before me, the raw drama of life and death had rung the curtain down in its stark reality. How foolish mortals are who go through life without a care, living only for the present moment, as if time would go on forever. A little more pleasure, a little more laying up of earthly treasure. Yet death comes, and as far as this world is concerned, it is the end of everything. The terrible irreversibility of death!

But people visit poorhouses after midnight for business and not for philosophical contemplation, and we must proceed in our grim duty. Today, the funeral-home takes care of everything. Not so in those days, for inmates of the poorhouse who responded to the call of the Rider of the Pale Horse. A coffin of rough pine boards had been prepared, and was now ready. It was plain, with no fancy satin lining, but was adequate and performed the chief function of a coffin. The dead man must now be placed in it. We picked him up to transfer him to the pine box. But now we met with a difficulty. The box had been made after death had taken place, so there had been a delay. In the meantime, rigor mortis had set in. The man did not fit well into his wooden shroud. There was nothing to do but to use force. Perhaps this may seem amusing, but there is nothing humorous about death. It is something with which we, all, must reckon and it makes no difference in the long run whether we are buried in a pine box or a silver casket.

Our job finished, we went to the home of the relatives. In the front yard a bonfire was burning — a custom observed among the poorer people of the South. It was called a wake. The coffin arrived behind us on a truck, and the friends watched through the night. Two other relatives had just come in with shovels. They had put in many weary hours out in the cemetery, digging the grave. I remember one of them cursing. He may have been partly intoxicated. How strange, I thought, that men in the sober atmosphere of death should profane the name of the God, who holds the lives and destinies of all men in His hand. Haughty man is only a heartbeat from death.

The following morning, a simple, graveside service was performed. I preached a few words, tried to comfort the widow, but fear I had little success. What can one say that will give comfort at the death of the wicked?

Today it is different. When the unconverted edges near eternity and fears arise, they are given morphine or some kind of tranquilizer. The dying are ushered into eternity as on a production line, with the minimum amount of trouble, and the maximum of efficiency. The feelings of relatives are soothed and anticipated. Morticians are skilled in the art of making the countenance look as peaceful as possible. The body is placed in a costly casket. The sweet perfume of flowers fills the air with its fragrance, and soft tones from an organ are in the background. The people pass by and observe that the departed looks so calm and natural. But death is just as real, just as stark, just as fearful, whether it is seen in a funeral parlor with the most costly appurtenances, or in the grim confines of a county poorhouse and the background is the wail of the bereaved one. The only true comfort for times like these are the words of the Nazarene, Who said,

"I am the resurrection and the life. He that believeth in me, though he were dead, yet shall he live." (John 11:25)

While in this town of Waynesboro, I stayed at the home of a certain family, who lived on the edge of the city. The family was the very personification of hospitality, giving me the best of everything, while I was in their home. But like many southerners (and northerners too), their deep hostility can be roused if for any reason the virtue of their women is impugned. The father had a young married daughter who stayed at the house. Not long after I had left, a colored boy apparently offended the daughter by some uncalled-for words. The father walked out on the porch, and sternly called the boy to account. The lad rather impudently denied the accusation — in fact, lied to cover up his wrong-doing. The share cropper ordered the boy to come to him, but instead he started running. The man took down his rifle and with a well-placed shot, killed the boy. He then got into his car, went to town and gave himself up.

A grand jury was called, and after due deliberation he was exonerated of blame. Such was the jury's sense of honor for womanhood. Their interest in the preservation of womanly virtue was to be commended, but I could not agree with their verdict even though the defendant had been a good friend of mine. The boy deserved punishment for his conduct, but the taking of human life is not be done lightly.

Mob law is a fearful thing when it gets out of hand. The lynchings that we used to hear about in the South, were a throwback to the confusion that followed the Civil War. One such lynching took place in Sherman, Texas, when we were holding meetings nearby at Farmerville. In this city was witnessed the fearful consequence of mob violence, when its passions were given unrestrained vent.

A negro had been accused of violation of a white woman, and was placed in a cell in the courthouse to await trial. In the meantime, a crowd gathered that soon numbered into the thousands. Certain self-appointed leaders began to stir up trouble and agitate for custody of the prisoner. To save him from the mob's vengeance, officers locked him in a large vault. When those set on a lynching heard this, there were angry mutterings and ominous threats made, indicating that they were not going to be thwarted in their purposes.

Late in the day, two youths and a woman appeared at the rear of the courthouse. The woman hurled a rock through a window, and the boys tossed a large can of gasoline through the opening that was made. A burning match which followed, did the rest, and soon the courthouse was a fiery inferno. Officers, bailiffs and stenographers, alike, rushed for the exits, some climbing out through open windows. There was no time to rescue the unfortunate prisoner in the locked vault who, would be apprized of the horror that awaited him by the gradually rising temperature in the vault that was to become his tomb! The courthouse was an old one and was especially inflammable. Soon the whole building was a roaring mass of flames and the crowd, now standing back at a respectable distance, watched in awed silence, the destruction of the courthouse.

The mob leaders were not yet satisfied. As soon as the ruins cooled, a crew appeared with acetylene torches and special equipment for cutting through steel. Slowly they bored their way into the vault. After many hours of labor, they broke through into the interior, and found the lifeless corpse of the negro. He was carried out and speedily hung on a tree. Negroes fled from their homes in terror. Then, as suddenly as it had begun, the mob's fury abated. The mob beginning to be ashamed of what had been done, slunk away to its homes.

The hoodlum leaders who were responsible for this outrage were not typical of the South, but their deed showed that mobs still had power to overawe constituted authority. It is a mistake, nonetheless, to suppose that such scenes were peculiar only to the South. A minister friend of mine lost his brother in a terrible lynching that occurred in the city of San Jose, not long after the Sherman incident. Every community, whether North or South, has a certain percentage of excitable persons, who can be hypnotized by fanatical and irresponsible leaders. Such men seem to have a strange power to whip up the passions of the people, so that they forget reason and are swept along by their spellbinding.

A lynching merely exposes raw, unregenerate, human nature which has been covered with a superficial veneer of civilization. It was the same spirit that caused the pagans to persecute and torture the Christians of the Early Church. It was the same thing that caused the popes to order the burning of John Huss and Savonarola, and decree the St. Bartholomew's massacre of 1572, or the Crusaders to massacre the Turks as they went to retrieve the Holy Sepulchre from the infidel — all done in the name of virtue and religion. Yet that which is said by the Nazarene when

He was taken by the soldiers to be crucified, is still true today, "They that take the sword, shall perish with the sword."

While in the West, during the previous winter, I had raised some money that enabled me to purchase a fairly, good-sized tent. Actually, I bought the materials and had the tent made. We pitched it in two or three towns, including Yazoo City north of Jackson. I was practically alone at the time, and I discovered that by the time I had gone through all the effort of getting the tent up and seating it, I was so exhausted I did not have the strength to properly carry on the revival. I felt that the meeting, as it developed, was not a success. Souls were saved, but we did not have the breakthrough for which I was looking. With finances limited, I decided to take the tent down. I loaded it on my trailer and drove out of town some ten miles, when the car stopped. Something serious had gone wrong, and I could not possibly repair the trouble. In two hours, it would be dark. To leave the tent on the roadside and go for help would be to invite theft. I was weary from my labors and almost without money. What could I do? There seemed to be no possible answer at that moment. I had only a few dollars — certainly not enough to send for help.

Then suddenly a voice seemed to speak to me, as it did to Elijah. It seemed to say, "Son, what doest thou here?" I had been preaching to others that we had an all-powerful God; yet, here I was discouraged and about to give up. At that moment, I knelt down in the middle of the road and began to pray in a loud voice, asking God to come on the scene and vindicate His Word, and get me into Jackson by dark with my trailer — by what means I knew not.

I really had no more right to expect to get the car and trailer into Jackson by sundown, than if I had asked to be landed on the moon. But when I arose from where I was kneeling, I expected a miracle to happen. But what kind of a miracle, I hardly knew. Even while I was standing there, a man with a brand-new Plymouth stopped by and asked if he could help. I told him I needed assistance, but I didn't know how he could help me. My own car was loaded down, and behind it was the trailer with the large tent, with poles, stakes, etc. He said, "Do you have a rope?" I answered, "Yes, but do you think your car could pull both vehicles?" My words apparently decided the matter. He had a new car, and undoubtedly my question was challenging its power. He backed his car up to mine and said tersely, "Tie it on." I did, and realizing the strain to which it would be subjected, I took the rope and doubled it back and forth as many times as was possible.

I got into my car, and he into his. In gaining traction, his back wheels whipped out a volley of pebbles, but finally we got into motion. What a strange procession it was, each vehicle pulling the other. I have never seen anything like it on the highway before nor since. Gradually we picked up speed, forty, fifty, fifty-five, sixty miles an hour! The dynamics of three vehicles each pulling the other, resulted in some very curious effects, not unlike those produced in the game, crack-the-whip, where several persons are hand in hand and the tail of the line is whipped from the opposite end.

As anyone knows who has ever pulled a trailer, any movement of the car has a double effect on the trailer behind. Now, when a third vehicle is attached, weighted down with a fair-sized tent, the effects are compounded many-fold, especially when travelling at a high rate of speed. I summoned all the skill I ever learned about driving, using the clutch, brakes, and steering wheel to counteract the complex motions set up by this curious arrangement. Hills rose and fell as we made our way to Jackson, the driver not once slackening his pace. We were not breaking any known law; legislators, who had thought of everything else, had not anticipated any such combination of vehicles operating on their fair highways!

At last we approached Jackson. As we slowed down, I could begin to relax from the strenuous effort required in keeping the trailer from whipping about so far, as to cause the car to get out of control. When we stopped, I went out to untie the ropes. I perceived that only two or three flimsy strands were left! I took them loose, but the significance was lost on the driver who was thinking only of the performance of his new car. With a triumphant voice he asked, "What do you think now, of this buggy?" I agreed with him, that he had a wonderful car. I offered him money but he waved aside the poor little amount I had to give him, and the Good Samaritan was on his way apparently, as highly pleased as I was, by the feat he had accomplished!

It all seemed very humorous after it was over, but I began to realize that I was not operating in a manner that could be considered sound, when miracles of such a precarious nature were required to keep me from coming to disaster. I had been preaching in the South for quite a few years. I was soon to make a decision to return to the West and to work in that area, perhaps to raise up some churches in California.

Before I left the South, an event took place that particularly impressed me. While in Louisiana, I had followed with interest the rise of one of the most amazing, political personalities of American history—Huey P. Long. Brilliant, astonishingly resourceful, irresistibly persuasive with the common man, and utterly ruthless, he appeared on the political horizon as a blazing meteor, and then as suddenly disappeared from the scene, as the result of an assassin's bullet. Many astute political observers claim he would have been president of the United States in 1940, and made it into a dictatorship as he did the state of Louisiana.

The working of the mind of Huey Long was amazingly swift, always anticipating any move of his opponent. Early in his political career his enemies, correctly discerning his dictatorial ambitions, laid plans to impeach him from his office of railroad commissioner. Before they could act, Long, by the force of his hypnotic persuasiveness, managed to secure enough of the state senators to sign a "round robin" which committed them to support him, regardless of what maneuvers his opponents might make. From that time on, the rise to power of Huey Long was irresistible. Soon after winning the governorship, he not only made a rubber stamp of the legislature, but every department of the state, including the police force, was brought under his thumb. With his deadly wit, he cut his opponents down and made a laughing stock of them. Having set up a dictatorship in Louisiana such as has been unknown in the history of America, he began holding political rallies in other states. One campaign, for example, was held in Arkansas. In that state there were six candidates for senator, and the one who had the least chance of winning was Hattie Caraway. But after Huey's spellbinding campaigning for her just before election, the people of Arkansas gave her a thumping majority. As leader of his delegation from Louisiana, his speech at the Chicago convention had much to do with the nomination and election of Franklin Roosevelt as president of the United States.

At that time, America was still in the throes of the Great Depression. Huey came out with a dazzling program which he called "Share the Wealth," which proposed confiscating the wealth of the rich for the benefit of the poor. Share the Wealth Clubs sprung up everywhere, and millions of people looked to Long and his nostrums as the salvation of the country.

The time was ripe for the political panaceas of the demogogues. Father Coughlin and Dr. Townsend were busy advocating their messianic programs, but it was the spellbinding personality of Huey Long who really moved the masses. It was no false alarm; political leaders, including President Roosevelt against whom Huey had turned his big guns, were frankly apprehensive. They foresaw a national rallying to this brilliant but unprincipled demogague which conceivably might thrust him into the White House.

One Friday night in September, I listened for a long time as Huey discoursed on the radio at great length, on his plans for taking over America. His speech was exciting and amazingly convincing. Facile of tongue, he spoke effortlessly and with apparently inexhaustible energy. The minister in whose home I was staying, a godly man but quite naive as far as political matters were concerned, listened approvingly. "People know that Louisiana is now on the map," he observed with pride. He, too, felt that Huey Long would be president by 1940, and was the answer to the Depression.

But some of the people of Louisiana who had opposed Long's political ambitions, were experiencing the consequences of his ruthless dictatorship. Huey knew how to take care of his enemies. Placed on his "blacklist" they soon found that opportunities to make a living, vanished. A man by the name of Dr. Carl Weiss was one of these. Some have come up with the theory that Weiss labored under the delusion that Long planned to charge his father-in-law, Judge Pavy, with having negro blood. At any rate bitter and brooding, Weiss carried a gun, met Huey in the marble corridors of the skyscraper he had built in Baton Rouge, and fired a shot that abruptly ended the career of the Louisiana Kingfish. Long was rushed to Our Lady of the Lake Sanitarium. The best surgeons were at New Orleans. They were called, but a car wreck prevented their arriving on time. The emergency operation that was performed, failed to take into consideration that the bullet had nicked a kidney. In thirty hours, Huey Long was dead.

That Sunday night I had preached, and then retired for the night. Not yet asleep, I suddenly began to be aware of voices in the distance. I soon realized it must be newsboys shouting an extra. I bought a paper which headlined the grim news: *HUEY LONG SHOT AND PERHAPS DYING!* Then I realized how men with their great plans are brought low, in a moment of time. Today they are here, tomorrow they are gone and are seen no more. According to Herman Deutch's, "The Huey Long Murder Case," among Huey's last words was the request, "Pray for me."

Huey believed the Bible and quoted from it often. He was familiar with the gospel message, and frequently referred to events in old-time-revival services he attended as a youth. It is interesting to speculate just what would have happened had Huey Long turned his enormous talents to the calling of an evangelist. Had those remarkable abilities been sanctified by the Spirit, he could possibly have won a million souls to Christ. But Huey Long had his hour. Surely these words are true:

"Only one life. 'twill soon be past.

Only what's done for Christ will last."

CHAPTER XVIII

How to Start a Church

My brother-in-law, L. D. Hall, was pastor at Coalinga, California. Twenty-five miles farther south was the new oil town of Avenal. Here a great oil field had been recently discovered and opened up. Some of the deepest wells in the world had been sunk there.

Having returned to the West and after waiting upon the Lord in the matter, I decided to attempt to establish a church in that town. I pitched my tent which I had brought from the South, and began meetings there in January. Ordinarily, there is little rain in that city, especially that time of the year. With the help of my brother-in-law, I got the tent set up and arranged it in as attractive a manner as possible.

We had one or two services in it, and then the storm struck — one of the worst I have ever experienced. I was sleeping in the tent, to insure its safety from molestation. Around midnight, the wind came up and then the storm struck in all its fury. Because the entire town is built on slanting ground, streams of water soon began pouring down the slope. The dirt barricade that had been provided around the tent was quickly broken through and the swirling water mounted until it was nearly a foot deep. My cot was on the platform, so I was safe from the water. But my apprehensions were not concerning the water, but rather the wind which had reached gale proportions. Instead of subsiding, it continued to increase in violence. I realized that the tent could not long stand the pressure of such a force, but I could think of nothing to do at the moment to better the situation. And then it happened! A particularly savage gust of wind lashed the tent, pulling out the stakes at one end. This was all that was needed, for the other stakes, one by one to give way. Tent poles and canvas came toppling down upon me!

I crawled out from under the canvas, fortunately unharmed. The rain was driven with a relentless force, and within five seconds I was soaked as much as I ever would be. There was only one thing to do. I gathered up as many of my belongings as I could put in the car, got the motor started, and drove to Coalinga.

Arriving at my brother's-in-law, I presented, I fear, a rather sorry appearance. Brother Hall got out of bed and going back with me, we salvaged as much as possible from the wreckage. Such are the problems one faces, when he attempts to establish a church in a new field.

I decided then upon another plan. We would buy a lot and build a canvas tabernacle in the center of the town. The Coalinga church helped us some, and in a few weeks' time we had a tabernacle with a canvas top up. We reinforced it heavily against possible storms in the future.

By the month of June, we had a fair congregation gathered — not large but sufficient to take care of a pastor. I then resigned and made plans to hold some evangelistic meetings, after which I would choose another community in which to establish a full gospel church.

It was while I was visiting Portland, that I saw Freda again. Several years had elapsed since she had been converted in our Portland meeting. She had been faithful in attending services and taking part in all the activities of the Portland Foursquare Church, pastored by the brilliant minister, Dr. Harold Jefferies. She also attended their Bible School. Later, she became president of the young people's Crusaders. After giving the matter several months of prayer, I asked her to become my wife. About a year later we were married. She proved to be a remarkably capable helpmate in the gospel work.

It had been my plan to establish a church in one of the cities in the greater Los Angeles area. Often young men just entering the ministry, wonder just how one goes about establishing a new work. So I will give a few details, in the case of the San Fernando church. Starting in a new field is not the easiest job in the world, but it has its rewards. In pioneering a new church, you become its founder. Your efforts make possible all that will take place in the future. In time, your name may be forgotten by the people who will enjoy the benefits of your labor, but not in God's book of remembrance. All that is done afterward, is accomplished because you sowed the seed!

After making some preliminary explorations of the situation, I decided to go to the city of San Fernando, a town about twenty miles north of Los Angeles proper. It was not long before I discovered that a very curious situation existed there. A man who had been in a psychopathic institution and had been released, was holding forth in a barn-like structure next to the railroad tracks. Naturally, the poor fellow made a very unfavorable impression upon the community. He was behind in payments of lights, gas and water bills, and was on the point of being ejected for non-payment of rent. In the community, there were a few saints who had attended for a time, but the situation was so unappealing that they soon quit, and with no income, the man could not pay the bills. After talking with him and reviewing the situation, I agreed to take over the hall, bills and all.

My next step was to visit the one family who had been faithfully attending the little mission, and from them I got the names of several families who lived in the area, who might be interested in coming to the services. They had come to the mission hall a few times previously, and were members of the same denomination I was. They were attending here and there, but had not really settled down anywhere.

I held a two-week revival in the old mission hall, with a fair attendance. Then I invited a young evangelist, Howard Clark, from my brother's-in-law church, to hold a meeting for me, while I made further plans.

As I have said, in taking over the mission, I had agreed to be responsible for bills that had fallen due. I also learned that this minister who had been in the psychopathic ward, had borrowed a considerable sum from his sister, who owned a walnut orchard south of town, to pay some of the bills that had been long overdue.

I have been amazed at the conduct of some ministers, who pile up debts and show a flagrant sense of irresponsibility in paying them. They do not seem to realize that by their conduct, they betray all for which the ministry stands. They seem to get by for awhile, and this encourages them to continue in their ways. The time finally comes, of course, when their manners catch up with them, and then they cannot understand why they have to pay the piper. Individuals who are irresponsible in making debts they cannot pay, have no place in the ministry. This statement, of course, does not include those who, when they get into financial difficulties, make an honest attempt to pay their bills. Nor do I suppose that it should refer to this poor fellow, who had suffered from mental troubles. Actually, he should not have attempted what was quite beyond his ability to accomplish.

It would have been easy to disregard the debt owed to this woman, but I saw no way of honorably evading it. So, I gathered up courage and drove out to her home. She was moderately well-to-do and could afford the loss. But whether she was a poor person or a millionaire, had no bearing on the matter. Arriving at her home, I knocked on the door. It was opened presently by a woman, with what seemed to me a most suspicious expression. Certainly, it did not give me any encouragement. I must have stumbled over my words in my poor attempt to introduce myself and give the reason for my visit. Upon learning who I was, she cut me short and what she had to say was aplenty. Her tongue was sharp as a razor, and she let me know in no uncertain terms what she thought of me and all the people who attended that mission. (Actually, there had been scarcely anybody attending it.) She went on to declare that they were nothing but hypocrites, who wouldn't pay their bills, but who claimed to have religion more than anybody else. Well, if that was religion, she wanted none of it. And so she went on, until finally she had her say.

I had no hopes of conciliating the woman. I simply said, "Madam, I am very sorry all this happened, but I have only been in the town a few weeks. Having learned about the debt that was made, I considered it a matter of honor to come and find out how much it was and make arrangements to pay it." I told her I did not have the money then, but would pay the debt off a little at a time, and would she be pleased to make a statement of how much was owed her.

If I had actually struck the woman, I could scarcely have achieved a more surprising result. She had been all set to dress me down further, but here I was acknowledging the debt and agreeing to pay it. Now, it was her turn to find it difficult to speak. Actually, she was a decent sort of woman but like most people, hated to be taken advantage of. It wasn't the amount of money at stake, it was the fact that she didn't want to be taken in.

Finally, she said, "Well, I am sorry that I talked to you the way I did. I see you are wanting to do the right thing." She hesitated a moment and then said, "By the way, I understand my brother left owing some other bills. How much are they?"

"Oh," I replied, "it is true there were some other bills but that is nothing for you to worry about." But she insisted that I let her know what they were. So I gave her a list. The total was less than one hundred dollars, which does not seem like much today, but was indeed a formidable sum to me then. She went out of the room for a moment, and came back with a check. It was made out to me for the exact amount of all the bills past due! Now she said, "Forget about what is owed me and take this check and pay all the bills, and do not think too hard of me for what I said."

When I recovered from the shock, I assured her fervently and sincerely that I thought she was a wonderful person, and that her unexpected generosity was something ,I never anticipated. When I realize how important her assistance was in helping me get started in San Fernando, I am still of the same opinion.

Within six weeks, we had gathered together a fair-sized congregation, but I knew we could not get very far in the shabby building we were using. We had no money with which to make a move, but still I knew that we had to do something. The secret of a good pastor is always to keep one step ahead of the people, whether it be a small or large congregation. They must feel their minister is going somewhere. Then, they will accept his leadership.

I had not been in San Fernando long, before I learned that in the very heart of town was a piece of property, almost a third of an acre, which had three buildings on it. Two were houses, while the third was a building that needed to be torn down. Nonetheless, it had a lot of good lumber in it. I had been informed that the owner wished to sell, and it had been put up for sale a short time back for $3,500. At today's prices, the same property would be worth at least fifteen or twenty thousand dollars. Perhaps more.

I remember going out in the moonlight and stepping off the property. In my spirit, I claimed it for God's work. We were not ready to buy it, and even to get an option, I would need a hundred dollars. And how to get the hundred dollars? This is what we did. At every service we had a "penny march." This fund gradually grew until we had our hundred dollars. I then had an option made out, ready to sign, so drove to Hueneme where the owner lived.

I felt that we just had to have this property. One of the houses could be used as a parsonage, and the other would help make the payments. The old building could be torn down and made into a temporary tabernacle. But were the people at Hueneme still of a mind to sell at their old price? A $3,500 debt would be about all we could dare take on. I drove to the city where the owners lived, met them and talked the situation over. They were willing to sell, but they wanted $4,500 now! My heart sank. I told them that with our limited resources, we could manage to obligate ourselves for the $3,500, but I did not think we could take on a debt of $4,500. The husband and wife went into another room and talked for a long time, while I remained in the parlor silently praying. It seemed that everything was at stake at that moment. After what seemed an interminable length of time, they were back and said they would sign. That is how we got the property.

I lost no time in tearing down the building. I worked long hours and got all the donated help I could. Two of our men were contractors, and they poured the concrete floor. I used a very unorthodox system in constructing the roof. Finding a lot of old cable in the building that had been dismantled, I took this cable and stretched it between the two walls. Then I used my car to supply the power to stretch it tight. When the cable was taut, I put on the brakes and secured the cables. This held the building together when the roof was put on. Of course the tabernacle would be a temporary affair, which would give way to a permanent church building later on.

And so it was that in a period of two months from the time we came to San Fernando, we had paid off the debt against the mission, assembled a congregation, secured an option on property which in a few years' time was worth at least $15,000, not to speak of the improvements that would be made. One of the houses made a good parsonage and the other brought in a welcome rental. In another month's time, we had the tabernacle up and were holding meetings in it. I recite these things to encourage others who feel called to launch out for God. There is an old saying which goes as follows, "Pray as if everything depended upon God, and work as if everything depended on you."

CHAPTER XIX

Marriage and Our First Meetings Together

In the fall, arrangements had been made for our marriage. I drove to Portland, my sister Fern accompanying me for the wedding. Freda had been president of the Foursquare Crusaders for some time, and the church almost outdid itself to make it a fancy wedding. I shall not describe it. The groom is the least important part of a wedding; the bride gets all the attention. However, he has this one consolation: They could not have the wedding without him.

My mother insisted that I follow protocol. I must wear a tuxedo. Since my wardrobe had never boasted any such luxury, I had to locate one. I discovered that there was a man in town that made a living by renting such outfits. With the assistance of my mother, who used pins at strategic points, she got it to make a pretty fair fit. Part of the ensemble buttoned down the back. At last I was dressed and presumably ready for the occasion. Rather uncomfortable in this pretentious outfit, I prepared for the great event, which was executed in due time. We then returned to San Fernando.

I may add at this point that Freda was to become a great asset to my ministry. She had taken several years of Bible School in Portland, and had hoped to complete her course in L.I.F.E. Institute, since she would require only six months to graduate. I felt it would be wise for her to complete her Bible School education, so I resigned the church at San Fernando and Carl Leonard took it over. For the next several months I continued in the evangelistic ministry.

It is of course, impossible to even mention the many cities in which we labored during the next few years, and the numerous, interesting events that transpired. In all, I probably held 150 campaigns during the course of my evangelistic ministry, before we launched out into the large city-wide meetings which reached thousands of people a night.

Shortly before Freda graduated from L.I.F.E., I was asked to take over a new work that had just been started in a northern city. I was there only a brief time until my wife joined me, and together we worked hard to get the church established. We did not succeed in making it a large church, but we did get it over the bumps, and through the years it has slowly grown.

There were a few incidents that happened in this city, that I must describe, which I believe will be of interest to the reader. I have related some of them elsewhere in my writings, but they will bear repetition.

At the crucial time, when we were putting forth every effort to keep the church from going under, there was a lady, the wife of one of the deacons, who had become seriously offended at the previous pastor. In spite of his mistakes, I was convinced that she herself was a difficult person with whom to deal. She felt that she had been insulted, and I could see that she thirsted for revenge. We needed every adult person we could possibly hold on to, if we were going to save the church. So I used every means within my power to conciliate her and to soothe her wounded feelings. At length, I saw that this was impossible, for she had predicted that the church was going to go to pieces, and so she was going to lend every effort herself, to make her words come true. We tried to be patient with her, and even conceded that she had some just cause for complaint. Finally, however, we were forced to admit that our most persistent efforts to win her sympathy had proven a complete failure. Moreover, we perceived her actions were steadily undermining the faith of other members of the church. Her husband, a good man, was on the verge of backsliding, and the whole church was being jeopardized by her conduct.

Realizing that further efforts to conciliate her were useless, and that the future of the church was hanging in the balance, I returned to my home one day and laid the matter before my wife. I told her that I felt definitely led to turn this woman over to Divine discipline, lest both she and the church should be brought to ruin as a result of her bitter implacable spirit. Kneeling down, we agreed in prayer that this offender in the church be bound in spirit, that she might know how serious a matter it was to trifle with the work of God. (1 Cor. 5:5)

What was the outcome? We recall the details clearly. In the matter of a few days, we received a call from the husband to come at once to their home. When we arrived, we were met with a scene that baffled description. This headstrong woman, who had so relentlessly sought to destroy the work of God, now lay on her bed, her eyes filled with stark terror. She plead with us to do something to help her. She believed a devil had taken possession of her, and that she was about to lose her mind. We looked at her frightened expression, and saw that she was indeed telling the truth. We told her that we would pray but gently reminded her that there was something for her to do. We left after a few minutes. But the next day or so, we were called again. This time we no sooner entered her room, when she began to pour out an awful confession of her rebellion. She accused herself of being the cause of every trouble the church had ever had. She went on to add that she had been given up of God, and that the devil had taken her over. The poor woman avowed that she had committed the unpardonable sin and that her case was hopeless.

We visited her a number of times, and now that she had repented, encouraged her to accept full forgiveness through the blood of Jesus. For quite a time she refused to believe that there was hope for her, but at length she came to the place where hope began to return. It was perhaps a month before she was able to get out of bed, but during that time, one by one, she called all the members of the church to her bedside and asked their forgiveness, which all were willing to do.

She was finally able to return to the church, and from that time on, proved to be a most humble and submissive woman, never again saying a word that in any way could adversely affect the welfare of the church.

The other incident concerned our young people's leader, one of the finest we ever had, whom I shall call Joan, although that was not her real name. She was an exceptionally beautiful young lady, talented, musical, artistic, but above all she had a real burden for souls. Through her efforts she held the young people's group together, which was the one bright spot in the church. She used to come to the house and have dinner with us on Sundays. And no more delightful person could be found.

After we left the city, we thought once or twice of inviting her to join our evangelistic party, but were reluctant to ask her, because we knew she was needed badly in the church where we had been. Occasionally, we heard from her and finally we received a note that she was going to attend Bible School in Los Angeles.

Now comes the sad part of our story. We did not hear from her for a number of years. Then, when we were holding the meeting in the Shrine Auditorium in Los Angeles, my wife saw her under the strangest circumstances. She has told the story in a previous publication and I give it here as she wrote it:

She was a beautiful girl — a rather tall, slender blond. Her grace and charm won her many friends. Her musical talent gave her an open door of service. When she stood before an audience, there was a natural poise about her, that was both fascinating and relaxing. But above and beyond all this, there was a genuine consecration to the cause to which she was dedicated — so much so, that she spent many of her Sunday afternoons, at the church praying for the young people, whose meetings she led at 6 P.M. Her entire family was spiritual and a credit to our church. To sum it all up, she was an outstanding leader, with a bright future, if she continued to wholly follow the Lord.

After knowing this girl for several years, our close contact with her was broken when we left that part of the country for other fields of labor for the Lord. We heard, indirectly, that she had gone to Los Angeles to attend Bible School.

But while in school, she made the mistake that many before her had made — that, of getting her eyes on people, instead of keeping them on Jesus. She became lonesome, disillusioned, and discouraged — a fertile field for the Devil to begin sowing his seeds of doubt and discontent.

Next, she began attending a church whose standards were considerably lower than those she upheld in her home town. Then came the report that the pastor was keeping company with this blond. How could this be? He, a married man with a family? But it was true! And finally, the news that they had run away!

But the wife had somewhat to say. Soon the police were on their trail, and shortly after, apprehended them. The minister was put in jail and convicted of stealing, as the car he had used to make his getaway, was in his wife's name and thus was her personal property.

And there in that jail was born one of the most satanic-inspired, false religions. The minister, instead of confessing and forsaking his sin, decided to go on a fast. To get an individual to repent is a Herculean task, unless the Spirit of God is given place to work. The guilty would rather do most anything than to confess and forsake his sin. It has been said that the two hardest words to say in the American language are, "I'm sorry." But God's Word says, "Obedience is better than sacrifice."

Finally, as he continued his fast, a voice spoke and said, "You must start a new religion. All other religions are wrong. The Christian faith is error. Christ is a bastard. You must overthrow them all. You must start this new doctrine now. Call this true religion Y—."

Immediately, he sent for his newly acquired wife. As he told her of his "revelation," a strange power came upon her — a strong delusion from hell — and she embraced this cult, utterly forsaking Christ! But he had to serve out his term in the penitentiary. Who was to carry on in the mean time? Why she, of course!

And so it was, after our party had just completed a large salvation-healing revival in Los Angeles which ended in the Shrine Auditorium, with some 7,000 attending in a single night, we picked up the local paper and there beheld an announcement of a Sunday afternoon service by this strange cult. I felt I must attend and see for myself, as the reports were hard to believe about one who had been so close to us.

Making my way into a large auditorium of one of the downtown hotels, I slipped into a seat near the rear of the room, breathing a prayer that I would go unnoticed. Several hundred people were present.

Soon the service began. Someone led some songs, all of which were unfamiliar to me. I looked anxiously for our friend. At last, she made her way to the platform. There she stood, beautifully clothed in a long, shining garment, with a cluster of flowers on her left shoulder. All eyes were upon her!

What I was to see and hear during the next hour, even yet brings cold chills to me, and will remain indelibly imprinted on my mind as long as I live! All at once, a spontaneous praise and worship of Y— broke forth from the people, as they rose to their feet with hands stretched toward heaven. This occurred again and again. I felt at times I must run from the building, so oppressive to me were the powers of darkness, but I decided to weather it, sitting silently with my hat somewhat pulled over my face to avoid recognition.

And then came the sermon — a bitter attack against Christianity. The blond mistress stood there and cursed and blasphemed Christ, again and again, calling Him "bastard," while the congregation shouted, "Praise Y—!" She read scriptures from the Bible concerning the Holy Spirit, the Virgin Birth, the Resurrection. She would describe the event in a lewd manner and pervert it into a sex joke, amid a mighty roar of "Praise Y—" from her adherents.

At long last, the service came to a close. Refreshments were served, but I could not partake as they were offered to "strange gods." Then it was that I stepped in line to shake hands with the speaker. When suddenly she recognized me, her face became an ashen white, and she began to tremble. Calling me by my first name (which she had never before done), she asked, "Were you in service?" I replied in the affirmative. I then asked her to accompany us to dinner, as Brother Lindsay was to join me momentarily. She declined with many and varied excuses, but I insisted.

Another hour passed, and it was apparent that our guest was stalling for time, hoping we would leave. She disappeared into a dressing room, outside of which we stationed ourselves, as the minutes ticked wearliy away. Finally, at long last she emerged with several "attendants," who, she informed us, must accompany her. We drove to Clifton's Cafeteria and there persuaded her to leave her "escorts" in the car while we went in to eat.

Once inside, there was a coldness in the atmosphere. Nevertheless, we tried to be friendly and encouraged her to talk. Finally, she opened up. She was, not too many years hence, to give birth to the true Messiah, out in the desert, in a haven that was even now being established. As for Christianity, she had forsaken it because it was dying.

Then it was that Brother Lindsay asked her if she had heard of the large meeting our party had just closed in the Shrine. No, she hadn't heard. Nor had she heard of other similar campaigns in various cities with many thousands attending. We assured her that the real Christian revival was just getting underway, thousands were getting saved and healed, and God was pouring out His Spirit on all flesh. Her face registered surprise and bewilderment as we continued to show her the error of her decision. Then nervously, she arose quickly, shook hands with Brother Lindsay, threw her arms around me, hugged and kissed me, and walked away to join her "escorts."

When we arrived back at our apartment, we prayed earnestly for her salvation if she had not already crossed the line, and asked God to bring a halt to this terrible delusion which was spreading as a new religion. We stayed in the city an additional two weeks. Each Saturday, we would look for her ad. Each time it stated, "Due to the illness of — (the young blond) — no service would be held." We learned later that week, from a relative of hers, that immediately after she left us, she developed a throat trouble and was unable to talk. We felt God had at least temporarily closed down the services while we were in the city.

For a long time we had no further news concerning this cult, though occasionally we got a letter in our office from one who had fallen into the Devil's trap. "Because they received not the love of the truth, that they might be saved. And for this cause God shall send them strong delusion, that they should believe a lie, that they all might be damned who believed not the truth, but had pleasure in unrighteousness." (II Thess. 2:10-12)

Now comes the most startling development: I had been seeking information concerning the status of this movement and also the sequel to what had happened to this young woman.

I was dictating a letter to a Los Angeles newspaper for possible information, when our secretary, who had recently been a resident of Denver, suddenly paused and looked up saying, "I know what happened to that woman!" This of course took me by surprise, that our secretary would have any knowledge of the matter. And what she told me, shocked me beyond words! Nevertheless, she affirmed that it was true, so we wrote to the Denver News from which we have gathered the following information.

We learned from this newspaper that at the time this young woman disappeared from our knowledge, she had entered the entertainment field, and in 1950, was known in Houston as the "Blond Bombsell," in the various night clubs, where she sang and played. After several years of nightlife, she decided to turn again to her strange religious delusion. However, by this time, and we quote from Denver's Rocky Mountain News, March 4, 1957, "she separated from her husband — and divorce proceedings were under way.

"Miss — leased her offices in Denver, a week ago with plans to lecture and write on psychic phenomena stressing the use of extra-sensory perception. She planned to establish headquarters here for the Kingdom of — , a religious cult.

"She told police she was working late Friday when she was accosted by a tall Negro man. She said the man raped her after smashing a pop bottle over her head and striking her in the mouth and stomach. The assailant then knifed a janitor who came to her aid.

"One day later, on Sunday morning, Miss — was found by her hostess, with her feet resting on the bed and her head and shoulders on the floor. It appeared she suffered a convulsion. Death occurred at 6:30 A.M."

The Rocky Mountain News carried inch tall headlines on the front page of Monday's paper — with a seven inch photograph — saying, BLOND MYSTIC DIES AFTER ASSAULT. So ended the career of one who might have been greatly used of God, had she followed in His footsteps.

CHAPTER XX

We Pastor in Ashland

For several years my wife and I engaged in evangelistic work. During that period, a daughter and son were born to us, Carole and Gilbert. For a time we traveled with both children, which is not the easiest way to engage in the ministry. We were in Wickenburg, Arizona, when the attack on Pearl Harbor occurred. I realized that America was in for a trying period. People were allowed little gas for their cars, and this circumstance became an added hindrance in the holding of revival meetings.

While we were in Nevada, we received some very sorrowful tidings. I was summoned to the phone on a long distance call from Mother. She acquainted me with the sad news that my niece, Elaine, youngest daughter of my sister Gladys, and her husband, had been killed in an accident. She was a favorite niece of mine, vivacious and full of life. A man operating a road-grader offered her a ride, although it was strictly against all rules for him to do so. Somehow, as he was engaged in conversation with her, he failed to notice an approaching train. The locomotive plunged into the road-grader, and both he and the girl were instantly killed. My brother-in-law was working on the roof of his church, when a man who was one of his members drove up. He owned an ambulance, and it had been summoned to the tragedy. Now he must break the sad news to his pastor, and he hardly knew how to do it.

My brother-in-law saw him and asked him what he wanted. "Better come down at once," the man said. "There has been an accident and your little girl has been involved." "Is it serious?" the father asked, vaguely suspecting something dreadful had happened. The man answered softly, "She is dead."

The world seemed to crash around Leon when he looked at her body, still warm. A few minutes before, she had been alive and well. Now, the terrible irrevocability of death crowded upon his mind, as he realized that shortly he would be looking upon the form of his little daughter, for the last time. To my sister, it seemed a nightmare from which she would surely wake up. But she knew that this was not to be. For awhile, she felt that she could never smile again. And the "ifs" began to torment her. If her child had not walked down the road just at this time. If the man had not broken the law and picked her up on his grader. If he had only looked, when he approached the railroad tracks. And the inevitable human cry, "Why, why, did it have to happen?"

There are some things that happen to all of us in this world, for which we cannot seem to find the answer. One thing is certain: this world is a very temporary place! Most of the human race acts as if it were going to be here, forever. Men strive and labor and sometimes sell their souls, in a desperate attempt to accumulate as much of this world's goods as possible. Yet, in a moment of time they are taken away from it all, snatched into eternity from whence they never return.

Bereavement often leaves those of this world confused, and in a state of hopelessness. But Christians have a consolation. They know that they shall surely see their loved ones again.

They know that beyond this vale of tears, there is a bright tomorrow. What consummate folly then, what monstrous madness, for a man to put off his soul's salvation, for the trifling baubles of time. Jesus told about a rich man who thought he had many years to live:

"And he thought within himself, saying, What shall I do, because I have no room where to bestow my fruits? And he said, This will I do: I will pull down my barns, and build greater; and there will I bestow all my fruits and my goods. And I will say to my soul, Soul, thou has much goods laid up for many years; take thine ease, eat, drink, and be merry. But God said unto him, Thou fool, this night thy soul shall be required of thee: then whose shall those things be, which thou hast provided?" (Luke 12:17-20)

While we were visiting in Grants Pass with my sister and her husband, we received a call from the church at Ashland, Oregon, to become its pastor. It was a small congregation, but we decided to accept the call. The church had a few excellent families, who had a real vision to see something done in that city, but it had a long record of being a small church. The Sunday School, the first Sunday we were there numbered just forty persons, although it had averaged somewhat more than that. One reason for which the church had remained small was that it was a community where many old folks came to retire. Moreover, there were quite a number of churches in the town, and therefore, interest was divided between them.

I believe, nevertheless, that a minister should not allow his attention to be fixed on difficulties. There will always be opportunities, and if a pastor makes the most of those that he has, he will find that he has a growing church.

My wife and I resolved that we would not allow an opportunity to build up the church, pass us by, and if we did not find opportunities ready-made, we would make them. Our first step, we knew, was to make new contacts. If necessary, we would start visiting the families of the community — a certain number of persons each day. We didn't follow this plan long, since our work soon gave us many contacts, and we found that the returns were much greater visiting prospects with whom the church had some contact, than just taking everybody as they came.

I soon saw that if our Sunday School was to be enlarged, we would have to dig a basement, to make more room. There was enough space under the building for several Sunday School rooms, as well as a young people's chapel. But since the finances were pitifully small, there was no use frightening the church by proposing that we put a basement under the whole building. Rather, we would start with two rooms. Later on, we would complete excavation underneath the whole church.

I am saying these things for the encouragement of the young minister, who usually must start in a small way. If he desires success, he must keep one step ahead of his congregation. On the other hand, he must not bite off more than he can chew. If he is going to be a good pastor, he must also be a good business man. Nothing disheartens a congregation more than to see that their pastor has wasted their money, because of the lack of proper planning. There has always been a controversy over how much authority a pastor should have, and how much a deacon board should have. I lean to the side of the pastor — that the leadership should reside in the shepherd of the flock. To maintain this leadership, the pastor must carefully plan his program with much prayer and waiting on God. If he proves slothful and incompetent, the board is gradually going to assert more and more authority, for they too have responsibility in protecting the interests of their congregation.

A pastor must demonstrate ability in the pulpit. He must be able to feed the people from the Word of God, and not be a purveyor of dull sermons void of windows. He must possess an evangelistic touch, if his church is to grow. The gospel, with its great issues of life and death, heaven and hell, with Divine healing and the miraculous is a tremendously dramatic thing. It is unfortunate for a church to be saddled with a pastor who preaches boring sermons. There is no place for a dull preacher, nor one who is too lazy or unimaginative to prepare messages that are directed straight to the needs of the people. A pastor, of all people, must be practical. He should learn how to help individuals with their daily problems. He should have wisdom to counsel them on the important decisions that they face in their everyday life. He should learn how to help individuals with their daily problems. He should have wisdom to counsel them on the important decisions that they face in their everyday life. He should be able to inspire them with faith for health and healing.

I would also say that a pastor should take a real interest in the church's youth, who are absolutely essential to its future growth. With all the advantages available at the present day — music, choir, orchestra, youth activities, gospel films, and special speakers, there is little excuse for not being able to keep young people interested and active.

Yet, all of this is of little avail unless we labor to keep apostolic ministry in the church. There must be the miraculous element. Men must be brought into personal touch with God. There should be a continual move of the Spirit in the assembly. Members must experience the supernatural in their lives, if the church is to be more than a human organization or a social club. But enough. I say these things to encourage and help young ministers, and to show them that there are great opportunities for them, if they have a vision and are willing to work hard, and will not allow themselves to become discouraged by difficulties. A young man and his wife who will make prayer a business in their lives, can build a strong church that is a real lighthouse for God. Such a congregation can become a tremendous power for good in their community.

In the few years that we were in Ashland, we had the joy of seeing the congregation double, triple and quadruple. How long we would have stayed in Ashland, I cannot say. As I have said, all through the years I had been expecting God to do something special, that there would be some outstanding move of the supernatural that would reach the multitudes — faith that would restore apostolic ministry in a way greater than ever before. I somehow felt that the time was drawing near, when I would begin to see these things come to pass.

CHAPTER XXI

William Branham Enters the Scene

I have mentioned elsewhere my friend, Jack Moore, of Shreveport, Louisiana, whom I met in the early years of my ministry. He is one of my most esteemed friends, a man with a great heart and love for God's work. For many years Brother Moore has been a business contractor, but was greatly interested in the spiritual needs of his city. He tried to help various ministers establish a work in his community, but when they failed, he at last decided to attempt it himself. He and his associates founded Life Tabernacle which has had a phenomenal growth and has been the dominant Full Gospel Church in that city.

In the month of March, 1947, we were engaged in a revival with Evangelist J. E. Stiles in which some fifty received the baptism of the Holy Ghost. At that time I was most singularly impressed that God would soon reveal to the Church a new ministry of power in which mighty signs and wonders would be manifest — that the vision that God had given us years before, would shortly come to pass.

On March 24, a letter was handed to me by my wife, which came from Jack Moore, and which read as follows:

Dear Brother Gordon:

I know you will be surprised to hear from me here in Oakland, California, but this is what happened. We had a Brother Branham of Jeffersonville, Indiana, a Baptist minister who has received the Holy Ghost, and has great success in praying for the sick on such a scale as I have never before seen. We had a meeting in Shreveport, the like of which has never been before. So Brother Young Brown and myself came along with him out here to fill some engagements he had made. We haven't found buildings large enough to take care of the crowds. Last night was our first night here, and the building was packed out and all standing room was taken. We shall be here through the 25th and then go to Sacramento for three nights. So we will be in this country for several days and I would surely like to see you and would like for you to see what this brother is doing . . .

With deep regards,
Jack Moore

I read the letter slowly several times with mingled emotions, and finally took it and read it to Brother J. E. Stiles. His own spirit witnessed with us on the matter, and we both determined to make the trip down to Sacramento and observe the unusual ministry of this evangelist about whom my friend had written. Within the next day or so, Brother Jack Moore flew up by plane to Ashland to pay us a visit, and the following day we all went by automobile to Sacramento, a distance of about 300 miles. When we arrived, we found the church where the meeting was to be held, though located out toward the edge of the city, already filled with people.

Certainly the service that we witnessed that night was different than any we had ever been in before. Never had we known of any preacher calling deaf mutes and blind people to pray for, and then to see those people delivered on the spot. The last one that was prayed for that night was a little cross-eyed child. I saw the mother and the girl sitting disconsolately at one side — there were so many to pray for, and it seemed the evangelist would never get to them. Time came for the service to close, with many yet desiring prayer. The evangelist was preparing to leave and had reached the steps of the platform, when he happened to look back and see the child. Instantly his compassion went out to her, and he took her, put his hands over her eyes and prayed a brief prayer. When the child looked up, lo, her eyes had come perfectly straight!

The following morning we had the pleasure of meeting Brother Branham. What we had heard and had seen the night before, and the impressions that we had when we met him, convinced us that here was a man, who, though humble and unassuming, had reached out into God and received a ministry that was beyond any that we had witnessed before. Here was a simple faith that brought results and seemed on the order of that which we had long considered necessary to bring about the revival that we were sure God intended should come to pass before the Coming of Christ.

In meeting our brother, we learned that Jack Moore had already spoken to Rev. Branham about me, and that he had looked forward to meeting me. Indeed Brother Moore, having witnessed the unusual power of the ministry of this evangelist, saw the advantage of the inspiration of such a ministry being made available to all God's people. For indeed, when the angel had given Brother Branham the charge, he straightly told him that his ministry was to be *to all people.* Because our associations had been in the larger Full Gospel circles, it had suggested itself to Brother Branham and Brother Moore, that perhaps I might be the one to introduce him to the ministers of these groups. Thus, it was that we found Brother Branham immediately willing to consider our invitation for him to come north and hold some campaigns the following fall, in Oregon and adjacent states.

We returned to Ashland, convinced that God was in our trip and that this was the ministry that would reach the masses. We began to look forward to the possibility of arranging several brief campaigns for Brother Branham in the region of the Northwest.

Up till this time, few union Full Gospel campaigns had been undertaken. Doctrinal differences and other reasons had caused one group to be suspicious of the other. If all were to get the benefit of these great services, we saw it would be necessary for the campaigns to be organized on the inter-evangelical basis, where all concerned would agree not to precipitate debate on controversial subjects, but would join together in a united effort to bring this message of deliverance to all the people. Could this be effected? We thought it could. Brother Branham was enthusiastic about the idea, for indeed the uniting of believers had been the burden of his heart from the time that the angel had visited him. And so it was that definite plans were made for a series of meetings to be held in the West that fall.

What was it, that had happened in this brother's life that had given him such an unusual ministry? The story of Brother Branham's early experiences and his meetings with the angel have been told many times, but it will bear repeating here. I give it even as I heard him tell it many times with his own lips.

* * * *

I must tell you of the angel and the coming of the Gift. I shall never forget the time, May 7, 1946, a very beautiful season of the year in Indiana, where I was still working as a game warden. I had come home for lunch, and was just going around the house taking off my gun, when a very dear friend of mine, Prod Wiseman, a brother to my piano player in the church, approached me and asked me to go to Madison with him that afternoon. I told him it was impossible as I had to patrol, and while walking around the house under a maple tree, it seemed that the whole top of the tree let loose. It seemed that something came down through that tree like a great rushing wind . . . they ran to me . . . My wife came from the house frightened, and asked me what was wrong. Trying to get hold of myself, I sat down and told her that after all these twenty odd years of being conscious of this strange feeling, the time had come when I had to find out what it was all about. The crisis had come! I told her and my child good-bye, and warned her that if I did not come back in a few days, perhaps I might never return.

That afternoon I went away to a secret place to pray and read the Bible. I became deep in prayer; it seemed that my whole soul would tear from me. I cried before God . . . I laid my face to the ground . . . I looked up to God and cried, "If you will forgive me for the way that I have done, I'll try to do better . . . I'm sorry that I've been so neglectful all these years in doing the work you wanted me to do . . . Will you speak to me someway, God? If you don't help me, I can't go on."

Then along in the night, at about the eleventh hour, I had quit praying and was sitting up when I noticed a light flickering in the room. Thinking someone was coming with a flashlight, I looked out of the window, but there was no one, and when I looked back, the light was spreading out on the floor, becoming wider. Now I know this seems very strange to you, as it did to me also. As the light was spreading, of course I became excited and startled from the chair, but as I looked up, there hung that great star. However, it did not have five points like a star, but looked more like a ball of fire or light shining down upon the floor. Just then I heard someone walking across the floor, which startled me again, as I knew of no one who would be coming there besides myself. Now, through the light, I saw the feet of a man coming toward me, as naturally as you would walk to me. He appeared to be a man who, in human weight, would weigh about two hundred pounds, clothed in a white robe. He had a smooth face, no beard, dark hair down to his shoulders, of rather dark-complexion, with a very pleasant countenance, and coming closer, his eyes caught with mine. Seeing how fearful I was, he began to speak. "Fear not. I am sent from the presence of Almighty God to tell you that your peculiar life and your misunderstood ways have been to indicate that God has sent you to take a gift of divine healing to the peoples of the world. IF YOU WILL BE SINCERE, AND CAN GET THE PEOPLE TO BELIEVE YOU, NOTHING SHALL STAND BEFORE YOUR PRAYER, NOT EVEN CANCER." Words cannot express how I felt. He told me many things which I do not have space to record here. He told me how I would be able to detect diseases by vibrations on my hand. He went away, but I have seen him several times since then. He has appeared to me perhaps once or twice within the space of six months and has spoken with me. A few times he has appeared visibly in the presence of others. I do not know who he is. I only know that he is the messenger of God to me.

Needless to say, I started praying for the sick people. I do not claim to take the place of a doctor . . . I know that doctors are able to assist nature, but they are only men . . . God is Almighty. The great things which have taken place during these months are too numerous to ever be recorded, but God has confirmed the angel's words time after time. Deaf, dumb, blind, all manners of diseases have been healed, and thousands of testimonies are on record to date. I do not have any power of my own to do this . . . I am a helpless human until I feel His presence. Many people who have attended these meetings know that their diseases and sins have been told them, right from the platform. Please do not misunderstand my poor, illiterate way of trying to convey all this to you. I say it that you might have a clearer understanding of how to take advantage of God's gift. He told me to be sincere and get the people to believe, and that is what I am trying to do. God always has something or someone to work through, and I am only an instrument used by Him. No mortal can take credit for performing a miracle, and I am just a mortal. I do not know how much longer God will permit me to do this, but by His grace, I intend to serve him the best that I know how by serving His people as long as He allows me to live.

* * * *

It is interesting to note the reactions of those who heard Brother Branham tell the story that first night I heard it in Sacramento. The people, as a whole, received his message with great interest. But one skeptical minister pointed out that his claim to have seen an angel was a sure sign that the man was under an hallucination! It is strange, indeed, that we have gotten so far away from apostolic ministry. Mary, the mother of Jesus, saw an angel. Christ's disciples were visited by angels. Peter was released from prison by an angel. Paul relates of angels appearing to him. Certainly, if God's plan has not changed, there should be angelic visitations today. Another individual pointed out that if God were going to do something special, he would do it through a Pentecostal preacher and not through a Baptist minister. We must not forget, however, that God looks at the heart, and not at the denominational name. Only a generation ago, the Pentecostal movement was small and humble. It worshipped in churches on the other side of the tracks, and in store buildings. Today, the movement has become large and has commodious houses of worship and a vast following of people. If we are not careful, we shall become exalted by our prosperity and numbers, and fall into the same error of denominational pride, as others before us.

The time came for us to begin the northwest meetings that had been planned. I left the work at Ashland in the hands of the Lorne Fox evangelistic party, which I must record, in passing, gave the City of Ashland one of the most outstanding campaigns it ever witnessed.

The first meeting was in Vancouver, British Columbia. Although, it lasted only four days, it was an outstanding success. One of the local ministers described it in the following words:

"Scenes of indescribable glory were witnessed during the all-too-brief, four-day, city-wide campaign with Rev. William Branham. As in other cities, so in Vancouver, the largest available auditoriums were inadequate to accommodate the teeming multitudes that waited on the ministry of our brother. Surrounding towns and villages seemed to literally empty into Vancouver, until the whole city was conscious of the spiritual impact of thousands of praying, believing people. Ministerial delegations from various cities attended with a view to securing the ministry of Brother Branham for similar meetings in their various fields of labor. Thousands were unable to gain access to the meetings, and this in spite of a transportation strike involving all streetcars and buses.

"The Vancouver meetings were preceded by three mass prayer meetings, and three great preparation services on the day before the meetings commenced. Right from the beginning of negotiations for the coming of Brother Branham to Vancouver, a salutary spirit of unity and cooperation prevailed among the Vancouver ministers. This gracious spirit continued, and in fact increased throughout the meetings, and is yet very much a reality, finding expression in fellowship groups and meetings. We have noted this to be one of the outstanding features of Brother Branham's ministry in other cities, also. And how desperately it has been needed."

CHAPTER XXII

The Evil Intruder

The next meeting, which was in Portland, Oregon, began on Armistice Day. Services were held in various auditoriums, but no building was found that was able to take care of the crowds. For the last three nights, the Municipal Auditorium was engaged, but on the final night, even this spacious place was crowded out. Hundreds of ministers attended and religious services in Full Gospel circles, practically ceased except at the auditorium, while the meetings were going on.

On the third day, an event took place of a dramatic nature, that showed the people the power of faith. I have related it in the book "William Branham, a Man Sent from God." I quote from it here:

"The services of the first two nights aroused tremendous interest; and now on the third night the building was filled with people waiting again for the speaker to appear. The writer, who was directing this brief campaign, in preparing to turn the service over to the evangelist asked the people to stand to their feet and sing the chorus, 'Only believe, only believe, all things are possible, only believe.' While the great congregation sang, a slight little man with modest demeanor and a friendly smile entered, then came and stood behind the pulpit. The singing ceased, and a hush fell over the audience as it listened intently when he began to speak. As he proceeded, .it was apparent that the listeners were impressed by the graciousness of the speaker as well as his evident sincerity and humility. The evangelist, taking the thought of faith inspired by the chorus that had been sung, began the theme of his message. 'Yes,' said he, 'All things are possible to him that believeth. There is nothing that can stand before faith in God, and if the people here tonight will believe God with me, we shall see that God will honor that faith and confirm it before the eyes of this entire congregation.'

"As the audience listened with rapt attention to the slight little figure on the platform, no one anticipated the startling drama that was about to unfold. Certainly, I had no such intuition, and the interruption which was about to occur could not have been more unwelcome. For suddenly, our attention was directed to a man far back in the building who was making rapid strides, apparently in the direction of the platform. At first we supposed that some emergency had arisen; perhaps, someone had fainted or had taken seriously ill in the auditorium. But as he drew near, we observed with no little misgiving that his countenance bore a demoniac grin, as to suggest that the man was demented, or violently insane, and apparently had broken away from those who had him in their care. We were to learn later what indeed would have been more disturbing had we known it at the time, that the man was not insane, in that he did not know what he was doing, but was a notorious and vicious character who had previously run afoul of the law for disturbing and breaking up religious services. Jail sentences had not taught him a lesson, and now seeing his opportunity to cause a large commotion and again break up a service, he had come forward for that purpose.

"Up the steps he strode without pausing. Now he was on the platform assuming a menacing attitude that by this time was attracting the attention of the entire congregation. Two sturdy policemen standing in the wings, becoming aware of the distraction, were about to come forward and lay hands on this disturber, but we could see that this would result in a scuffle and the excitement created could well ruin the service. Moreover, the evangelist had apparently put himself on the spot for he had just declared that all things were possible to him that believed, and that God would always back up His servants who put their trust in Him. Indeed, the meeting had reached such a high state of expectation, that reliance on the officers of the law, though perhaps entirely justifiable in the present instance, did not seem to be the Divine order. We knew nothing else to do but to hastily wave the officers back, and call attention to the evangelist as to what was taking place. But he himself was already conscious that something was wrong. Speaking quietly to the audience and requesting that the people unite with him in silent prayer, he turned to meet the strange challenge of this evil antagonist.

"As he did so, the man with the evil gleam on his countenance, which reminded one of the hideous grins the heathen engrave on the faces of their idols, began to impudently accuse and curse the speaker. 'You are of the devil, and deceiving the people,' he shouted, 'an impostor, a snake in the grass, a fake, and I am going to show these people that you are!' It was a bold challenge and every one in that audience could see that it was not an idle threat. As the intruder continued to revile the evangelist, hissing and spitting, he made motion to carry his threats into execution. To the audience it appeared to be an evil moment for the little figure on the platform, and most of them must have felt exceedingly sorry for him. The officers attempted again to come to his aid but were waved away, and now in rejecting their assistance, the speaker had deliberately accepted the challenge of this wicked antagonist whose size and fierceness had convinced the audience that he was well able to carry out his boasts. No doubt, critics who had slipped into the auditorium out of curiosity, expected a swift and pitiful conclusion to the unexpected drama that was now coming to a climax. Certainly, they could see that there was no room for trickery. The man on the platform would have to have the goods or else take the consequences.

"In the moment of suspense that followed, one could not help being reminded of the story of the challenge of long ago, when the bold Goliath cursed little David in the name of his gods, and boasted that he would tear him limb from limb. The startled congregation, as the hosts of Israel must have been in their day, looked on the scene with wonder and amazement, hardly knowing what to expect next, but fearing the worst. The gathering of ministers on the platform reviewed the situation with no little dismay, knowing that unless God did a very unusual thing and backed up the speaker in a supernatural manner, the evil intruder, who had successfully broken up religious services in the past, would now do so again. Some were much disturbed that the policemen had not been permitted to take charge of the situation, and believed that this error of judgment would allow this demon-possessed man not only to ruin the meeting and thus bring reproach on the cause of Christ, but also might actually result in physical injury to the speaker.

"The seconds passed, however, without the awaited climax happening. Presently, it appeared that something was hindering the challenger from carrying out his evil designs. For some reason he was not proceeding with the execution of his boasts of physical violence, but was rather contenting himself in hissing and spitting and uttering the most fearful imprecations. Softly, but determinedly, the voice of the evangelist now could be heard rebuking the evil power that dominated the man. His words, spoken so quietly that they could be heard only a short distance, were saying, 'Satan, because you have challenged the servant of

God before this great congregation, you must bow before me. In the name of Jesus Christ, you shall fall at my feet.' The words were repeated several times. The challenger ceased to speak, and it was evident that it was now he who was laboring under a strain. Strong as he and the wicked forces were that controlled him, strengthened by every evil spirit in the building, apparently they were gradually succumbing to another Power that was greater than they, a Power that responded at the whisper of the Name of Jesus! Soon it was evident that the man realized he was being overcome, but nothing he could do apparently could reverse the situation. A tense battle of spiritual forces now summoned every bit of strength that he had in him. Beads of perspiration broke out on his face as he put forth a last desperate effort to prevail. But it was all to no avail. Suddenly, he who a few minutes before had so brazenly defied the man of God with his fearful threats and accusations, gave an awful groan and slumped to the floor sobbing in an hysterical manner. For quite a while he lay there writhing in the dust, as the evangelist calmly proceeded with the service as if nothing had happened.

"Needless to say, the great congregation was awed by the scene that had transpired before them, in which God so signally vindicated His servant, and loud praises to God filled the spacious auditorium. The policemen too, startled by what they had witnessed, openly acknowledged that God was in their midst. Need we record that in the healing service which followed, a wave of glory was manifest that will never be forgotten by those who were present. Many miracles of healing took place that night as a multitude of people were ministered to in the prayer line."

* * * *

From Portland we went to Salem. The large armory was packed out and so were all its separate lower rooms which were fitted with loud speakers.

From Salem, we went to our own city of Ashland where the local armory seating 1,200, was jammed out. The following week, the party drove over to Boise where a powerful three-day campaign filled the largest auditorium in the city. In the 14 days of services, with only a comparative small amount of newspaper advertising, some 70,000 people had heard the gospel of deliverance and at least 1,000 of these were ministers.

Early in the year 1948, Brother Jack Moore and I were called to go with Brother Branham to Miami, Florida. It was there that we met the famous evangelist F. F. Bosworth, who had held great healing campaigns attended by thousands of people some years earlier. In meeting the brother, we were particularly impressed by his sweet and godly spirit. Brother Bosworth, commenting on the meeting, had said that God had given him campaigns of tremendous magnitude, but he had never witnessed miracles take place with such consistency so early in the campaign. Brother Bosworth found it possible to be with the party in several campaigns.

We made arrangements to hold the next campaign in Pensacola, under a large tent cathedral. An incident took place in this meeting that was of such interest that I will record it in some detail. It concerned the deliverance of a violently insane man. I give the incident as I wrote it at the time.

* * * *

"Because strong winds had forced lowering of the tent, one service of the campaign was held in the local arena. An insane, young man had been brought from a state institution to the meeting that night, to be prayed for. At the close of the service, those who had brought him tried to lead him from the building, but he refused to go. When our attention was called to this, we secured the services of a half dozen men and took him from the building by force. So strong were the powers that possessed him, that it required no little exertion to accomplish this, but at length we had him safely seated in the automobile, so we thought, and left him, supposing that there would be no further trouble. Imagine our dismay, when a couple of minutes later there was heard a hoarse cry, and turning we saw him dash from the car toward a group of women and children who were standing and talking near the door of the arena.

"His headlong dash occurred so suddenly and unexpectedly that we scarcely knew what to do. Fortunately, the people at the door fled in every direction before he reached them. Then furiously he turned and charged, with arms flying, toward me, as I had not been able to get out of the way in time.

"Demons have power to break chains, and to do other superhuman feats, but fortunately they are powerless before the Name of Jesus! Though struck at time after time, I was not harmed nor even touched, no not by a single blow. Something supernatural parried every thrust made by the demon-possessed man! How long this might have continued, it is impossible to say, but just at that moment two policemen who happened to be in the vicinity, hearing the shouts and cries of the women, rushed up, and seeing what they supposed was a common brawl, began questioning us both. At this moment, however, the insane man, with fierce imprecations, charged the officers, and they soon found that they had more than their hands full. Over and over on the grass they rolled and tussled, and finally the officers had to resort to rather stern measures before they could handcuff and subdue their refractory assailant. A call to the police brought out a squad car, and finally the man was secured and taken to headquarters, where he was placed in a special cell for the night.

"After they drove away, we shall never forget the tears of the unfortunate man's sister, who had been responsible for bringing him to the meeting. She came and plead with us with anguish of soul that Brother Branham would pray for him. Of course, it was impossible for Brother Branham to respond to the multitude of calls that came daily from those who would desire him to visit sick and confined people. But so urgent and griefsticken was the sister, that finally Brother Jack Moore consented to tell Brother Branham about the case in the morning.

"The following morning, Brother Moore started to relate the story of events of the previous night to Brother Branham. Then occurred that marvelous manifestation of the gift of the Spirit, by which our brother often witnesses events that take place at a distance, and even before they happen. We are indeed reminded of the exploits in Elisha's ministry, when he beheld the plans of the King of Syria even before they took place. Or of Christ, Himself, when He saw Nathaniel at a distance by other than natural sight. In this case, God had already shown Brother Branham this insane man, that he would pray for him that day, and that the man would be healed. The scene of the deliverance was identified by him in the vision by the presence of a red-appearing car, and the manner of the clothing worn by the man who would be delivered.

"Arrangements were then sought with the Pensacola police for the release of the young man. But they, remembering the trouble that they had had the night before, perhaps could be pardoned for their refusal to let him go unless he were taken outside of the city limits and never returned. So finally, a rendezvous was arranged on the Gulf beach, where all the parties concerned would meet. But when Brother Branham arrived and looked carefully at the cars, he made the remark that all was not what he had seen in the vision. While he hesitated, Brother Moore decided to drive his new De Soto up some little distance from where the insane man was, as his daughter and another sister were in his car. Brother Branham then got out and walked to where the young man was standing. He noticed at once that his clothing was exactly the same as what he had seen in the vision, so he told him to get back in the car and wait. Then a peculiar thing happened. As Brother Branham told it afterward, 'I looked back toward Brother Jack's car. Most of the beach was of white sand. But where the car had just been parked, there was a bank of red clay. The sun reflecting from the red clay on the highly polished tan sedan caused it to appear red. I knew then that this was exactly what I had seen in the vision. I went over and pronounced the words to the young man, "Thus saith the Lord, the evil spirit shall leave you now, and you shall get well." Instantly the young man was delivered and entered into a normal conversation.'

"This was an impressive testimony to the police officers of Pensacola, as they realized that God had done something wonderful in their midst. It caused many to praise God for this manifestation of His compassion for the man whom Satan had so cruelly bound.

"Some months later, the young man who had been delivered, sent in his testimony and it appeared in an issue of THE VOICE OF HEALING. (July, 1948) His testimony reads as follows:

" 'When I was two years old I had polio. My parents carried me to many different doctors. I spent some time in crippled children's hospitals. All of them did no good. I got worse all the time. Finally my condition was so bad that I became insane. I had been in the state institution nearly seven months when my people heard about Brother Branham's healing service in Pensacola. I was carried over there and that night I was put in jail because the Lord wasn't through with me. He used me as an example to show the people that He has more power than the devil. When my sister came to see me the next morning, I was perfectly contented because God had shown Brother Branham that He had healed my body. I am now 25 years old and have a good job. Thank God for His healing power.' "

* * * *

From Pensacola, the Branham party went to Kansas City, Kansas, to the Memorial Hall. U. S. Grant was chairman of the local committee, and had made admirable preparations for the meeting.

When we arrived, he was glad to see us, but expressed some

anxiety concerning Brother Branham, who he said had not yet arrived, though he had received communication that he would be there earlier in the day. Rev. Grant said he knew that he had not arrived, as only he had knowledge of the location of the hotel where we were to stay — this being always of necessity a closely guarded secret. (On one occasion when the location of Brother Branham's hotel became known to the public, a long line of sick formed at his door, seriously disrupting the business of the hotel.)

We ourselves were just a trifle disturbed as we knew that Brother Branham should have arrived by this time. But there was nothing to do but await further word, and we ourselves went to the hotel. We were not a little surprised when we learned from the night clerk that he had arrived and had already retired. When later we asked how it had happened that he had not gone to Brother Grant's place first, his reply was that he had been very tired and thought that perhaps it best to go to bed early and get as good a rest as possible. But we said, "How did you know to come to this hotel?" "Well," he said, "I just seemed to know." That was all the satisfaction we could get, and perhaps all he could give us. Time after time, we had similar experiences, when his perception reached out, and he knew things that did not come to him through the avenues of his five senses. We shall not forget how non-plussed Brother Grant was when we told him what had happened. We do not wish to give the impression, however, that Brother Branham had the ability to use this gift at will, but only at such times as the Spirit of God would specially move upon him for its manifestation.

Within three days, the Memorial Auditorium was completely filled.

It was while I was at Kansas City, that I became acquainted with a most unusual young man by the name of Oral Roberts. He had just held a campaign in a church in Kansas City, Missouri, and had stayed over to witness the Branham meetings. Since he did not have his car with him, he asked me to drive him to the place where he was staying. I was very glad to do this, and in fact, we spent time each evening after the meetings together. I was particularly impressed by the vision and call that Brother Roberts had. He believed that God had a great work for him to do. Subsequent events proved that the vision he had received from God was true. His ministry was to have a tremendous impact upon America.

From Kansas City we went to Sedalia, Missouri, and then to

Elgin, Illinois. After Elgin the party went west to Tacoma, Washington, for a six-day campaign. The great Ice Arena was jammed to the doors. The temperature outside was near freezing, and the building was unheated. To attempt to hold religious services in an unheated building seemed unthinkable, but so closely packed were the people that the arena was found to be very comfortable. At the close of the campaign, there was a noon luncheon given in which Brother Branham spoke to the ministers. After the luncheon, one said to another, "When this meeting is over, and while these wonderful things are still fresh on my mind, I want to get away a few days and be alone with God."

CHAPTER XXIII
Events of the Year 1948

To understand developments of this year, we must go back a few months.

At the close of the Boise campaign, Brother Branham expressed himself that he was very happy over the outcome of the meetings that had been held in the Northwest, and said he felt it was God's will that in the future his meetings should continue to be conducted on the same inter-evangelical basis. He asked me if I would go to Shreveport, Louisiana, to confer with Brother Moore as to the possibility of arranging other campaigns on this basis. I consented to go, for I dared give no other answer to this but an affirmative. My church again was very gracious in permitting me to go. The congregation was fortunate in securing the services of Evangelist Velmer Gardner during my absence, and the church moved along at high tide. Indeed, Brother Gardner was to receive a great inspiration from the campaign we later held at Eugene. Shortly after that a new ministry of healings and miracles began to follow the campaigns held by this evangelist.

Whether to leave my church permanently, and follow the work that seemed providentially indicated, was becoming a matter of increasing concern to me. It was not easy to make a decision to leave those one loves, especially a church that you have seen grow from a small struggling group to a strong and vigorous assembly. God seemed to be leading, still I hesitated. Finally in prayer, God spoke directly and told me to go ahead, nothing doubting, and He would see that I should be led step by step in my part of the great work He was beginning to do over the land. Once the decision was made, I never for one moment have had reason to doubt that God led me in making it.

Shortly after the first of the year, I arrived at Shreveport, Louisiana, and talked the entire situation over with my friend, Brother Jack Moore. Together with Young Brown, we drove to Jeffersonville, Indiana, where Brother Branham was resting at his home for a few days. He seemed glad to see us, and we had an inspiring time of fellowship. There were some problems to be worked out. Previously, Brother Branham's meetings were being publicized in a magazine edited by a good Christian brother in Texas. The problem that had arisen was this: Brother Branham realized that since the meetings in the Northwest, his campaigns had reached a scope that believers from all the various groups were now attending. Any magazine that would be used in the meetings would go into the homes of all these groups. If the campaigns were to be organized on an inter-evangelical basis, it was evident that the magazine used must also be of the same character.

We parted for the evening, and all of us placed the matter definitely in the hands of the Lord. In the morning we met Brother Branham again, and he seemed to have received a peaceful assurance. He said that he had heard from heaven that night. We carefully listened to what he told us, and in the months which followed we indeed witnessed the exact fulfillment of those words. For the next six months that we were with him, God mightily blessed the ministry of William Branham. Then he was to find it necessary to leave the field for many months.

In the meantime, events moved swiftly. *The Voice of Healing* was born, and it fell upon me to be its editor. Its purpose was not to argue over doctrine that might precipitate division and confusion among God's people, but rather to proclaim the message of the Great Commission, to minister healing to God's people, and to prepare them for Christ's coming. This policy of the Voice of Healing has been continued through the years, and will be perpetuated until Jesus comes.

At the time the *Voice of Healing* was being brought to birth, it was considered only as an organ of Brother Branham's meetings. But even as our first issue was published, Brother Branham's strength had so deteriorated that he was forced to announce his intention to go off the field. One day while we were in Tacoma, Brother Branham called Young Brown and me into his room. He said, "How long has *The Voice of Healing* been published?" I replied, "Just one issue has been printed." He then said, "I know this will be a disappointment, but because of my weakened condition, I am going off the field, and I may never return. You will therefore have to carry on the magazine as you see fit, or discontinue it."

I gave the matter considerable thought and prayer. Finally, I got the go-ahead signal from the Lord. Brother Moore's daughter, Anna Jeanne, an extremely talented young lady, became as-

sistant editor, and gave her invaluable services to the work for
several years. The Voice of Healing will always owe a debt to
her for her devoted labors. As Brother Branham was now off
the field, we began carrying reports of other evangelists. Thus it
was that almost from the time of its inception, the magazine came
to represent the deliverance ministry as a whole.

From June until the following year, Brother Branham went
through a Gethsemane that few ministers have experienced. The
evangelist had reached out into spiritual realms that had pro-
foundly disturbed the kingdom of hell. His battle with the enemy,
together with his great exertions which went beyond his physical
strength, caused him to have a nervous breakdown. Physicians
advised him that he would have to leave the field indefinitely.
Nevertheless, as we shall see, his faith triumphed over the dire
predictions of the physicians, and God gave him a glorious deliverance. But that was to be yet some time in the future.

Shortly after Brother Branham made the decision to return to
his home for an extended period of rest, I met Evangelist William
Freeman in Oregon. This young man had gone through a series of
unusual experiences a year or two previously. He had a serious
heart attack, and thought he was finished. Not long after that, he
found that he had cancer. All these things drove him to prayer.

Then one night, the Lord appeared to him. In the vision, he
saw the Lord standing upon a cloud. As he continued to watch,
he saw the scene change, and he stood before a great congregation. Then he saw himself praying for the sick for hours, before
vast crowds of people.

This experience caused him to spend much time waiting before
the Lord, and in meditation. Then one night, he was awakened
from his sleep, and a great light shown around him. In that light,
an angel suddenly appeared in "a white robe whose appearance
was strong and his vision penetrating." The angel touched him
and told him that God had given him a gift of healing to take to
the people. He was to tell them that Jesus was coming soon, that
many were sleeping and slumbering, and that they must be
awakened, for a great darkness was already upon the land.

He then resigned his church in Porterville, California, and went
into the evangelistic field. It was at this time that I met him. He
asked me if I would work with him on the field. After some
prayer, I felt it was the will of God. We began organizing campaigns in various cities in California. Each campaign proved to
be larger than the one before. In Oakland, the Civic Auditorium

was filled. In Watsonville, the building was packed to the doors. A tent pitched in Salinas, was filled to capacity.

It was at this time that I felt definitely led to resign my church in Ashland, Oregon. Although I was absent from the church at least half the time during that year, the congregation was most sympathetic and co-operative. They had been hoping that I would return to the church, but they realized that God had called me to a special ministry, and that all of us must be resigned to His will. During our few years in that city, we had witnessed hundreds of conversions and many baptized in the Holy Spirit. The church had enjoyed a four-fold growth. When we got ready to leave, the church gave us lovely gifts, and there were tears in our eyes when we said our final farewells. We did have the satisfaction of knowing that a very able pastor, Rev. O. C. Klingsheim was following us.

A few months after we left Ashland, I received a letter from a skeptical clergyman whom I had known in that city. In his letter he made a tirade against Divine healing, speaking of it as associated with "primitive magic, fetishism, and money-making possibilities." He denied that any miracles were taking place.

In answering him, I gave him a test case to investigate which had occurred in his vicinity. The young man in question was given up by the doctors to die of nephritis. In addition, he had developed a condition which resulted in his becoming stone blind. Being bedfast from this illness, he couldn't even walk. The man had been brought to the meetings in an ambulance, but after prayer, received his sight and was able to rise from his bed, healed by the power of God.

I told this minister to investigate this case. If what I said was not true, then to let me know. I never heard from him again.

During the time we were with William Freeman, we held a brief campaign with my friend, Jack Moore in Shreveport. The news of the campaign attracted considerable attention in that state. There was a young minister pastoring a church in the southern part of the state, by the name of W. V. Grant. At first he was disturbed by the reports, and warned his congregation against the meetings. Notwithstanding, after prayer, he decided to make the trip himself. What he saw in the service produced such an impact upon him, that it revolutionized his life. He began holding campaigns of his own, in which many were saved and healed and hundreds received the Baptism of the Holy Ghost. Later he began writing books and achieved quite a ministry in this.

During the summer and fall, we had other campaigns in Richmond, San Francisco, Portland, and Bakersfield. In each place, the auditoriums were filled to capacity. The final meeting in which we labored with William Freeman was in Los Angeles, where we moved from auditorium to auditorium with the final services conducted in the Shrine Auditorium, seating over 7,000, with two thousand turned away at the doors.

It was in the Los Angeles meeting that I first met Demos Shakarian. He had recently helped plan a large Hollywood Bowl Rally of Pentecostal young people, and he was recommended to me as the one to help us organize the Los Angeles meeting. That was the beginning of a friendship that has lasted for many years. Some three years later, Brother Shakarian told me God had laid on his heart a Full Gospel Business Men's Fellowship, and discussed it with me in considerable detail. I told him that I felt it would be a wonderful thing, and a substantial step toward bringing about the unity of the body of Christ. In the year 1954, The Voice of Healing held a convention in Philadelphia, which filled an auditorium seating some four thousand people. The Full Gospel Business Men co-operated, and at the same time organized a chapter in that city. From year to year, the Full Gospel Business Men's work has grown until it has become a powerful force in America. Demos Shakarian has become one of the significant figures of our time. He is one of California's leading business men, yet at the same time a humble Christian, who believes in the moving of the Spirit.

CHAPTER XXIV

Testing the Deliverance Ministry in Mexico

For two years, we had witnessed the mighty power of God in action in America, with great auditoriums filled to capacity and thousands of persons saved and healed. The time had come, when we felt that this message was needed on the foreign fields. We had always been interested in missions, but had felt that the methods employed were not getting the job done. Jesus had said to preach the gospel to every creature, but He also added, "These signs shall follow them that believe." The present methods that were being used, were just too slow. At the rate we were going, the growth in population was increasing far more rapidly than the evangelizing of the heathen was progressing. Missionaries visiting our church during the years I was pastor, repeatedly told us of the overwhelming difficulties that they faced on the field.

Early in 1949, my wife and I decided that we ourselves, must make a trip, to a foreign field, to test out the ministry of deliverance. Unannounced, we arranged to go to Mexico. No one would know we were coming. There would be no special advertising. We would test the effect of this ministry upon the people ourselves.

Arriving in Ciudad, Victoria, we arranged to hold some meetings in a local church. The pastor, Florentino Flores, was rather apologetic about the situation. A meeting held some time earlier by an American evangelist had resulted in disorder and some violence. Stones had been hurled and windows broken. The pastor hoped that this would not be repeated. The first services passed uneventfully, until the beginning of the healing service. When the people began to see the miracles, their eyes opened wide with wonder. At first they were stunned, but soon recovering, they entered enthusiastically into the meeting. Indeed, the hearts of the audience were completely won by the demonstration of the power of God, as large numbers knelt at altars for salvation.

In Monterrey, the same enthusiasm was repeated. Many were prayed for and healed. On Sunday morning they carried in a man who was in a most pitiable condition. He was completely paralyzed and absolutely helpless, his hands shaking with palsy. Gently, they brought him to the platform so he could be prayed for. I asked him if he were healed, would he live for Jesus? The poor creature nodded with an effort and said weakly, "Si, senor." Prayer was made, and at the command, the man slowly straightened up. Everyone believed the Lord would touch him, but no one expected the swift drama that was about to unfold. The man now reached out his hands, pushing away those that were attempting to support him. So they left him alone. He moved toward the end of the platform, rather than to the steps! What was he going to do? Suddenly, he leaped into the air, and came down to the auditorium floor. But he landed on his feet, raced up the steps and leaped again! Several times he did this, crying, "Gloria a Dios!" Then he and those who brought him fell at the altar, and weeping gave praise to God.

Another case was that of a little child. It was very sick and had been brought to the church to be prayed for. Somehow, the parents whose name was Parra, could not get to me for the crowd. The child weakened and they left the church; the little thing gave a shudder, rolled its eyes back, and all life apparently ceased. Those who examined it, declared it to be dead. At someone's suggestion, they came back to the church, and this time a path was made. Amid the noise and crowd, my interpreter said to me, "The child has died." I thought she said, "The child is dying," so I prayed. Suddenly, life came again into the little body, the pall of death left, and soon its eyes were bright with life, to the great joy of the congregation. Then I learned that the child had really been dead.

We returned back to America, convinced that the ministry of deliverance was God's ordained method to reach the masses in foreign lands. Our trip was merely the vanguard of many great overseas revivals, that were to reach millions of people.

Despite the remarkable miracles that were happening throughout the land, opposition arose from different quarters. Soon after we returned from Mexico, a man who was an official in a so-called deaf fellowship, wrote me a letter challenging the testimonies, and questioning that any genuine healings of deaf mutes were taking place. And he claimed to be Pentecostal.

Of course, there was only one way to answer such unbelief. Present to this man a test case for his examination! Over the years, we have published instances of healing of deaf mutes, but for this test case, we chose the Batey girl, healed in the Wilbur Ogilvie meetings. This girl had been sent to some of the world's leading specialists. They said there was no chance of helping her. Nonetheless, Brother Ogilvie prayed for her, and she was wonderfully healed. The mother, Mrs. Batey, in a written statement, after describing the hopelessness of the case, wrote of the miracle:

"We then took her to Brother Ogilvie and he prayed for her, and God healed her! I sent her to the Chowchilla, California, public school and she passed two grades in four months. She could read and write in two weeks. Before she was prayed for, I had to run and catch her when I wanted her for anything. We had to make signs with our hands; she could read lips a little.

"A county nurse came to take the little girl to the deaf school. At first, she would not believe she was healed, and demanded that the girl be allowed to go to school. My little girl then talked to the nurse, and you can imagine how amazed she was.

"She is now in the third grade and expects to pass into the fourth in a week. She is saved and loves to go to church and Sunday School."

We published this testimony, and presented it as a test case to this man who challenged the healing of deaf mutes. We never heard from him again. Apparently, he wasn't happy about the miracle!

While the healing of a deaf mute is a comparatively simple thing, teaching him to talk is an altogether different matter. Individuals who come from foreign countries, and who have the best of hearing, often find it difficult to adapt themselves to another language.

There are authentic records of two children in India, who were reared by animals. They made noises just like animals. When discovered and returned to civilization, they could only learn a few elementary words.

In most cases, the deaf who are healed do not receive sympathetic treatment from people, who often regard them as a curiosity. The deaf have a serious inferiority complex and when they are told to talk, they can hear but of course do not understand what they are being told. Although they may have a high intelligence, the very word "dumb," in the public mind, has come to mean someone who has little intelligence. These persons are extremely sensitive to the remarks of others, and are not able to match wits with the world. After their deliverance, they can hear the sounds but do not recognize the meaning of the words. There are no schools for the purpose of teaching deaf persons who have been healed.

After a few unpleasant experiences, these people may lapse back into their old methods of communication. Nonetheless, despite these snares that confront those suddenly healed of deafness, there has been a good number of them who have learned to use their newly awakened faculties, and have developed into completely normal persons.

In happy contrast to the skeptical official, was the case of the photographer and reporter who came to the Gayle Jackson meetings in New Orleans. I was present at that particular occasion. These men had been authorized by LOOK magazine to investigate the Divine healing meetings. We had dinner with them, and they appeared to be of an open mind, but wanted proof of the healing of such persons as deaf mutes and cripples. Brother Jackson at that moment spied a young man and his mother who were standing near by. He called them over, and asked the mother to explain to these reporters what had happened in their family. Whereupon, the mother told them that her boy had grown up a deaf mute. The medical profession had been unable to do anything for him. She had brought him to the Jackson campaign the previous year, and Brother Jackson had prayed for him. The young man's ears had been instantly opened, and during the ensuing year, he had learned to talk quite well. The astonished reporters then carried on an animated conversation with the young man, from whose lips they learned the details of the wonderful story of his healing. While his speech still lacked the fluency that a person, who has been talking all his life, possesses, the young man spoke remarkably well. The reporters from LOOK carried a very favorable report of the Jackson meetings in that magazine.

The Voice of Healing magazine had met a special need in the Church and by the year 1950, it had reached a circulation of nearly 100,000. Consequently, many evangelists whose faith led them to enter into apostolic ministry, began to send in reports for us to publish. Since it had been our purpose to encourage the deliverance ministry, we began carrying a number of these reports. The meetings of these men in various parts of the nation was spearheading a revival with special emphasis on supernatural ministry. Soon there came a great flow of material to our office, documenting the most marvelous miracles, including healing from total blindness, invalidism, from organic diseases, and afflictions of every kind.

In December, 1949, it was suggested that we have a Voice of Healing Convention. There were only a few days to announce it, and we decided to hold it in connection with a campaign that was being held. There were a number of evangelists and notable figures present including William Branham, Raymond T. Richey, Gayle Jackson, Velmer Gardner, Clifton Erickson, H. C. Noah, F. F. Bosworth and son Bob, Jack Moore and others.

At the close of the convention, Brother Branham called Jack Moore and me to a private conference. He told us that since he was now completely healed and restored in strength, he wanted us to join him in a series of new campaigns, the first of which was to be held in Houston, Texas. After some consideration and prayer, we felt that it was the will of God for us to accept his offer. We believed God would continue to bless the unique ministry of our brother, but we were hardly prepared for the phenomenal event that would occur during the Houston campaign.

CHAPTER XXV

That Amazing Photograph

In January, 1950, I went to Houston, Texas. At that time, I was writing Brother Branham's life story, and as I was in the midst of gathering source material, it helped me to have Brother Branham nearby. F. F. Bosworth and Jack Moore were also with the party at the time.

The meeting soon attracted an unusual attention in the city. The city auditorium was filled to capacity, and the newspapers took note of the Divine healing ministry. It was not long before the services were a common topic among the people of the city.

From night to night, God's power was revealed, and in the case of practically every person dealt with, Brother Branham was able to discern not only the affliction, but anything that was interfering spiritually with the person seeking healing. Unconfessed sin was promptly called out. This action of the Spirit revealed to the audience how important it was for those seeking healing, to surrender their lives completely to God.

During the campaign, a hostile clergyman by the name of W. E. B ---- raised a great hue and cry against the meetings, claiming that the days of miracles were passed. He said that those who prayed for the sick were fakers and challenged the evangelist to a debate on the subject of Divine healing. Brother Branham refused the offer to debate, but F. F. Bosworth accepted the challenge. So it was that on the night of January 24, some 8,000 people were in the Sam Houston auditorium to witness the proceedings. There never was any doubt that night, as to which one had the sympathies of the vast crowd. Dr. B ---- had nothing to offer the people. He told the audience that God no longer was interested in healing the sick.

Nevertheless, Dr. B ---- thought to capitalize on the meeting by having his picture taken as one of the speakers. He hired a Mr. Ayres, a professional photographer, who worked with the Ted Kipperman Studios, to take pictures of him.

Although Brother Branham refused to take part in the debate, he was however, prevailed upon at the close of the service, to say a few words to the audience. Mr. Ayres although told not to take any pictures of Rev. Branham, nevertheless, slipped forward to get the shot. We could have stopped him, but decided to let him go ahead.

Back at the studios that night, Mr. Ayres tried to develop the photographs taken of Dr. B - - - - . For some mysterious reason, the negatives all turned out blank! Rather surprised at this result, since his camera was in perfect working condition, Mr. Ayres now tried to develop the shot taken of Rev. Branham, though naturally he expected it to be blank also. Imagine his surprise, when he found that the film was not only good, but there appeared on the negative over the head of Brother Branham, a flame of fire in the form of a halo!

In the morning, the astonished photographer came down to our hotel where we were staying to report on the strange result of the negative that had been taken on the night before. There could not be any doubt that the photograph was genuine, but to anticipate skepticism, we had the negative taken to Mr. George Lacy, a professional examiner of questioned documents, who made a scientific examination of the film.

After giving it a careful analysis over a period of two days, Mr. Lacy gave a signed statement that in his opinion the photograph was absolutely genuine.

THE EXPERT'S REPORT OF THE NEGATIVE

A part of Mr. Lacy's written report was as follows: "Rev. Lindsay requested that I make a scientific examination of the aforesaid negative. He requested that I determine, if possible, whether or not in my opinion the negative had been retouched or 'doctored' in any way, subsequent to the developing of the film, that would cause a streak of light to appear in the position of a halo above the head of Rev. Branham." Then followed his scientific analysis and conclusion. He said, " . . . Based upon the above described examination and study I am of the definite opinion that the negative submitted for examination was not retouched, nor was it a composite or double exposed negative. Further I am of the definite opinion that the light streak appearing above the head in a halo position was caused by the light striking the negative."

The appearance of this remarkable phenomenon on the negative was, of course, a startling confirmation of the authenticity of Brother Branham's ministry. The fact that the shots taken of

Dr. B - - - - , turned out blank could only be interpreted that God was rebuking and discrediting this presumptuous minister.

The incident had a powerful effect upon everybody, including the photographers. Mr. Kipperman, convinced that the photograph indicated God's hand upon Rev. Branham, travelled with the party for a season. We believe that it was God's call to Mr. and Mrs. Ayres and her ten year old son, Douglas Ashley. However, the family were Jews, and as we all know it is a very difficult thing for a Jew to suddenly accept Christ.

Alas, if they had only known what they know now, they would surely have given themselves to God at that time.

There were many interesting incidents that took place during the next few months while we were holding meetings in various cities of America. In almost all cases the auditoriums were filled to capacity or near capacity by the second night. The people were especially impressed with the remarkable operation of the gifts of the word of knowledge and of discernment. I do not recall a single error that was made when the anointing of the Spirit was upon our brother. At no time would Brother Branham look at the prayer cards, but in every case he would by the Spirit discern the afflictions that were the most important. Usually some other word was spoken that would encourage the person to believe. Sometimes he would tell them their name, or the city where they were from. He usually noted and mentioned the fact if they were a minister or a minister's wife.

In almost every case when the Spirit spoke, there would be a reference to something vital or important in the person's life in which they needed either correction or encouragement. It is significant that if the person used tobacco or drank intoxicants, he was reproved by the Spirit and asked to quit these habits before receiving healing.

This functioning of the gift of discernment to expose evil plans of men, brings to mind an incident in the Branham campaigns. Two men who attended one of the campaigns in Canada, and had witnessed the unusual manifestations of the word of knowledge, explained it all as a scheme to hoodwink people and get their money. They further declared that the evangelist's ability to discern the exact physical need of each individual who came to be healed, to be so much trickery.

These men agreed between themselves to a scheme by which they would trap the evangelist. During prayer for the sick at the next service, one of these men came forward in the prayer line. He had a list of afflictions written on his card. The evangelist glancing at him, waved him on saying, there was nothing the matter with the man. The imposter protested, however, stating that there was a long list of things written on his card.

Suddenly, the evangelist paused. He then began to speak in a stern tone.

"What is this!" he cried. "I see two men sitting across from each other at a table, making plans. Yes, they are plotting to come up on this platform, and pretend they are sick."

"You are one of these men!" the evangelist said accusingly. "How is it that you have agreed to commit this great sin? How is it that you have planned together to lie to the Holy Ghost?"

The color drained away from the man's face, and his brazen spirit vanished. Terrified by this exposure by the Holy Spirit, he fell on his face and begged for mercy.

The powerful manifestation of the gifts had the effect of producing a deep sense of the presence of God. People had the feeling that by the time the service was over they had met with God. The calling of the altar was usually left to me and it was not unusual for several hundred people to respond to a single invitation.

CHAPTER XXVI

The Meetings in Scandinavia and the Raising of the Dead Boy

Shortly after the strange event in the Sam Houston Auditorium, Brother Branham made the decision to go to Scandinavia. He had been receiving invitations from the country for about three years. During the month of January, when I rejoined the party, Brother Branham asked me to make the arrangements for the trip to Finland. Early in April, Brother Branham, Jack Moore, Howard Branham, J. Ern Baxter and I, held three days of services at Glad Tidings and Manhattan Center in New York, and then prepared to leave for Europe. It was April 6th, Brother Branham's birthday, when we took off for London.

The following morning, the party landed at the London Airport. Several days were spent in visiting historic buildings and shrines of one of the world's largest cities. The climax of the party's stay in that great metropolis was the visit to Wesley's chapel. While there, we also saw the Wesley residence, entering last of all the room in which John Wesley prayed every morning at five a.m. Before leaving, we all knelt down and had prayer. It was a moment not to be forgotten.

After two days in Paris, which were spent visiting the historic landmarks, we continued our journey to Finland via a Scandinavian airliner. On the 14th of April, we landed at Helsinki, where we were met by several ministers including Pastor Manninen, who had given us the invitation, and Sister May Isaacson, our American-born interpreter, whose knowledge of the Finnish language contributed greatly to the success of our meetings in Finland. The first service at the Messuhalli, witnessed a crowd of 7000 in attendance. After that, several thousand waited outside all afternoon, standing in a line four deep and a half mile long, so that they might be assured of a seat in the largest auditorium in Finland.

During a five day interlude, when the auditorium could not be obtained, the party went north to Kuopio which is not far from the Arctic Circle. Faith was very high in this city and some marvelous miracles took place. One of these was the healing of little

Veera Ihalainen, a war orphan. She was marvelously delivered from wearing a brace and using crutches, after she had in faith touched the coat of Brother Branham as he passed by. Two or three evenings, the people just passed by and Brother Branham said a brief prayer for each one. By the time each service was over, there was a good-sized pile of crutches and canes which had been discarded. Brother Baxter spoke at the afternoon services, and his messages were received with great interest. Brother Moore and the writer took the morning services, and prayed especially for the deaf mutes and the blind. As many as seven or eight were healed at a time, one after another. One boy learned words so fast that he was used as an interpreter to communicate with the others who were prayed for. One incident that highly intrigued the audience was that the deaf mutes, when their ears were opened, could learn English words as fast as Finnish.

One event, which will never be forgotten by the members of the party, and which happened while we were at Kuopio, was the raising to life of a child that was run over and killed in an automobile accident, the circumstances of which had been previously shown to Brother Branham in a vision. We shall let Pastor Vilho Soininen, of Kuopio, relate this remarkable incident:

*   *   *   *

"On Friday afternoon, a remarkable and startling incident took place which meant much to Brother Branham and to those of us who happened to be its witnesses. Three carloads of us made an unforgettable trip to nearby Puijo Observation Tower, situated on a beautiful scenic elevation. The outing was one of the most precious I can remember, because of the blessing of God upon us. Then as we were returning from Puijo, a terrible accident occurred. A car ahead was unable to avoid striking two small boys, who ran out into the street in front of it, throwing one down on the sidewalk, and the other five yards away into a field. One unconscious boy was carried into a car just ahead of us and the other, Kari Holma, was lifted into our car and placed in the arms of Brother Branham and Miss Isaacson, who were sitting in the back seat. Brothers Moore and Lindsay were in the front seat with me.

"As we hurried to the hospital, I asked through Miss Isaacson, the interpreter, how the boy was. Brother Branham, with his finger on the boy's pulse, answered that the boy seemed to be dead, since the pulse did not beat at all. Then Brother Branham placed his hand over the boy's heart and realized that it was not functioning. He further checked the boy's respiration and could detect no breath. Then he knelt down on the floor of the car and began to pray. And Brothers Lindsay and Moore prayed, too, that the Lord would have mercy. As we neared the hospital, about five or six minutes later, I glanced back, and to my surprise, the boy opened his eyes. As we carried the boy into the hospital, he began to cry, and I realized that a miracle had taken place.

"The other boy had been brought in a little earlier and was still unconscious. As I was taking my guests back to their hotel, Brother Branham said to me, 'Do not worry! The boy, who was in our car, will surely live.'

"At that time Brother Branham had no assurance that the other boy would live, but on Sunday evening he assured me on the basis of a vision which he had seen early Sunday morning, that he, too, would live. At the exact time that Brother Branham was telling me this at his hotel, the boy lay dying at the hospital. However, according to the statement of the doctor, that night there was a change for the better, although on the 28th of April as I write this, he still occasionally lapses into unconsciousness. (A later statement received declared that the boy had fully recovered.) The boy, who was in my car, Kari, was dismissed from the hospital in just three days, and is feeling very well considering the circumstances.

"In the Friday evening service, Brother Branham told us about the vision he had seen in America two years ago, and which had been fulfilled that afternoon when he had prayed for the dead boy. The angel had appeared to him that evening before the service, and had reminded him of this vision which he had seen two years earlier, and which he had at that time told to thousands. Now it was fulfilled. Brother Branham's coming to Kuopio was in the eternal plan of God! We of the Kuopio Elim Assembly wondered why the Lord was so good to us that He granted to just us the gracious privilege of receiving His servant."

The night we left Kuopio, a great crowd of people assembled at the station and sang in their usual minor key, the beautiful Finnish songs. As the train pulled away from the depot, the singing gradually died away, but the pleasant memories of the days spent in Kuopio will not be soon forgotten.

Returning to Helsinki, Brother Branham continued services for several more days in the Messuhalli. One morning, we ventured out to the edge of the "Iron Curtain." At one point, we were only six hundred yards from the Red soldiers. The Finnish guard surrounded our car and warned us that this was no place to be. We were glad to return to our hotel. The Communist element strongly opposed our meetings, and indeed demanded our arrest. A former Chief of Police of Kuopio, a very influential man, was present and intervened for us, and we were permitted to continue the services without interruption. Three days were spent in resting at the close of the campaign, in a castle owned by a wealthy Christian lady. We were treated as kings while there. However, when the Moscow news broadcast was turned on one evening, we were startled by the announcement (interpreted for us) which declared that American spies were operating under guise in Helsinki. We knew to whom the Moscow radio was referring, and were by no means elated over the notoriety which was being given us. In the case of a sudden outbreak of hostilities, we knew that all gates of exit would be closed immediately, with Russian guns only ten miles from the capital. Once a rumor was circulated that a break had come between America and Russia, over the shooting down of an American plane by the Soviets. It proved to be only a rumor, but it kept us uneasy. Fear dominates Europe, and most of the Finnish people fear that it is only a matter of time until the dam of Communist power will sweep over the boundaries, and push the world into the throes of Armageddon.

On the day that we left Finland, we received a special letter from one of the ministers of the State Church, informing us that there had been a mass meeting of the ministers of the church, and that after considerable discussion, the body as a result of the inspiration of the Branham meetings, had voted to accept the ministry of healing. Brother Branham wrote in reply, a letter of thanks, and encouraged the brethren to believe God for mighty things within their ranks. Though we were given to understand that the whole group who had gathered had voted to accept the truth of Divine healing, we knew that did not necessarily mean that every minister in the State Church had endorsed it. That some opposers might later appear could be expected, but the overwhelming sentiment in favor, which appeared in the letter we received that last morning was indeed encouraging to us, and made us feel that our journey to Finland had not been in vain.

After a last farewell to our kind friends in Finland, we boarded a plane and two hours later were in Oslo, Norway. There we found a similar interest among the people. Unfortunately, there had been reaction in the government circles against the ministry of Divine healing. The Health Administrator had clamped down with a ban against praying for the sick, and we being foreigners, knew that the moment we would disobey this prohibition, we would be expelled from the country. Nevertheless, there was an unexpected and remarkable result of the ban. The city's ministerial group in a mass protest meeting of two hundred ministers, "took only one minute to literally shout their unanimous agreement that protest should be made." The following protest was then drawn and signed by some of the most illustrious names in Norwegian religious life.

To the Norwegian Government
Oslo
Sirs:
Healing through faith and prayer is an inherent part of the Gospel, and is as an anchor in the life and work of Jesus Christ. Throughout the ages, this doctrine has had a firm position in the commonwealth of Christian life and preaching.

The Christian population of Norway principally stands as one man in this matter, even if details and ways of procedure may differ in churches and countries.

The undersigned, therefore, vividly regret the measures taken by our authorities and form a protest against the prohibitive regulations given, endeavoring to exercise censorship over Christian preaching. This procedure is of a nature to offend fundamental human rights in a free country, and disputes the principle of free worship.

We suggest that the prohibitive restrictions be immediately repealed, imposed by act of the Oslo Chamber of Police.

Oslo, May 5th, 1950.

To get ahead of our story, we may state that the Divine healing ban was indeed lifted, and several years later, we had the privilege of preaching in Oslo to a packed auditorium.

From Norway, we went to Sweden, where several services were held at Gotenburg, one night at Jonkoping, and then for five days at Orebro where is located the famous Evangelipress, which sends out a steady stream of Christian literature. A crowd of five thousand attended the first service which was held open-air in the park. Our stay in Orebro was in all ways very pleasant and we trust profitable.

From Orebro, the Branham party went north to Ornskoldsvik which lies only a short distance south of the Arctic Circle. Some 6000 people, it was estimated, jammed in and around the tent. It was said, and we have reason to believe that it is true, that this was the largest religious gathering in the history of the world, near the Arctic Circle. Although at that time it was yet in the middle of the month of May, it was sufficiently light at midnight to take a picture of the tent!

From Ornskoldsvik, we traveled south to Stockholm where is located the largest Pentecostal Church in the world of some 6500 active members, and a Sunday School of about 5000. Our visit with Brother Lewi Pethrus and his son, Oliver, who was our interpreter while there, was a highlight of our stay in Stockholm. Utterly unassuming in appearance, yet endowed with wisdom by which he has guided to a great extent the fortunes of the Full Gospel movement in Sweden during the past forty years, Brother Lewi Pethrus charmed all of us as we listened to him in private conversations, as was our privilege on two afternoons. Brother Pethrus has a simplicity of faith, and yet a spiritual shrewdness that has enabled him to build on strong foundations, until today the Full Gospel work in Sweden is renowned throughout the world. Brother Branham's ministry was well-received in Stockholm, and indeed when it came time to leave, Brother Pethrus expressed the hope that Brother Branham would find it possible to return again soon to Sweden. And so the trip overseas came to a close. Brother Branham and all of us had enjoyed our stay in Europe, but we must admit that we were glad when our giant airliner took off from the Stockholm field, and we began our journey home.

CHAPTER XXVII

The Summer Campaigns in America

Returning to America, I found that a large amount of business had piled up during my absence, and I was undecided whether I could continue in meetings that summer.

Jack Moore informed me that he was having a large tent constructed for Brother Branham's meetings that summer. However, Brother Branham had been depending on some money that was promised him, in order to pay for the tent that was almost constructed. This money, which Brother Branham expected, did not materialize. Brother Moore then asked if the Voice of Healing would purchase the tent. This would, of course, require my handling the tent and being on the field. After some consideration I consented, although this would mean that I would have to work on a tight schedule that summer. The wonderful results that came from those summer campaigns, showed that God was in the plan.

There is not space to enumerate the many interesting events that took place nor the remarkable gifts manifested by Brother Branham in those meeting. The word of knowledge and the gift of discernment came forth in almost perfection, as nearly a hundred per cent perfect as it was possible for them to be.

In one case, I recall that a little deaf boy came to be prayed for. Unfortunately, he was so far back in the line that by the time he got near Brother Branham, the service was closed. This lad and his mother looked so sad and disappointed that Jack Moore turned to me and said, "Why don't you pray for him? He may never get to Brother Branham." So I went ahead and prayed for him, and God delivered him. But that was not the end of the story.

The next day, he and his mother were there again. By some chance they were given another prayer card in the afternoon service. Well, the mother knew that the boy could now hear, but she thought the card was too valuable to be wasted. So they got into the line. As we saw them in the line again, I looked at Brother Jack Moore and he looked at me. Then he said, "I guess it doesn't do us any good to pray for the people. They aren't satisfied unless Brother Branham prays for them. We watched with interest, nonetheless, to see how Brother Branham would handle the case. When the boy came to him, we were startled to hear him say, "Go, your way. A man of faith prayed for you last night and you are healed."

*   *   *   *

In Cleveland, Ohio, an incident took place which the people who attended, will never forget. It was an insolent attack by the Cleveland News against the integrity of the meetings, practically accusing Brother Branham of fakery and hoaxing the people. The story of what happened was carried in the October, 1950, issue of the Voice of Healing. We reproduce it here:

The location of the tent for the Branham campaign on the shores of Lake Erie, and almost within the shadows of Cleveland's skyscrapers, was most admirable and convenient for the thousands who attended. To the west, and a little farther from town, was the immense grandstand of the Cleveland Indians' baseball park.

We were informed that union meetings in Cleveland had not proved overly successful in the past. One such effort in the spring, sponsored by scores of churches, drew only fair attendance on the best nights. But during the entire 17 days of the Branham campaign, the large tent was filled, and often there were many hundreds on the outside.

Newspaper reporters attended the first night of the campaign and gave very fair write-ups of the meetings. Nevertheless, several days later, a reporter from the Cleveland News, notorious for his hostility toward religion, began a series of infamous articles against the meetings. Since a large number of Cleveland churches were sponsoring the meetings, it was, in effect, a bold attack on the religious faith of thousands of solid, Cleveland citizens.

It has been the considered opinion of the writer that such attacks on the Gospel should not be let go unchallenged, nor should those who engage in such practices be allowed to believe that they can continue to do so, with impunity. In the article written by this reporter, the central assumption was that no actual healings were taking place, and therefore the campaign was a fake.

Our first action in meeting this attack, was to go down that same evening into the audience and bring a test case to the platform. The one chosen was little Bobby, who had been brought to the meetings by his mother. This child had been totally blind, but had received his sight during the campaign to the degree that he could get around by himself. The mother's testimony was as follows:

"Bobby was born with weak eyes, and at the age of six months cataracts formed on them. When Bobby became two years old, the Lions Club raised two thousand dollars to have an operation on one of the eyes, performed by Dr. Culler, a noted specialist of Columbus, Ohio. The operation was not successful. Infection set in in the other eye, and Bobby became totally blind, and since then has had to be led around by hand.

"A few days ago, a registered nurse, Mrs. Mildred Galbraith, of 2120 E. Meade, Yakima, Washington, who was healed of a cancer in the Tacoma meeting, suggested to me that I bring the child to the Branham meetings. When Bobby was prayed for on Wednesday, he instantly received his sight. The miracle took place before a large number of people who were attending the service. Now Bobby is able to see, and no longer does he have to be led about. The circumstances of this miracle are known by thousands of people who are attending the meetings."

Our next step was to take this child with the mother, and the registered nurse to the office of the Cleveland News and present the circumstances to the City Editor. He seemed to be quite a reasonable person, and asked us to write an article for insertion in the Cleveland News. However, the main editor was not present, and in a later conversation with him on the phone, he informed us in tones of extreme arrogancy, that he had no intention of apologizing for the attacks that had been made. Instead, he made further threats against the meeting, intimating that other such articles would appear.

But he reckoned without host. That night in the tent, the situation was presented to the people of Cleveland. Was this insolent attack on the religion of thousands of citizens of Cleveland to be done with impunity? The people of Cleveland gave the answer. The congregation rose en masse in condemnation of the newspaper articles, and what is more, they put their protest into action. Phones began to ring continuously. Nothing like that had ever happened to these men. The lines to the Cleveland News were clogged with protests of angry citizens. Telegrams were sent and notification of cancellations of the newspaper flowed in. Finally, in desperation, the editor appealed to the police department to see if they would do anything to stop the mass protests. But evidently the police department had no desire to waste their sympathy on a newspaper that had so well deserved the condemnation of the public. As a matter of fact, one of the captains of the department brought down one of their own cases for healing.

No more vicious articles appeared in the paper. Moreover, the Cleveland News hastily inserted the article that they had requested from us, but had failed to carry. We bore no ill-feeling toward this editor, and trust he thoroughly repented for his conduct, but we do believe it is time that those who contemptuously assail holy things, shall find that they must face the just penalty such conduct rightfully incurs. (We understand that the newspaper has since failed and has discontinued publication.)

* * * *

Whenever Brother Branham was under the anointing, the most remarkable happenings took place. It would seem that the omniscient knowledge of God would be manifest. Hidden things in the person's heart would be revealed. The Spirit was always gentle with individuals unless there was presumptuous, unconfessed sin. Then it would often be exposed and rebuked. Those who used tobacco or liquor were urged to give up these things. The mighty presence of God effectually kept such persons from showing any resentment, and those that were dealt with often would be quite broken up.

When Brother Branham left the tent, I would usually make the altar call. Under the circumstances, this was not hard to do, and often several hundred would come forward.

The remarkable healing in the Branham meetings, of former Congressman William D. Upshaw was of such a nature, and the circumstances were so well-known, that skeptics were hard put to explain it. It was more than a healing; there was a work of creation done in his body which enabled him to walk again, after 66 years a cripple. The former Congressman served four terms for the state of Georgia. Once he ran on a minority ticket for the presidency of the United States. He was an unusually gifted speaker, and his name was known to millions of people.

When young Upshaw was 18, he fell on the crosspiece of a wagon frame and fractured his spine. For seven years he was a total invalid. By dint of his own exertions, he finally learned to walk by the aid of crutches. When I first met him after he had used the crutches for nearly sixty years, he was able to make his way about in a painful and tedious fashion, supported by crutches. He had been attending our salvation-healing campaigns in Los Angeles, where thousands were being saved and healed.

One day, during the meeting, he asked to see me. He told me about the injury which kept him on crutches all these years. The accident had evidently severed certain, vital nerves. Apparently, a creative work would have to be done before he could walk. I encouraged him to continue to attend the healing services. I told him God could heal him, but his faith needed to grow until it could take hold of the promise for the needed miracle. I do not recall whether he was prayed for at that time or not, but I know he continued to attend the meetings regularly.

Two years later, I was present in the Branham meetings in the same city. Brother Branham told me that in a vision, he had seen the healing of a statesman. The following night as he left the platform, and while still under the anointing he said, "The Congressman is healed." William Upshaw's heart leaped, and believing that what was told him was true, he rose to his feet and started walking! In his own words he said, "I laid aside my crutches and started toward my happy, shouting wife . . . and the bottom of heaven fell out! Heaven came down our souls to greet me, and glory crowned the mercy seat."

For several years after that, the Honorable William D. Upshaw criss-crossed the country, giving his testimony in many cities of America, including Washington, D.C., where he had spent many years as Congressman. His testimony was published in a number of America's leading newspapers. As the blind man who washed in Siloam and came seeing to the astonishment of many, so likewise the miraculous healing of this statesman became one of the most outstanding testimonies of God's power in the Twentieth Century.

CHAPTER XXVIII

The Deliverance Revival Spreads to Overseas

Various of our associates began to hold overseas meetings. In October, 1950, Evangelist Clifton Erickson asked me to go to Lima, Peru, with him for a campaign. Brother Erickson, himself, had had a remarkable testimony. While he was doing some work on a truck, a piece of steel broke off and struck him in the eye. The steel pierced the eyeball and lodged in the pupil. He delayed having it examined, and when finally the steel was removed, the eye had become infected. The condition of the eye steadily grew worse, and the pain became so excruciating, he could scarcely bear it. He was suddenly faced with the possibility that he would be blind the rest of his life. At that point he determined not to return to the physician but to trust God.

There was a Bible Conference at Wenatchee, Washington, and he decided to go there to be prayed for. After he was ministered to, he felt God had touched his eyes, but the following day the pain seemed to be worse than before. Friends came to sympathize with him, but he refused their pity. God was dealing with him. At that moment, he felt God calling him to the ministry. Previously he had refused the call. Now he was willing to do what God had asked him to do. Within two weeks after he began to preach, the pain was all gone and his eyes were perfectly normal.

Brother Erickson asked me if I would be willing to go to Lima, Peru, a few days early, to get things started. I said I would. Arriving in the city, I was met by the missionary, Walter Erickson, who asked me if I would speak to the congregation that was at the church waiting for me. Although I had been up all night and would like to get some rest, the thought of the congregation waiting, caused me to consent.

Brother Walter Erickson proved to be one of the finest of missionaries, but he thought that faith would have to be built up considerably before any miracles could take place. He suggested that I preach a few days before there was any praying for the sick.

After I had finished speaking to the people I said that I would pray for a few persons. Again the missionary let me know that he was not sure that the people were ready. He was all for the deliverance ministry but thought that more preparation was needed. I asked if there was a deaf mute present, and somebody led one forward. I noticed out of the corner of my eye my missionary friend was a little troubled. He so wanted the meeting to be a success, and he feared that if things didn't develop as we had hoped, we might get discouraged and leave. However, we went ahead and rebuked the deaf spirit, and in a moment the woman's ears were opened. She was able to keep time with the music, and her expression showed that something wonderful had happened to her.

That night we had a powerful service. I saw that faith was strong in the people. We called for those who wished to be healed to come forward. Near the head of the line was a man who had been stone blind for twenty-five years. Ordinarily, I would not permit such serious cases to be in the front of the line until a number of miracles had taken place, which would in turn quicken their faith. A person stone blind often falls into a condition of such hopelessness that he has no active faith. But on this man's face was an expression of such faith that I told them to leave him in the line. In a moment I prayed for him and then told him to open his eyes. He began looking. "Can you see?" I asked. The interpreter repeated my words but the man said nothing. He was not yet seeing, but I saw a confident look on his face. I knew that the man had the necessary faith. "Let him stand right where he is," I said, "and tell him to keep on looking."

I then began to pray for others. But only a few brief moments lapsed until there was a great shout from the audience. I turned to see the cause of the excitement and lo, the man was pointing out the lights. "Uno, dos, tres, cuatro, cinco, seis!" He was counting them. The people stood to their feet and as one person began to shout, "Gloria a Dios, Gloria a Dios!"

Then suddenly the man dropped his hand. There was a puzzled look on his face. Everyone stopped. Something seemed to be wrong. "Ask him what is the matter," I said. The interpreter talked to him and then relayed his words back to me. "He says that he can see good, but something is wrong with the lights. They are big long things!"

What happened was that at the time he went blind, twenty-five years before, there were no fluorescent lights! The matter was explained to him, and a broad smile came on his face.

By the following night the church was packed out. Within a few days Brother Clifton Erickson came and we moved into the arena, seating some 5,000 people. Within another week the arena was nearly filled and hundreds, perhaps thousands, responded to the altar calls.

It was necessary that I depart before Brother Erickson did. After leaving Lima, he ministered in another city in Peru. By this time the State Church was roused and Brother Erickson was, in fact, arrested and put in jail. He was released the next day but had to discontinue further meetings in the country. Nevertheless, the revival spirit that had begun, continued.

Brother Walter Erickson in writing about the meetings said:

"After two glorious weeks in the Coliseum, with ever increasing crowds, the State Church suddenly woke up, and by political pressure caused the great meetings to be stopped, but the revival is by no means stopped, nor can it be. People by the thousands stormed the Coliseum until it was necessary to put police all around it, and finally to rope off the streets leading to it. All Lima is in a ferment over the revival which has reached into the highest brackets of society, because we find that the wealthy are just as keen about God and His healing power, as the poor. The matter has reached the Minister of Government, and finally the President of the nation; we believe it will not stop there. It has produced a spiritual upheaval such as Peru has never before known, and I believe that people will no longer be satisfied with any empty profession after they have seen the reality of God. This is Peru's great opportunity, and I am sure the nation will never be the same again as they are able to open their hearts and receive this great visitation from the Spirit of God.

"I have been a first-hand witness of these blessings, because I have served as interpreter for the brethren, Gordon Lindsay and Clifton Erickson, in every meeting from the very beginning, and have been an eye witness of all of these great miracles as I stood on the platform at their sides as they prayed for the sick and afflicted, and cast out unclean spirits in the name of the Lord Jesus. The thing is of God, and to Him we give all the praise and glory in the name of Jesus Christ His Son."

I describe this meeting in Peru, because I was present in it. However, it was only one of many. Scores of campaigns were held by our associates in many different countries. Audiences numbered from 5,000 people on up. On a few occasions they went as high as fifty to a hundred thousand.

CHAPTER XXIX

Jack Coe and the Great Kansas City Flood

I first met Jack Coe during his tent meeting in Castro Valley, a town located near Oakland, California, while I was still with William Freeman. I have regarded Jack as perhaps having as great ability as any contemporary evangelist, to reach the common man with the gospel. In the short period of about eight years, he left his mark upon America as few evangelists have.

Jack was brought up in an orphanage. He had to fend for himself and he had none of the benefits of home training that most of us get as a matter of course. Nevertheless, he possessed certain innate talents that appear in an evangelist only once or twice in a generation. He was a rugged individualist to the last degree, yet at the same time he desired fellowship, and could not live without it. Nonetheless, his ineptness at times would work against the very thing he desired the most. Despite his obvious shortcomings, we felt that his untimely death was a distinct loss to the evangelistic field. He possessed such a unique personality that it was days after his passing, before people could accommodate their thinking to the fact that he was gone.

While William Freeman and I were in Oakland, California, word came to us that a preacher by the name of Jack Coe was holding a meeting in Castro Valley. He was apparently having considerable success, but we were informed that his preaching was marked by the taking of potshots at any who incurred his disapproval.

Indeed, we were not left out. It appeared that our great error was in having prayer cards. "Did Jesus have any prayer cards printed?" Jack would demand of his audience. The logical conclusion was of course that we were using an unscriptural method. Jack had many a smile with me over this later. A year or two afterwards, when his own crowds became many times larger he found it quite necessary to use them, himself. Of course as everyone knows, the prayer cards are used merely to maintain order in a large meeting. It would not do to have several hundred people battling one another to get to the evangelist to be prayed for.

Even Jesus, when He fed the five thousand, had the people sit down in companies of fifties, so that the bread and fish could be passed out in an orderly way. (Luke 9:14) One Sunday night, when we were not in services, we decided to go and hear Jack. When we entered the tent we did not make ourselves known, as we wanted him to be free to preach in his own way.

As I listened, my reaction was a mixture of emotions. Although before Jack got through, he made his usual attack on card-using evangelists, I saw that here was a man with great potential as an evangelist. I realized that beneath his unpolished exterior, there lay an enormous ability to reach the common man. Jack's vocabulary was not extensive, but nevertheless, he could express himself with remarkable clarity and forcefulness. He always had the right word and could take an incident that seemed commonplace to other observers, and make it come alive in a way as to leave the listener sitting on the edge of his seat in suspense. He used short homespun expressions that would drive his thought home with more pungency than a silver-tongued orator could who had twice the vocabulary.

Months later, William Freeman and I went to San Francisco. We got a call from Leland Keyes asking if we would come to Glad Tidings Temple to hold a campaign. I asked him how many the Temple would hold. He replied, "We have more room than you will need. Even Dr. Charles Price could not fill our auditorium." I replied, "Brother Keyes, before the week is out, the people will be standing in the street trying to get in." He was rather skeptical about this, but being a polite man he did not argue the point. It was not long, however, before he found that my prediction came true.

While we were at San Francisco, two brethren, C. M. Ward and Claude Weaver from Bakersfield, came to the services and asked to see me. Could our party come to Bakersfield? The ministers there, they said, were ready for a city-wide meeting. They felt that this was the time to emphasize the Divine Healing meetings. Then they added that in a nearby city there was an evangelist by the name of Jack Coe who had a good ministry, but he was so tactless in his preaching that they feared it would have an adverse effect on the Divine healing ministry in that area. Brother Freeman felt inclined to go. And so a week or two later, we went to Bakersfield. A few days later, Jack closed his meeting and left town.

I believe that this was a turning point in Jack's life. He began to see that direct onslaught on everyone in particular, was not the way to reach the people. He saw that our meeting reached many thousands of people, and yet we did not resort to severe criticism of our brethren.

A year later Jack Coe came to see me. I thought that perhaps he might still hold a resentment against me because I had disagreed with methods he was using. Instead, he was very friendly and told me that he had learned many things during the past year and he would like me to help him. He wanted to be a part of the fellowship of the Voice of Healing. Jack was now attracting large crowds, but many pastors seemed leary of him. Like others, I was impressed by his personal magnetism, and before he left I promised to attend one of his meetings. In fact, he became one of the speakers at the Kansas City, Voice of Healing Convention, and his colorful personality together with his unusual manner of speaking, captivated the audience.

Shortly after that, Jack asked me to write his life story for him, and I consented. I had him tell it in his own way and at his own convenience — which was usually after midnight. I smoothed the most rugged parts of his story, but as far as possible, tried to preserve his own inimitable style. The book promptly became a best-seller.

I attended a number of Jack's meetings while preparing the book. Just as I was completing it, a most dramatic event took place in Kansas City. An unprecedented disaster struck in that city where he was holding a tent campaign.

For weeks rain, had been falling in unprecedented quantities in the Midwest area. The Kaw River was steadily rising. The terrific downfall caused the ground to become water-soaked, but still a capacity crowd attended the meetings. Hundreds were being saved and filled with the Spirit. Although the river kept rising, still nobody thought a flood would occur that would be called a billion dollar disaster.

Some three months before the Kansas City meeting, Jack had a dream. Relating that dream he said, "It seemed as if our tent were sitting in the middle of the flood, and the water was closing in on every side. I could see the muddy water, and the waves dashing in and curling under. The dream troubled me, and I mentioned it to my wife. Some time later, we went to Wichita, and one night there was a violent storm. During the storm the whole top of the tent was ripped. The waters overflowed the banks of the Little Arkansas, but they didn't come near the tent. I thought this incident was the meaning of the dream that had been troubling me. I went on to Kansas City . . . "

Although the meeting in Kansas City was going well, Jack continued to be burdened. He couldn't sleep. The dream kept coming back to him. On Tuesday, he was at a cafe having lunch with several brethren. Suddenly he said, "Something tells me that I ought to take the tent down."

He and some of the brethren walked out to the trucks, which were all stuck deep in the mud. Jack set the men to work getting them out on to the pavement. Then he and Brother Barnett got into a car and went down to look at the dikes. Everything seemed safe. The water was still five feet from the top. They noticed also that the business establishments were still carrying on their work as usual. One minister remarked, "If there were any danger, it looks as if they would be moving their goods out."

Jack went back to the trucks. Everything was so wet that they had to get "hot shots" to get them started. Some of the ministers came up to him and said, "What are you doing, Brother Coe?" He answered, "I am getting ready to take the tent down. A few minutes ago the Lord spoke to me and told me to take it down."

It was then about 4:30 P.M., and everyone that came to the tent was put to work. While they worked some ministers said, "Don't take the tent down. God can take care of the tent." Jack replied, "I know God can take care of this tent. That's the reason I am moving." About 10:00 P.M. they got the tent down. Just as the last stake was being lifted, the stake puller jammed and would not pull another stake. They finally got all the canvas rolled. Then suddenly, every whistle and siren in town began to blow. I am letting Jack tell the exciting story that followed, just as he told it to me when I was writing his book:

*   *   *   *

A cry went through the street, "The dikes are breaking!" There I was ready to go if I could get the canvas in the trucks, but I found that the A-frame was broken, and I couldn't get the heavy sections loaded unless I had a lot of men.

When the whistles started blowing and the cry came that the dikes were breaking, the men that had helped me began to leave. I got up on a large box that was behind the tent and plead, "Men, don't leave me now. The tent is rolled up, don't leave me." One spoke up and said, "Man, if you think that I am going to stay here and drown, you're crazy." I said, "The flood's not coming yet. I am sure it's not coming yet." By that time the bridge was clogged up. People grabbed what they could and rushed for safety, and traffic on the bridge was snarled up as panic-stricken people tried to make their way over. The men saw the people struggling to get over the bridge, and they wondered if they were making a mistake in delaying, but I stood there with tears in my eyes and plead with them not to leave me. Then one spoke up and said, "Brother Coe loves God, and he isn't afraid to stay here and get this stuff out, and we ought to be men enough to stay here and help him. If he isn't afraid of drowning, I surely am not."

When the man said that, about forty of them came forward and said that they would help. It took every man there to carry one of those large sections, but finally all the rolls were loaded. We started the trucks up, and one of them got on the bridge, and ran out of gas. Then another got on the bridge and it ran out of gas! The truckman had failed to fill the tanks, so we had to go and get gasoline and put in the trucks, and finally we got them moving, for they were blocking the whole bridge leading away from Armourdale. Since some of the trucks wouldn't run, we had to use tractors to get our equipment over.

I helped Brother Barnett take his furniture from his house and stack it in his church. The earlier cry about the dikes breaking was false, but we knew that they were leaking, and Brother Barnett went back to see how things were. I had just taken a bath and cleaned up, when he came rushing back to tell us the worst. He cried, "Come quick, the flood's coming!"

The dikes were not far away, and he had gotten there just in time to see them crumble, and a wall of water moving down toward him. He ran back and jumped in his car. In his excitement, he couldn't find his key. Then he said to himself, "Now look here, Barnett, you have to get hold of yourself." He found the key, but the car wouldn't start. The water was drawing nearer, but finally, to his great relief, it started and he whirled around and down the street he went, and got back to the house.

I rushed to the truck, backed it out and started for the bridge. The sirens were blowing continuously, but some people had thought it just another false alarm and stayed in their homes. I saw them sitting on their porches. A patrolman drove by and saw a man with his wife and two children, and he shouted angrily, "You fools, you were told to get out of here." He didn't even try to pick up the children, but put his car in gear and took off. We picked up the family and got them in the truck just in time. As I turned the corner to go up on the bridge the water started to come up on the wheels!

As I pulled up on the bridge, the river began to rush through. The first thing I saw coming on the surging waves was a hundred gallon oil drum. Soon there must have been over a thousand of these things bouncing on the whirling torrent. As the water rose, I saw a Model A Ford going down the street, just as if someone were driving it. It turned the corner, and I could see that there was no one in it.

Brother Barnett was with me in the truck. He had wanted to stay with his church, but I said, "Man, you are not staying, you're getting in this truck." By this time, the water had risen rapidly, house trailers, houses and everything started to wash down.

As we had started up the bridge, we saw people who had gathered at the filling station. They started to scream as they saw the wall of water coming. Some escaped in time and ran up on the bridge, but others were cut off and were now screaming for help. One woman, a little distance, away, was crying out, "My God, help me, help me." They tied ropes around some of us and others held the ropes and we got the woman. On a roof top, we could see a man and woman and two children. Another man was also on a housetop, but not so far away. A little motor boat started out to get them, and they rescued the man, but as they turned to get the family, the house turned over in the water and the people disappeared.

We looked over toward Brother Barnett's Church, and the water was up about seven feet. Suddenly we heard some one screaming in the house across from the Barnetts'. But it was over near where the box cars were, and the water was coming in so fast you couldn't get in there with a boat. A Coast Guard cutter came along and tried to get over there, but they were never able to get to that house. Finally, the cry subsided. Whether or not they drowned, we'll never know.

As the water rose up the sides of Brother Barnett's Church, he said, "If it reaches the windows, everything I have is gone." As the water kept rising, and reached the windows, he turned to me and said, "Let's not stand and watch it any longer; I can't stand it." By that time, his six or seven buses had washed away. As the water poured into the windows, he knew that everything that he had was gone.

As we started on across the bridge, he said, "I have no home, nor place to hold services. I guess I'll have to leave Kansas City." He paused — "But I can't leave all those people that way. I owe it to them to stay." I looked back one more time, and by this time the flood had come up 22 feet, where the tent had stood, and only a little part of the church was showing. I turned back, and we walked to the other end of the bridge, leaving America's greatest flood disaster in its history, behind us.

(Brother Barnett and his congregation recovered from the flood and built a new church. He now has one of the largest Sunday Schools in the city.)

CHAPTER XXX

The Miami Court Trial and the Passing of a Great Evangelist

In the year 1952, we moved the Voice of Healing office to Dallas, Texas. That summer, Jack had a camp meeting in the interest of his Children's Home which he was establishing. A number of the churches of Dallas cooperated.

One evening a few weeks later, Jack was in the office with me, with a prominent official of a religious organization. This official had taken a strong stand against the deliverance ministry. He had explained to me that he had two children who had died because he had not taken them to the doctor, and as a result, authorities had almost succeeded in putting him in prison. This experience had given him a distorted and a decidedly prejudiced view of the ministry of healing. He no longer believed that Divine healing was in the atonement although his denomination believed it, and the Scriptures directly declare that it is. (Matt. 8:14-17) In the sorrow of his personal loss, he had developed a strong antipathy against those who emphasized the healing ministry, and as he claimed, financially profited from it. The faults and failings of those who preached the gospel of healing and ministered to the sick became greatly magnified in his eyes.

That evening, however, as he talked to us he was very congenial. He did not mention the many shortcomings of evangelists that had been his wont, but he did say something that was to have a great effect upon Jack Coe's future. He said, "The thing I can't understand about the deliverance evangelists is this: In the revivals of Dr. Charles S. Price, Aimee Semple McPherson and Smith Wigglesworth, many churches sprang up following their meetings. But," he continued, "I do not see this in these present revivals. It seems to me if this move were really heaven-sent, there would be new churches established as a result."

I was disturbed by his statement. The situation, as I saw it, was altogether different than in the days of those evangelists. Since then, thousands of Full Gospel churches have been built all over the country. In Dallas alone, there are sixty or seventy Full Gospel churches and more being built every year. There was no need for evangelists to start new churches, but rather to send new people into those which already existed. But, as I feared, Jack took him very seriously. He said, "Brother S——, I believe you are right. I have thought about this but I wasn't sure whether this was the thing that I ought to do. Now I am going ahead and start a church in Dallas."

I remonstrated and called attention to the fact that the local cooperating churches would not share this view of the matter. But the official who made the suggestion would not retreat from what he had said, and Jack began plans forthwith to establish a church in Dallas. Of course, his act created serious repercussions. It caused Jack for a long time to be out of fellowship with nearly every Full Gospel minister in the city. This nearly broke his heart. He always wanted fellowship, and could not understand why if the leading official of those churches recommended that he start a new church, that everyone should not be happy about it.

Several years passed and Jack came to see me many times. Once he said, "I need fellowship. I am made that way. The preachers in Dallas avoid me like the plague." Then he said, "Gordon, will you speak at my Children's Home Camp Meeting this year?" I was about to say, "No," but the Spirit seemed to check me. Something said, "What about that seventy times seven? Shouldn't the ministers forgive their brother after he admits that he has done wrong, and wants to come back into the fellowship?" I found myself saying, "Yes, I will speak for you." Jack, in his forthright way, put the announcement at once into his newspaper advertisement. There was many a raised eyebrow when they saw the notice of my participation. However, I felt that I had done right.

Not long after that, a remarkable thing happened. A pastor of the city was in my office. He was an official of a large religious organization, and I had always thought of him as a strong organization man. But he turned and said something that startled me. "God has been speaking to my heart, and I feel that the time has come to strive for the unity of the whole Body of Christ. I believe in being loyal to our own churches, but I am also convinced that we must reach out beyond this and work for the unity of the whole church. I believe we should start doing it right here in Dallas."

The effects of this stand by this man of God were to be far-reaching. Soon, a Full Gospel Ministers' Fellowship was formed, and men who had never spoken to each other in their lives became good friends. Once each month, a luncheon was held at some selected spot. There would be a speaker and the goodwill resulting from the fellowship brought the Full Gospel ministers close together. Several times at the Voice of Healing offices, we had over a hundred ministers and their wives present at a special luncheon.

The fellowship has had some remarkable results. While the ministers in many cities are divided into hostile camps, with feuds, rivalries and bitter controversies disturbing the peace, the policy of "live and let live" has been a shining example for other communities to follow. True it is, that we have opportunists in Dallas as in other cities. Ministers come to town with doubtful ethics. But the law of sowing and reaping is allowed to take its course in a normal way, and the Full Gospel churches in Dallas are far better off than in those cities where an open feud is going on. It was a matter of great regret to us when this ministers' fellowship was discontinued.

So it happened that I was awakened one night by a long distance call from Jack at Miami, Florida. He was in trouble. I shall give the story as it later appeared in the current issue of the Voice of Healing:

* * * *

A few weeks ago at about two o'clock in the morning, we received a long distance call from Jack Coe, who was at that time holding a revival campaign in Miami, Florida. He was not long in coming to the point. "I have," he said, "been arrested on charges of practicing medicine without a license, because I pray for the sick. Before they released me from jail, I was forced to raise a $5,000 bond. If they can make this charge stick, they can sentence me up to five years in prison."

A day or two later he called again, and this time he had his attorney, Mr. Chertkof, talk to me. The lawyer explained the gravity of the situation. Evil and determined forces, he said, were rallying every weapon at their disposal to make the charge of practicing medicine without a license, stick, and that Brother Coe needed all the assistance that *The Voice of Healing* evangelists could give him. The attorney requested that if it were at all possible, I should come to Miami. After realizing the significance of the situation relative to the future of the healing ministry in general, should such a charge be proved, I dropped everything and made arrangements to go.

Arriving in Miami, we quickly learned the story of events that had been leading up to what would prove to be a historic trial in the divine healing ministry. There have, of course, been minor ef-

forts from time to time in various parts of the country, to employ
legal action against those who pray for the sick. But none of these
have occasioned national interest. In this trial, however, the attention of the whole nation was focused upon it. Newspapers headlined it in distant cities. Moreover, one of the strangest alliances in
religious history formed the opposition. First and foremost, in fo-
menting the persecution, was Joseph Lewis, leader and champion
of the Freethinkers of America, one of the most deadly and sinister
organizations in our country. Mr. Lewis, himself, is a blatant
agnostic who publicly defies God and insults all religion. Allied in
this opposition were certain religious groups whose opposition to
Divine healing has long been notorious. And third was the newspaper, the *Miami Herald,* which also joined hands in this strange
alliance of infidels and professed Christians.

Events leading to this violent attack on the ministry of Jack
Coe began early in the campaign. A reporter from *The Miami
Herald* attended the meeting and decided to run a series of articles
in the paper, claiming the healings were fakes and that the evangelist was a religious racketeer. The violence of his attack was
sufficient to result in an article in the *Time Magazine.* This was
before the arrest of Rev. Coe.

Rev. Coe answered the attack of the Miami Herald by producing hundreds of written testimonies of miracles of healing. But
these testimonies were to a great extent ignored. The Miami Herald picked out one or two which claimed the person was healed
of "a cold" or some very minor ailment, and pointed to them as
typical. Testimonies which mentioned healings of organic diseases
were purposely given no attention.

Joseph Lewis, whom we have mentioned, prince of the infidels
of America, sat in his home in Miami Beach and read with un-
disguised pleasure the attack of the Miami Herald on Jack Coe.
That worthy successor of the notorious agnostic, Robert G. Inger-
soll, could not resist the impulse to join forces with the persecution. After making a search, he learned of a woman who had
brought her child to the tent to be prayed for — apparently without result. According to the woman's testimony (later in the
court), Mr. Lewis visited her, and promised free medical help for
the child if she could be prevailed upon to sign a warrant against
Jack Coe. The distracted woman fell for the bait.

Actually this woman knew nothing about the conditions upon
which Divine healing is based. She had heard that miracles were
taking place in the tent, and she had only one thought, and that
was to get her child in the healing line. When she was told to

wait her turn, and to receive instruction for healing, she became hysterical, soundly abusing the workers for not letting her get her boy into the healing line at once. She was to later testify on the witness stand, that she belonged to a nominal church but had not attended for eight years.

Because she made herself such a nuisance in trying to get her child prayed for, the workers permitted her on the second night to get her child in the line. There were hundreds to be ministered to that night, and Brother Coe, when he came to the woman, told her (witnesses differed in the exact words), "If you believe Jesus heals the child, take the braces off, and leave them off." This was an act of faith, commonly called for even by Jesus when He ministered to the sick. But no minister of Divine healing makes a guarantee that people who are not serving God, will be healed, neither they nor their children. Divine healing is the "children's bread."

The parents were disappointed and voiced their dissatisfaction to the neighbors because a miracle did not take place. As we have said, the news reached Joseph Lewis, President of the Free-thinkers. As the woman later testified in court, she was approached by this infidel, who told her that he had come to help her. He informed her that Rev. Jack Coe was a religious racketeer, and if she would sign a warrant against the evangelist, he promised to see to it that she got free medical treatment for her child.

Thus, came about one of the strangest associations in the history of religion. First was *The Miami Herald* staff writer who began the persecution with a series of vicious attacks in the newspaper. He inferred that Rev. Coe was a religious fraud, and a racketeer. He added that Coe's profits during the campaign would "top $30,000." He further said that no miracles of healing took place.

Second, the local Council of Churches banded together and issued a statement that they regarded Jack Coe as a quack, and that his praying for the sick "smacked of religious racketeering." The Churches of Christ issued a statement that anyone who practiced Divine healing was a religious mountebank and that they, as a church, had taken a stand that all claims of Divine healing were false.

The last member of this strange trio was Joseph Lewis, the country's most notorious freethinker and infidel. *The Miami Herald* in its February 10th issue, took note that this man was the leading spirit behind the prosecution and that he was financing the legal cost involved. The disclosing of this information was something *The Miami Herald* was later to regret, for it showed that *The Herald* and the Council of Churches and agnostic Joseph Lewis, were in alliance to destroy the ministry of Divine healing.

The warrant for Jack Coe's arrest was sworn out by Judge Duvall. Word came to Brother Coe that he would be arrested. The constable, a fine gentleman, who came to take him from the pulpit, told him with tears, that this was the hardest thing that he had ever had to do in his life, and was certainly not in sympathy with the persecution. At the court of Judge Duvall, Jack Coe was arraigned and placed behind bars until he could raise $5,000 in bail. A hearing was set for February 17th, to see whether the case should go to trial in a criminal court. The charges of practicing medicine without a license, if conviction were obtained, called for a sentence up to five years in the penitentiary.

A Historic Trial

Well, it had happened at last! There have been various minor brushes with the law in small towns, over praying for the sick, but never had an evangelist who commanded a national hearing, been arrested for this cause, and charged with the violation of law for practicing medicine without a license. At least it had not happened since the days of John Alexander Dowie who fought the matter through successfully in the courts of Chicago in 1894. This, therefore, was to be an historic test of whether ministers could still obey the command of Jesus which says that believers "shall lay hands on the sick and they shall recover."

The opposition had skillfully planned its attack. The *Miami Herald* carried malicious articles against Rev. Coe on its front pages, assuming that the courts had already proved him guilty. The little polio boy was put on television in an effort to inflame public opinion against the evangelist. City authorities in Tampa where the evangelist was to go next, cancelled the permit, on the grounds that Jack Coe was a religious racketeer. Tampa newspapers carried lurid front page stories of developments in Miami.

This was the situation when we arrived in Miami. The attorney, Mr. Chertkof, later told us toward the end of the hearing, that so strong was public opinion against the evangelist in the beginning, that he had been advised by many of his friends to have nothing to do with the case. But when he learned the whole circumstances, he entered enthusiastically into the fight, being convinced that the attack had been inspired by men who hated religion.

The Lord fought for us. The disclosure that Joseph Lewis, the agnostic, was behind the persecution, was the first step in the un-

·doing of the opposition. An "open letter" was drawn up, quoting excerpts from his blasphemous attacks upon Catholics, Protestants and Jews alike. When newspapers refused to take the statement as advertising, 40,000 circulars were printed and distributed on the streets of the city.

This open letter was as follows:

RELIGION AND COE GOES ON TRIAL ... YOURS MAY BE NEXT!!!

An open letter from Rev. Jack Coe to every Catholic,
Protestant and Jew.

CATHOLIC "Do you want me to tell you why God did not save the life of the little Bobby Greenlease? I will tell you. Because — there is no God! Away with the myth of Heaven; But when Bobby was kidnapped he was wearing a religious medal — which is usually 'blessed' by a priest, and sold at an exorbitant price — which itself is a barefaced religious fraud."

PROTESTANT "It is impossible for me to believe in the Bible God. My mind rebels against it. I cannot help but look upon this God as an inhuman wretch, incapable of pity, void and empty from any dram of mercy, an ignorant force that has stupefied the brain of man and paralyzed the intellect with fear. I denounce this God with all the energy I possess, and if this be blasphemy, then make the most of it."

JEW "But if Palestine is historically the Hebrew Homeland, then why does not Israel's God deliver it to them so that the persecuted may live their days in peace, NOW! I will tell you why. Because there is no such God as the Bible deity."

Who made these statements? Joseph Lewis in his books Atheism
and Other Addresses and The Ten Commandments.

Who Is Joseph Lewis???

The Miami Daily News on February 9, 1956, said, "Lewis, 66, is president of the Freethinkers of America ... Lewis told the News that he first became interested in Coe several weeks ago, when the evangelist opened his faith healing tent headquarters, here. 'I decided that even if I had to spend a large sum of money I was going to expose him as a religious fraud,' Lewis asserted.

The Miami Herald on February 8, 1956, said, "When the Clarks' experiences with the Rev. Mr. Coe came to light through medical circles, they were offered help by Joseph Lewis of 4444

Prairie Avenue, Miami Beach. Lewis, a wealthy retired Northern businessman, said he entered the case because he believed 'somebody ought to do something about' the evangelist. The Miami Beach man hired Floyd Miner, private investigator, to study the Clark case and probe the entire operation of the Rev. Mr. Coe BEFORE Tuesday's legal action was taken."

Are Joseph Lewis and the Freethinkers using our courts and the Miami Herald in an underhanded effort to impose their views on our churches and believers in a Biblical God?

Who is behind this religious persecution? I believe in God. What do you believe?

Signed,
REV. JACK COE.

This exposure of the blasphemous character of the man who was the main spirit of the oppposition became a leading factor in opening the eyes of the citizens of Miami, to the sinister nature of the persecution.

God began to work. Christians in the Full Gospel churches rallied nobly to the cause. Jack Coe's call to the men of THE VOICE OF HEALING to help him in the battle did not go unheeded. Richard Vinyard, Gayle Jackson, Raymond T. Richey, Philip Green, Sam Todd, and others carried on revivals in the various churches during the week before the trial. Other noted evangelists such as John Meares, Clifton Erickson, and Roy Wead were present. Over twenty ministers and evangelists from out of town were sworn in during court session as men standing behind the evangelist in this historic trial. The pastors of the local Full Gospel churches to a man, stood behind the defense. These ministers by their noble efforts proved themselves worthy of the highest commendation. Nightly they gathered in the Evangel Temple of which Rev. Mac Intosh is pastor, to discuss strategy for the defense.

But beyond all this, we believe that the greatest help came from the people who prayed and fasted for a successful outcome of a trial which could effect the freedom to preach the Gospel of salvation and healing for years to come. It was a case that commanded national attention.

But the time the trial opened on Friday, February 17, public opinion had changed to no little extent. Nevertheless, the prosecutors were confident of victory. They presented their cases in a belligerent manner. Mr. Coe, they declared, had committed a flagrant violation of the law. He had taken advantage of the misfortunes of people to fraudulently practice medicine without a license. All in all they denounced the evangelist in no uncertain terms.

The parents who had signed the charges, however, made poor witnesses for the prosecution. Trembling and almost ready to collapse, the father was led away from the stand. The mother, an almost pathetic case, went through the examination and cross-examination revealing visibly her misery in the situation into which she allowed herself to get. It clearly appeared that she was but a tool of the crafty and pitiless Joseph Lewis.

The woman admitted on cross-examination that she had no idea that when she signed the charges that she might send the preacher to jail. Moreover, she confessed that she did not know what she was signing. In fact, she admitted that she had no idea as to what the charges were. Joseph Lewis had not promised her actual cash, she explained, but she understood that free treatment would be given the child if she would sign the warrant for Coe's arrest. The unhappy prosecutor turned a sickly pallor at these unexpected confessions of his star witness.

Joseph Lewis, the agnostic, failed to show up at the trial. A subpoena had been issued for him, but having become aware that his despicable attempt to put the evangelist in prison was about to fail, showed his true colors by leaving his miserable victims to suffer alone the disgrace of their actions. He absconded to a safe place where he would escape the indignation of the God-fearing citizens of the community.

The outcome of the case hinged around whether in praying for the sick, Rev. Coe was "engaged in the practice of the religious tenets of the church." The defense realizing the weakness of its case, made desperate attempts to keep out any testimony which showed what the tenets of the church were. Rev. Mac Intosh of Evangel Temple, was put on the stand and made a very excellent witness, although the prosecution succeeded in getting many of its objections sustained. The defense attorney then put the writer on the witness stand. Again objections were raised which prevented testimony from being given in the courtroom concerning our beliefs in Divine healing. Just before we were taken from the stand, the attorney revealed the fact that *THE VOICE OF HEALING,* of which the writer is president, was an association of evangelists of many denominations and therefore, represented the views of many organizations on Divine healing. Whether this influenced the judge or not, at any rate on the second day he reversed his previous action and overruled most of the objections of the prosecution.

The following day, Rev. Ogburn of the Pentecostal Holiness Church, was put on the witness stand, and he also proved an excellent witness. The Lord enabled him to speak with great freedom on the part that the local churches played in the meetings, and of the churches' beliefs in Divine healing. When the court recessed it was recognized that the case was now turning in favor of the defense.

Immediately after recess, the writer was again called by the defense as a witness. This time the judge permitted him almost complete freedom in answering the lead questions of the defense attorney, Mr. George Chertkof.

The Aftermath

It was necessary for me to leave Miami just before the close of the hearing. The prosecution now could see the handwriting on the wall. The judge realized that the case was far more than putting away an itinerant evangelist who was unable to defend himself. The modernist churches which had joined up with Joseph Lewis and *The Miami Herald to* form a united opposition had now faded into the background, embarrassed and confused when they realized that their champion was the leading infidel in America. As an interesting sidelight, many thousands of people in Miami signed a pledge promising to discontinue taking *The Miami Herald* until the newspaper apologized for its actions.

It was not surprising, therefore, that on the following Monday, Judge Duvall threw the case out of court on the contention that Jack Coe had been only praying for the sick according to the tenets of his faith. It was a great victory for Apostolic religion in America. Indeed the trial is a historic one. Had Jack Coe gone to the penitentiary, it would have placed every minister in America who prays for the sick, in peril. A final ironic note for the opposition was that immediately upon vindication, the arresting officer who was a friend of this ministry, made Jack Coe a deputy sheriff of Dade County!

The following is from notes taken while I was on the witness stand in the Miami court trial.

* * * *

QUESTION: Do many Christians today believe in Divine Healing?

REV. GORDON LINDSAY: By far the largest proportion of Christians in America believe in Divine Healing and miracles. For example, in a recent issue of the COSMOPOLITAN MAGA-ZINE there is an article which tells about the miracles of Lourdes. Catholic authorities avow that miracles of all kinds have taken place there. Whether these miracles are authentic or not, makes no difference. The point is that the Catholic church, the largest denomination in America, believes in miracles. There are many other denominations in America, some large and some small, that believe in Divine Healing and practice this belief in religious services, similar to those conducted by Evangelist Coe.

QUESTION: Name some denominations that pray for the sick in public services.

GORDON LINDSAY: There are the Assemblies of God which number nearly half a million members. There are the Church of God, the Foursquare, Pentecostal Holiness, Open Bible Church, Christian Missionary Alliance, and many other denominations which practice the ministry of healing in public services.

QUESTION: Do any of these churches regard prayer for the sick as medical treatment?

GORDON LINDSAY: They do not in any sense of the word, and in fact, seriously object to any use of the term in relation to their ministry to the sick. The word "treatment" is not used in the Scriptures, and moreover in praying for the sick, ministers do nothing that resembles medical treatment. They merely pray for the sick in obedience to Christ's command in the Great Commission.

QUESTION: What is the Great Commission?

GORDON LINDSAY: The Great Commission is recorded in Matt. 28 and Mark 16. In the latter chapter, Jesus commanded His disciples to go into all the world and preach the Gospel to every creature. He then added that these signs shall follow them that believe, one of which is, "They shall lay hands on the sick and they shall recover."

In James 5:14-15, there is also another command given concerning prayer for the sick: "Is any sick among you? let him call for the elders of the church: and let them pray over him anointing him with oil in the name of the Lord. And the prayer of faith shall save the sick, and the Lord shall raise him up, and if he have committed sins they shall be forgiven him."

(The strategy of the prosecution was to prove that Rev. Coe had no right to tell anyone, after prayer, to drop their crutches nor remove their braces, and to do so was prescribing medical treatment. Therefore the defense attorney now turned his questions in this direction.)

QUESTION: Then those who pray for the sick give no medical instruction whatever?

GORDON LINDSAY: That is correct, sir. None whatever.

QUESTION: What would you call it then, if a minister tells a person after he has been prayed for, to drop his crutches? Or to arise from his bed and walk?

GORDON LINDSAY: That would be an act of faith, or putting faith into action. If a person is healed, he ought to be able to rise from his cot, even though he were unable before that. There are many cases of Jesus' demanding an act of faith on the part of the person receiving healing.

There was the case of a man with a withered arm who came to the Lord. Jesus told him to lift that useless limb and stretch it out. It was impossible for him to do that, but as he obeyed the command of the Lord as an act of faith, God gave him strength to do the impossible. (Mark 3:5)

There was the case of Peter's mother-in-law, who was confined to her bed with a fever. Jesus put out his hand to lift her up. She cooperated and arose from her bed and was healed. This is an illustration of an act of faith.

Nor was Jesus the only one who demanded an act of faith when ministering to those who needed healing. When Peter met the lame man at the Beautiful Gate, he told him in the name of Jesus to rise and walk. Then he and John encouraged the man by lifting him to his feet. The man cooperated and as a result he was healed.

There are many other cases in which an act of faith was required. For example, Jesus singled out one man at the Pool of Bethesda and told him to, "Rise, take up thy bed and walk." He immediately obeyed the words of Jesus and arose and took up his bed.

QUESTION: Did lack of faith keep Jesus from healing some?

GORDON LINDSAY: Yes. At Nazareth, people were skeptical of Christ's ministry. "And he could do there no mighty work save that he laid hands upon a few sick folk and healed them. And he marvelled because of their unbelief." (Mark 6:5)

QUESTION: How do you account for some people failing to get healed in these meetings?

GORDON LINDSAY: No claim is ever made by any responsible minister that all the people get healed that are prayed for. Ministers are commanded in the Great Commission to lay hands on the sick. It is God's business to heal them. God also commanded ministers to preach the Gospel of salvation in the Great

Commission. No responsible minister claims that all who respond to his invitation to be saved, get saved. In both cases there are conditions to be met.

QUESTION: Does Jack Coe claim that he has supernatural powers to heal?

GORDON LINDSAY: Absolutely not. I have never heard and I am sure that no one has ever heard Jack Coe say that he, himself, possessed supernatural power to heal the sick. Rev. Coe or any other minister who prays for the sick is merely carrying out the command of the Great Commission to lay hands on the sick, so that God may heal them. The Scriptures plainly state that no man may take the glory for healing. Where Paul and Barnabas commanded a certain cripple to walk in the name of Jesus, the people who beheld the miracle began to call them gods. The apostles remonstrated against this in the most vigorous terms, saying, "Sirs, why do ye these things? We are also men of like passions with you." (Acts 14:15) God is the healer. Jack Coe prays for the sick and it is God that heals them.

THE CROSS EXAMINATION

MR. MARSH: Do you believe a child three years old can exercise faith?

GORDON LINDSAY: It can neither exercise faith nor unbelief.

MR. MARSH: Then the child had nothing to do with its healing?

GORDON LINDSAY: That is correct, sir.

(Interposed by defendant's attorney, Mr. Chertkof.)

MR. CHERTKOF: If it was not the child's fault, whose fault was it that it did not get healed?

GORDON LINDSAY: When the Syrophenician woman came to Jesus, she urgently besought Him to heal her daughter. At first Jesus did not answer her. But at length after many entreaties, Jesus told her that Divine healing was the "children's bread" inferring that it was not for sinners. The Syrophenician woman at length saw she needed to get on healing grounds and she acknowledged Jesus as her Lord. As Lord, Jesus could and did heal her daughter. Here as plainly as can be stated, we are told that there are conditions to healing. The Syrophenician woman could not exercise the proper faith until she accepted Jesus as Lord. Divine healing is the "children's bread."

MR. MARSH: You speak of the faith of the parents, or that

the parents should have faith for the child. If the parents have faith will their child be healed?

(It was obvious that the prosecution was setting a trap. The mother of the Clark child had claimed she had faith, but her child was not healed.)

GORDON LINDSAY: The child would have been healed if the parents had had Bible faith.

MR. MARSH: Bible faith? Do you mean there is more than one kind of faith?

GORDON LINDSAY: Yes, there is devil's faith. "The devils also believe and tremble." (James 2:19) But such faith does them no good. Devils do not obey God. Only people who obey God have Bible faith.

MR. MARSH: Would the fact of going to a doctor hinder one's faith?

GORDON LINDSAY: In many cases it probably would. Physicians serve a valuable purpose and, of course, we are not opposed to them. Doctors are able to give valuable advice as to the care of the body, proper diet, etc. The Bible teaches that we should obey the laws of health. There are instances, however, when God is specifically dealing with an individual to get him to put his trust in Him. Relying on medical drugs might in that case weaken his faith. Such was the case of Asa. "And Asa in the thirty and ninth year of his reign was diseased of his feet, until his disease was exceedingly great; yet in his disease he sought not to the Lord, but to the physicians. And Asa slept with his fathers." (II Chron. 16: 12, 13)

MR. MARSH: Do you believe that God is a good God, an all-wise God, a kind God?

GORDON LINDSAY: I do one hundred per cent.

MR. MARSH: Then why would not God heal the child even if its parents did not have the faith?

GORDON LINDSAY: We have to let God set the rules.

MR. MARSH: Witness dismissed.

* * * *

Jack appreciated what we had done and appeared with us in several of our conventions. Once, he flew through a violent storm in his private plane to be present at our convention in Erie. Late in the year, he came to our office. We were about to have our Voice of Healing Convention in Angelus Temple, in Los Angeles. Jack mentioned that he had some commitments, as he was soon going on television, but that he would be in Los Angeles to speak.

Jack had been going day and night in an exhausting program he had set for himself. He was holding some great campaigns, some of the largest in American history. Radio programs, and a projected television network were all occupying his attention. Jack had already suffered a couple of serious physical collapses. It was time he took a rest. But, he didn't see the handwriting on the wall.

Jack and I at that time had never been closer. He wanted to help us in our extensive missionary program that we were then developing. We shook hands and he left the office, expecting to see me in Los Angeles in a few days. I never saw him again, alive.

While we were in Los Angeles, we received a telegram that he had had a stroke. Subsequent news was not good. He was not responding. Had we been in Dallas, we would no doubt have had an around-the-clock chain of prayer for him. But his illness came at a time when we were all occupied. By the time we returned to Dallas, he had been taken to a hospital, and no one was allowed to see him. When the news of his death came, it was difficult for us to believe it.

Many questions came to us in the mail, as to why Jack Coe was taken in the height of his ministry. It was easy to see the good he would have done, if he had stayed, and not easy to see what had been gained by his going.

Some wondered why a man who had such success with Divine healing would be taken in the prime of his life. However, Divine healing was never meant to keep a man on earth forever. While in most cases, it is the will of God that man should live out his three score and ten, yet we have various cases in the Scriptures in which God took a consecrated person in his early years. John the Baptist, among the greatest "born of woman," was cut off at the age of thirty. Stephen, a young man mightily anointed of God, whom the Lord was blessing with great miracles and signs and wonders, was also cut off in the prime of his ministry.

When we come to answer the "whys" and the "wherefores" of these things, there is something that we usually ignore. We think of this world as the only place in which God has something for a man to do. That is certainly a false assumption. Heaven is not a place of idleness but one of joyous service. While full activity for the saints will come only after Jesus returns, is it not probable that the righteous have certain activities in paradise? Perhaps they are receiving special training for duties in the age to come. Notice that both Moses and Elijah appeared at the Mount of Transfiguration and talked about the approaching death of Christ. (Luke 9:30-31)

There is a definite time in which we have to labor for Christ. A time to live and a time to die. God grant that when He beckons us home, we shall have fulfilled our task and like Paul of old be, able to say: "I have fought a good fight, I have finished my course, I have kept the faith: Henceforth there is laid up for me a crown of righteousness, which the Lord, the righteous judge, shall give me at that day: and not to me only, but unto all them also that love his appearing." (II Tim. 4:7, 8)

CHAPTER XXXI
The Literature and Prayer Crusades

"And the gospel must first be published among all nations." (Mk. 13:10)

The power of the printed word is something recognized and shrewdly exploited by the evil forces of this world. Communism for example, spends hundreds of millions of dollars annually to disseminate its atheistic and ungodly propaganda. The cults and isms send out a steady flow of literature calculated to influence and brainwash the people into accepting their false and deceptive philosophies. The pornographic press turns out an avalanche of the vilest and most corrupt kind of reading matter, flaunting it unashamedly on every newsstand.

Only the Church has been slow to take advantage of the power of the press, to spread its message of salvation and deliverance. Especially has this been true as far as the Full Gospel message has been concerned — at least until a few years ago. Religious magazines seemed to be made to appear as dull and unattractive as possible, their pages usually unbroken by illustrations and photographs. Very few well-written books appeared, that effectively set forth the Pentecostal position.

When, therefore, The VOICE OF HEALING began its publication, one of our immediate aims was to publicize the Full Gospel message attractively, and on as large a scale as possible. The Voice of Healing was sent without cost to missionaries and gospel workers all over the world. Sending the magazine to these missionaries brought the news of the deliverance message to key persons on the mission fields. The missionaries in many cases were stirred, and began praying that God would send a deliverance revival to their field. This resulted in many overseas invitations coming to evangelists who were associated with us, and salvation-healing campaigns were conducted in numerous countries. The meetings often had audiences of a size unprecedented in the history of missions.

Special editions of 50,000 or more copies of THE VOICE OF

HEALING, were prepared in various languages, for such countries as Jamaica, Latin American nations, the Philippines, Israel and Japan. These proved quite effective in spreading the message by the printed word, in connection with the mass salvation-healing campaigns.

In the year 1954, it was impressed upon our hearts to take an important step in the publication ministry. The plan was to establish a printing plant that would specialize in the publication of faith literature on a large scale. As we did not have sufficient money available for such a large project (at least $100,000 is required to set up a modern plant), we sold our home and loaned the money to the printing department. God blessed the plant and made it a success. We have consistently printed religious literature at a substantial savings over commercial prices that were in effect before we started the shop. Literally millions of faith books have been published since 1954, and every year, millions of magazines go through the presses.

By the year 1954, we had published around thirty or forty books, a few of which have had circulation of fifty to a hundred thousand. Quite a number of others have had a circulation of between ten and fifty thousand.

In May, 1959, the Lord led us to take another major step — the establishing of a World Correspondence Course, which now has approximately 11,000 enrollees. I might say that whenever the Lord has impressed a certain course of action upon my heart, and I have prayed through on it, invariably, His blessing is upon it. However, if I attempt something on mere impressions, or if I rely upon another who may not have received the same direct leading of the Lord, then it may be a different story.

How important it is for us to be led by the Spirit. The great accomplishments during the Church Age have been made by men who have prayed through and received a personal revelation of what God wanted them to do. They went ahead regardless of obstacles, and God saw them through.

Many times letters have come to us from pastors, asking us to send them an evangelist. This I have usually refused to do. To send a man to a certain city or country, unless he has the call, himself, may be to invite great disappointment. In the end, if the outcome did not come up to expectations, we would get no thanks from either the evangelist or the one who sent the invitation.

I have, nevertheless, put evangelists in touch with certain pastors, and asked them to pray through on it, and be led accordingly.

In some cases, the evangelist has been led to accept the invitation and the results have been very satisfactory.

So after much prayer about the World Correspondence Course, we felt definitely led to make a start. I had long been aware of the fact that many persons have regretted that they were unable to go to Bible School, circumstances being such that they found it impossible. There are literally thousands of such individuals. Now, there are a number of courses available, which are quite suitable for certain purposes. However, most of them have a theological slant which does not lend itself for easy reading to the person who is not a scholar. What was needed, it seemed, was a series of courses on the great dynamic subjects of the Scriptures, prepared in a simple, easy-to-understand style. Each course must have a practical value dealing with every-day problems, and not remote theological speculations. They also should include subjects that have a particular current importance. As examples of what has been prepared, the course now includes such subjects as Satan, demonology, prevailing prayer, and Divine healing. Because of the unusual current interest in the Book of Revelation, a total of sixteen volumes was prepared, covering the entire book. At the time of the present writing, the ten volumes on the gifts of the Spirit have been written and published. Now a new series carrying the reader through the entire Bible in character sketches, has been initiated. It has attracted unusual interest. Examinations are sent out monthly, and when a course is completed, a certificate is given.

Believing that these books would have a wide circulation, we felt that they should meet certain standards in their preparation. We would not claim for them unusual literary merit, but at least they have been carefully checked for factual accuracy. There is no place in religious literature for ludicrous scientific blunders. Witness some books that have been put out which went as far as to claim that the flying saucers were bringing little men to earth from Mars or in one case, from the back side of the moon!

Realizing that the Scriptures are not of private interpretation, we felt it important to establish a research library of several thousand volumes, which would include the principal evangelical writings of the Church Age. This research library is used in connection with the preparation of the World Correspondence Course. The thousands who receive this course may therefore know that these lessons contain the substance and essence of available Bible truths, from the Full Gospel standpoint. Novel theories and fanciful speculations or doctrines with a strong sectarian slant, are avoided. We have found that to a surprising degree, there is a basic unanimity of belief respecting the great doctrines of the Scriptures. Actually, the teachings of the Pentecostal groups, which for many years were considered to be extreme and unacceptable to the historic denominations, closely parallel their teachings. Both believe about the same thing with this conspicuous exception — the Pentecostal people hold that apostolic teachings are still relevant and in effect today. The old-line denominations have held to the tradition that Divine healing, the gifts of the Spirit, and the Baptism of the Holy Ghost were only for the apostles. This major difference is now rapidly vanishing, as hundreds of ministers in these denominations are receiving the Baptism of the Holy Ghost with speaking in other tongues, and are now regularly practicing the ministry of Divine healing.

* * * *

About the same time that our literature program got underway, the Lord impressed something else upon me. We had given ourself to prayer and fasting for several days, and each day the impression became stronger. That was, the importance of inaugurating a World Prayer Band, which would daily pray for world revival.

Thousands of people at that time were receiving a new spiritual vision, as a result of the deliverance revival. Even as in apostolic days, the people rejoiced in the mighty works that the Lord was doing, so today, many rejoiced with us in the way God has been showing forth His power and blessing. But now the Lord was revealing something else. The miracles and healings were wonderful. The literature crusade was needed. But all of this was to no avail unless God's people united and prayed as they never prayed before. We saw there must be an army of prayer warriors behind this revival, or much of the results would be lost. At that time God spoke to us in the following words. It was not all given at one time, but it came to us on different occasions.

* * * *

"Thou shalt begin to pray that I will assemble people, and that I will bring people all agreeing together. And thou needest to intercede and to pray with Divine prayer and divine supplications and intercessions. And the angels of the Lord shall be camped around thee to protect thee against the violence of Satan. And the Spirit within thee shall teach thee how to pray and when to pray. For a regular hour was established in the temple of the Lord, and so it shall be established in Israel. For My people are like scattered sheep. The people of My Body have not come together, even yet.

As one people they are not united fully. For they shall know that My Spirit shall cause them to pray day and night. For I shall have a world-wide prayer band. And they shall pray alone and pray together, and there shall be ones and twos and threes, and there shall be thousands that pray daily."

PRAYING INTO THE PLAN OF GOD

"And now shalt thou know that I have worked this out beforetime, even immemorial. Yea I have worked this out even before the foundation of the world. I would have you to work into My plan. Yea by prayer ye shall work into this plan. Yea, take this not for granted to coast as it were. But thou shalt persevere, thou shalt press in daily until thou shalt find the very vein of prayer, as it were in a gold mine.

"And now the Lord thy God shall see that the harvest is completed. And there shall be a great seething. Oh My people shall cry, My people shall pray, My people shall work. Now is the time to encourage those, who by sorrows, are oppressed by those circumstances that are coming on the earth. Yea they shall seek Me, they shall seek Me early. Yea they shall pray the Lord of the harvest. Thousands, many thousands of souls shall be rescued before the end of the harvest comes, when they shall say the summer is ended, the harvest is past and we are not saved."

Realizing the urgency of the matter, we sent out a call for men and women to become a part of this World Prayer Band. A call for those who would pledge themselves to pray daily. Who would lay hold on the horns of the altar, and reach out into the heavenlies and wrestle against the forces of darkness that were seeking to prevail against the Church:

"For we wrestle not against flesh and blood, but against principalities, against powers, against the rulers of the darkness of this world, against spiritual wickedness in high places." (Eph. 6:12)

We have long realized that any man who preaches the gospel, must develop a solid prayer life or else be open to devastating attacks of Satan. Those who have a ministry of the gifts of the Spirit are especially vulnerable. But ordinary Christians are not safe either, if they have not established a consistent prayer life. An assurance against dangerous onslaughts of the enemy is only possible if we build a bulwark of prayer around us.

The response to our appeal was most gratifying. Thousands of men and women now belong to this Prayer Band and we are dependent more than they can ever know upon this great band of praying people; nor is there a place for a let up. We must continue to pray until God gives us a spiritual break-through, a revival that will reap the harvest that is waiting for us as the age draws to a close.

I might add that we have tremendously appreciated the prayer ministry of Anna Schrader in the prayer crusade. Her wonderful prophetic gift has brought inspiration and guidance on a number of occasions at just the right time.

CHAPTER XXXII

The Rendezvous at Greenwich

In connection with what has been said in the previous chapter about the Pentecostal revival spreading into the old established churches I must tell of that remarkable meeting we had in the year 1956. This was with the leaders of the historic denominations in a retreat located at Greenwich, Connecticut. For several years, David du Plessis was secretary of our Winning the Nations Crusade. He had previously done a remarkable work as one of the organizers of the Pentecostal World Conference, of which he had been secretary for many years. At the time he was with us, God laid it upon his heart to bring to the historic denominations the Pentecostal message. He carried on a considerable correspondence with their leaders and in fact, visited many of their churches. He suddenly discovered that God had opened a remarkable door to him. Though he spoke in churches, some of which had a reputation of being strongly "modernist," he was, nevertheless, permitted full freedom to preach unhindered, the message of the Baptism of the Holy Ghost. In fact, a number of leading churchmen received the Baptism of the Holy Ghost as a result of his labors.

News of Brother du Plessis' ministry spread through the country, and finally the leaders of the main Protestant denominations of America invited him and me to meet with them in a retreat in Greenwich, Connecticut, not far from the City of New York. This proved to be an historic occasion. We had been asked to come and tell them the story of the great Pentecostal outpouring, and explain the phenomenon that accompanied it. Of all the varied experiences it has been my privilege to have, this was the most unexpected and unusual of them all. I had looked upon the historic denominations as men almost of another world with whom we had neither part, nor any point of contact. To receive an invitation to spend a day explaining the Pentecostal faith to these men, seemed as remote a possibility as a visit to the moon. I had thought of them as men totally without interest in a supernatural gospel. The thing I failed to take into consideration was, whether in my own thinking, I would have been different from them if I had not seen Pentecost in action. Well, anyway, the fact was that we had received this letter from them asking us to come and explain in detail the message of Pentecost. And, the exact words in their letter included the phrase, "be devastatingly frank!"

What happened to bring about this remarkable inquiry on their part? Of course David du Plessis' work had played an important part in the matter. They, too, had been aware of the tremendous effect that the salvation-healing revivals were having in foreign lands. During one campaign, 200,000 people had attended from night to night! Undeniable reports of actual miracles had been brought to their attention. Hitherto, they had thought of Pentecost as something under a tin roof on the other side of the railroad tracks. It had become apparent that Pentecost, as a movement, was growing up. A significant part of the nation's population was now accepting the Pentecostal message. Full Gospel Churches with large congregations were springing up in many cities and this they could no longer ignore. The question before these men was: What was the secret of Pentecost? Was Divine healing, the experience of the Baptism of the Holy Ghost, and the gifts of the Spirit, real after all?

I shall never forget that morning as these thirty-five or forty men, the spiritual leaders of the lives of forty million people — turned their chairs around, facing David du Plessis and me, and telling us that the floor was ours.

Brother du Plessis was the first speaker. He took nearly two hours and what he said was a masterpiece — a convincing proof of the reality and genuineness of the movement. God anointed him to present the Full Gospel message in such a way that his distinguished audience gave absorbed attention, measuring every word that he said. I saw these men listening intently to a story that not many years before, by their own testimony, they would have considered so fanciful as not worthy of a second thought.

Finally, it came my turn to speak. I related how we had been led of the Lord to found The Voice of Healing. How it and our associates had brought the gospel to hundreds of thousands of souls in America. I told them of the outstanding miracles of healing that had taken place, that could leave no room for doubt that the days of miracles were still here. I recounted how men of faith had come to heathen lands and preached to tens of thousands of people, and that whole nations had been moved Godward. As I spoke, I saw that I had never had a more attentive audience.

Soon, the morning was spent and we went to lunch. Afterward, we reassembled and the time was given to questions. And what questions they were! There was not the slightest trace of opposition nor cynicism evidenced by any man present. Through it all, there was a spirit of fellowship, good will, courtesy, and honest inquiry.

What were the questions? They involved the Baptism of the Holy Ghost, the speaking in other tongues, Divine healing, the gifts of the Spirit, prophecy, and other kindred subjects. For example, one minister asked whether the gift of prophecy was to be considered on the same level as the inspiration of the Scriptures. We explained that Paul taught that men were to prophecy and to let other prophets judge. (I Cor. 14:29) That the Holy Scriptures were in existence for many years before the Church decided which books were canonical, and which were not. That a currently spoken prophecy was to be received as edifying the Church, but not to be placed in the same category as the Scriptures.

They asked about the speaking in other tongues; should the gift come forth at any time during a service? We replied that the apostle set forth certain rules governing the exercise of the gift in the assembly, and that he was not the author of confusion, but of peace. That certainly there were times when those that spoke in tongues should not interrupt the order of the service.

Many questions were raised that all of us ask, when we are first convinced that the gifts of the Spirit have a basis in reality, and are not just fanaticism. They had us explain just what the experience of the Baptism of the Holy Ghost really was.

Next, they wanted to know what could be expected of a person who had been filled with the spirit. Did the experience make him an exceptional saint? We pointed out that one of the great purposes of the infilling with the Holy Spirit was that we should bear fruit. For this reason one's responsibility to live a holy life .was vastly increased; yet, it was no guarantee that he would do so. Man still had the power of free choice. We called attention to Bible characters such as Balaam, Samson, and Saul who received a measure of the Spirit, but who, notwithstanding, walked in the flesh.

And so, during the whole afternoon there were similar questions that were asked and discussed. I believe that God gave Brother du Plessis and me, wisdom for that hour to give them, at least to some degree, satisfying answers.

Having observed during the day the earnest attention that these men gave to the subjects we discussed, and their favorable response, the temptation was too great for me not to ask them a question. I said, "How can your receptive attitude toward these truths be reconciled with the teachings of the well-known divine Dr. X—, who professes to represent your views and who denies the virgin birth, the ministry of the supernatural, the miracles of the Bible, and the inspiration of the Scriptures?"

They smiled, and said that this at least was in their favor — that while in some organizations there were those who spoke authoritatively for their constituents, but that they themselves allowed no man to speak for them, notwithstanding the fact that some assumed to have claims to that privilege!

As the day came to a close, these men, the spiritual leaders of many millions of people, reached a conclusion. They agreed that they would adopt a change of attitude respecting the Pentecostals:

(1) That their official attitude would no longer be hostile, but friendly to the Pentecostal people.

(2) That they would be open to the Pentecostal truth themselves, as God let the light shine on their pathway.

(3) That any of their ministers who received the Baptism of the Spirit in their pulpits, should be free to continue their ministry in the churches without fear of penalty or interference.

(4) That they would even encourage their missionaries to cooperate with us in the large united efforts overseas.

The meeting broke up in the best of spirit. One man came to me privately and said, "I need healing. The doctors give me no hope, but I believe God can heal me." I warmly assured him that the Lord would.

Now what was the sequel to all this? Ofttimes, dramatic incidents take place that make an interesting story, but no real permanent results accrue from them. But in this case it was different. We hold no brief for men who rationalize the Bible and seek to destroy faith in the Scriptures. They will go to their own place in due time. But we found that in the most unexpected places, God's Spirit moves and performs His great work. The fact was, as subsequent years were to prove, that God was giving a spiritual break-through into the historic denominations. On the other hand, among many of the fundamentalists we found, sad to say, an antagonism to the truth of the Baptism of the Holy Ghost, often denouncing it in bitter terms.

Not many weeks passed before one of the most prominent churchmen in America, who was present at the meeting, wrote an article in Life Magazine on the subject of Pentecost. It was entitled, THREE FORCES IN CHRISTENDOM — CATHOLICISM, PROTESTANTISM, AND PENTECOSTALISM!

On the whole, it was a fair and friendly article. The writer declared that a few years before, he regarded the Pentecostal movement as a sect composed of more or less illiterate people, a religious movement which was not to be considered more than a transient contemporary phenomenon, catering to emotionalism, with an appeal only to the ignorant classes. Now, it suddenly became evident that it was more than this. It was, in fact, a revival of apostolic dimensions. That although there was much chaff among the wheat, nevertheless, there was much that was genuine, and that Pentecost must be recognized as a major force in Christendom. So wrote this leader of Protestantism.

I might add that David du Plessis had been invited at the Greenwich meeting, to write a major article for their publication. This he did and it was published, word for word, just as it was written.

Overseas, we began to get co-operation from some of the missionaries of these denominations. Sam Todd held campaigns in Chile for a number of groups, of which the bishop of the Methodist Church was chairman.

I reproduce the writeup of the campaign that was sent me by Pedro Zotelle, Chairman of National Council of Churches in Chile and pastor of the First Methodist Church.

"Once again God has sent the visitation of the Holy Spirit to Chile in revival. For two weeks, beginning Oct. 26, thousands have been gathering in the great military Park Casino for services led by Evangelist Sam Todd of the United States with most efficient assistance from the Rev. John Andresen as interpreter.

"Night after night hundreds and sometimes as many as one thousand or more stood to make public confession of Christ as Saviour and pray the sinner's prayer of repentance. Churches are already reporting increased attendance and interest as a result of the meetings. More than 40 Protestant churches of Chile's Capital City united in sponsoring this revival. As the Gospel went forth in the warmth and anointing of the Holy Spirit, men were cut to the heart and openly wept and cried in conviction and repentance.

"Also, God's mighty power was present to heal. As the multitudes obeyed the word of God, the Park at times seemed literally saturated with the healing presence of the Christ. It almost seemed as though the Master Himself were walking among men as of old. Almost every kind of malady was reported healed. Thousands beheld in amazement night after night as God stretched forth His hand to heal. Deaf mutes heard and spoke. One night (Thurs. Nov. 5) more than 40 cases of either partial or total deafness reported healing. A committee of ministers tested case after case and reported complete deliverance. Blind eyes were opened. One infant, 6 months old, blind from birth and scheduled for an operation after the consultation of six doctors was seeing normally as its mother left the park weeping for joy. The enthusiasm of the crowds became almost uncontrollable as paralytics arose and walked. A woman, crippled for 20 years left the audience and walked to the platform; a boy who had walked only with the aid of crutches for five years discarded his crutches and walked to the platform to thank God for deliverance; a boy of three, paralyzed by polio at the age of 6 months, leaped from his mother and began to run — the audience was almost hysterical with joy. Another boy of 4 who had never taken a step in his life leaped from his father's lap and walked.

"Yes, God is visiting Chile — we feel we are re-living the book of Acts. As God worked in our midst, no one could tell the Methodist from Presbyterian or the Presbyterian from the Pentecostal. Faith was united as God's people united and Bible results were received."

I have quoted the report of this Methodist minister which is only one of many of its kind, as it will give the reader some idea of how the leaders of the denominational organizations have entered into and participated in some of these overseas campaigns.

Perhaps the greatest result that came out of the meeting that day was the generous and, we believe, God-inspired resolution of these men to permit their ministers to seek and receive the Baptism of the Holy Ghost without interference from ecclesiastical authorities. And indeed, they closed the door to persecution, for they themselves published an amazing document, calling for a week of prayer, that set the course. I reproduce part of this tract as it was published. Ten years ago, any thought that the leaders of the historic church would print such a tract would have been absolutely unbelievable.

* * * *

First Day (Apostles in the Church)

And God has appointed in the church . . . apostles
Read Ephesians 2:19-22 (also I Samuel 3)

As you pray think of the particular local congregation of which you are a member in your own country and generation; in the light of verses 21 and 22 reflect on the early Church and its origin in the witness of those who saw Jesus and testified to His resurrection

— on the Apostles as foundations of the Church, a source and strength of church unity and the forerunners of the Christian mission.

Second Day (Prophets in the Church)

And God has appointed in the church . . . prophets
Read II Peter 1:19-21 (also Jeremiah 20:7-9, 11)

As you pray think of these verses and how the Word of God does not come from human reason but from God's creative Spirit in man
—how a Spirit-filled understanding brings true light into the world's darkness
—how all prophetic utterance is to enlighten individuals, congregations, and nations, as men listen, hear and heed the divine Word
—how discernment is needed to distinguish between true and false prophets.

Fourth Day (Miracle Workers in the Church)

And God has appointed in the church . . . miracle workers
Read St. Mark 16:14-18 (also Isaiah 61:1-3)

As you pray for the renewal of the Church and the recovery of its wholeness think of the God-given unity of soul and body, of the spiritual and the material
—of God's power to create out of nothing and of His power to make all things new both in the Church and in the world
—of all things being possible with God and the unwillingness to believe as the greatest spiritual danger
—of the need of the new and miraculous for the healthy life of the Church.

As you pray remember that you are a member of the whole Body of Christ and in particular consider the place of new gifts of the Spirit and new ministries in the life of the Church as it is renewed in wholeness and unity.

Fifth Day (Healers in the Church)

And God has appointed in the church . . . healers
Read James 5:13-16 (also Jeremiah 17:13-15)

As you pray think of the meaning of these verses as they apply to a particular situation.
—on Christ's command to His disciples both to preach and heal

on the calling of church members to minister to the sick of the community, giving not only pastoral but bodily care

—on earnestly engaging in intercessory prayer and really seeking to share in the healing process

—on anointing of the sick both sacramentally and by acts of mercy, and inwardly by the fellowship of love and prayer

—on Christ's concern for the whole man spiritual and physical.

Eighth Day (Tongues and Interpretation in the Church)

And God has appointed in the church . . . speakers in tongues and interpreters
Read Acts 2:4-11 (also Genesis 40:5-8)

As you pray think of the meaning of these verses as they apply to your own particular congregation, remembering the significance of the unusual and extra-ordinary in the Christian Church as opposed to the normal and mediocre

—of the witness which does not come only from the intellect and transcends the understanding of man

—of 'speakers in tongues' who can continually challenge and disturb the Church which all too easily becomes complacent and self-satisfied and contented to remain as it is.

* * * *

What has happened since then is history. Literally hundreds of ministers of the historic denominations have received the Holy Ghost and continue to minister in their own churches. Not far from Dallas, a bishop of the Methodist Church has received the Baptism. Leading churchmen in the Episcopal, Baptist and Presbyterian churches have been filled with the Spirit and have not been slow to make known their testimony. Even while I am writing this manuscript, a leading Episcopal layman is a guest in our home. And what fellowship we have! Of course, not all ministers have gone along with this change of attitude by any means. Modernism, with its unbelief, still holds sway in many quarters as we might expect it to. Worldliness, lukewarmness and apostasy still have a great grip upon a large segment of the church, as Christ warned it would. (Rev. 3:14-22) In such churches the Lord stands alone, outside the door knocking. The prophecy of the lukewarm Laodicean Church must be fulfilled. Notwithstanding, we rejoice in the hunger that is being manifested in the hearts of many, and we pray God that it will continue to increase as the days go by.

There is no doubt that God has used David du Plessis in a

major way in opening the doors of the historic churches to the Pentecostal message. The leading theological seminaries have invited him to come and conduct classes on the Baptism of the Spirit and the gifts. He lectured in Princeton, Yale, Union Theological Seminary, and many others. Everywhere, doors were opened to him and hundreds of students and key ministers have through his ministry received the Baptism of the Holy Ghost. The fact that he should have these open doors, is one of the greatest miracles of the Twentieth Century.

Unfortunately, some good men within the ranks of Pentecost, but nevertheless churchmen of narrow views, protested the freedom that Brother du Plessis had taken in visiting these churches and the theological seminaries. They pointed out that many of the people who were supposed to receive the baptism of the Holy Ghost, still stayed in those churches instead of deserting them and coming over to the Pentecostal Church. Moreover, Newspapers, as they are wont to do, sometimes misquoted what Brother du Plessis said, and these misquotations were eagerly circulated in an attempt to prove that he was compromising with Modernism. Actually, there is no possibility of compromise with Modernism. The moment a man becomes convinced that the baptism of the Holy Spirit and the gifts thereof are real, the whole superstructure of Modernism topples to the ground.

Some have said that Brother du Plessis should not have gone into those churches and theological seminaries even to teach on the baptism. That he should preach only in Pentecostal churches. Others go further and would restrict him to preaching only in churches of their particular denomination. How far from the truth can we get? If the Pope of Rome should ask us to come and preach to him on the baptism of the Holy Ghost and the speaking in other tongues, should we not be willing to go? Scripture and verse? "And Jesus said, Go ye into all the world and preach the gospel to every creature." (Mk. 16:15) Who is he that would dare to challenge that command?

CHAPTER XXXIII

The Native Evangelist Crusade

Among those who attended the Portland meeting held in 1947, was a young lady, wife of a minister. She saw the miracles of healing that took place, and witnessed the judgment that fell on the man who had so rudely sought to interrupt the service. She returned home to tell her husband what she had seen. The next night, T. L. Osborn, for that was his name, came to the service and was duly impressed.

He had gone as a missionary to India and had some good results, but was so disheartened by the general lethargic condition on the field, he finally returned to America and began pastoring a church. But when he saw the type of ministry demonstrated by William Branham, he went back to his home, determined that he should have such a ministry for himself. Writing for the Voice of Healing, October 1949, T. L. Osborn said:

"Rev. William Branham came to Portland and conducted a healing campaign in the Civic Auditorium. I heard about the great miracles of healing and of the wonderful ministry, God had given to dear Brother Branham. I went, and sat in the balcony. I can never express the emotions of my heart in response to the operation of the Gifts of Healing ministered to Brother Branham by the angel he tells about.

"For three or four years I had been greatly stirred about the traditional methods I had been using in regard to the sick and demon-possessed. I continually said that we were on the 'wrong track' in our manner of dealing with the suffering people. I always had believed that it could and should be done the Bible way. We would call the whole church to pray for one person, hoping that some one might be able to pray the prayer of faith on the sick's behalf. I knew this was not the Bible way. As I watched Brother Branham minister to the sick, I was especially captivated by the deliverance of a little deaf-mute girl over whom he prayed thus: 'Thou deaf and dumb spirit, I adjure thee in Jesus' name, leave the child,' and when he snapped his fingers, the girl heard and spoke perfectly. When I witnessed this, there seemed to be a thousand voices speaking to me at once, all in one accord saying over and over, 'You can do that. That's the Bible way — Peter and Paul did it that way, and SO CAN YOU. START NOW — You can do that — that's what God wants you to do!'

"I went home in a new world. I had witnessed the BIBLE IN ACTION. It was the thing I had always longed for. At last I had seen God do what He promised to do. My entire life was changed that very night.

"Many days of fasting and prayer followed that night. My wife and I went before God, determined to be channels through which God might work His mighty works of deliverance, today.

"A few weeks of happy results followed, but still my heart was not satisfied. I notified the church that I would see no one nor speak to anyone personally nor by phone until I let them know. Mrs. Osborn assumed the pastoral responsibilities and I went into an upstairs room alone, to remain until God spoke to me. I remained there only two days and nights and at the middle of the third day the spirit spoke to me very clearly and distinctly, and at last God answered my question concerning the death of so many heroes of faith, and the awful need that still existed throughout the world for this great ministry of deliverance."

It was not until the summer of 1949, that I met Brother Osborn. I saw at once that he had real faith in God. A brother in Reading, Pennsylvania, by the name of George Foulk had asked him to come for a meeting, and after our conversations in Detroit, it was agreed that I should go on to Reading and secure the co-operation of the churches for a city-wide meeting. There were only a few Full Gospel churches in that area, but I succeeded in getting a nominal co-operation.

The campaign began rather inauspiciously, and with no particular fanfare. Yet, it was not long until the big 220-foot tent was filled to capacity. Hundreds of people, sometimes thousands, stood for hours around the tent. Approximately 2,700 people answered the strictly salvation altar call, and literally hundreds received marvelous healings.

There is no space to tell of the many wonderful miracles that took place, nor of the remarkable conversions that occurred. After the campaign, several evangelists who attended the meeting launched out in a faith ministry, and had notable success on the field. Among these ministers was Gerald Derstine, who since has had such remarkable results among the Mennonites. Large numbers of these good folk have received the baptism of the Holy Ghost under his ministry.

Following the Reading meeting, we labored with T. L. Osborn in two other campaigns. From that time on, Brother Osborn's ministry took on an international aspect. Because of his interest in the foreign fields, he began conducting healing campaigns abroad; in fact, the previous winter he had had a successful campaign in Jamaica. Tens of thousands of people attended his campaigns in Cuba and other countries.

Then in the year 1953, Brother Osborn drove to Dallas and talked to me about a new missionary project. The missionary field had been much on my heart, and God had been speaking to me about placing the resources of the Voice of Healing behind a missionary program that would accelerate the spread of the deliverance message. We had already instituted missionary plans which included the inauguration of a radio program, the distribution of faith literature, and the sponsoring of some overseas campaigns. Yet, we did not feel that we were doing all that God wanted us to do.

Brother Osborn outlined a program of supporting native evangelists. He pointed out that the nationals were already overseas, and a small support would put one on the field. We discussed the matter thoroughly. There were lots of problems to be worked out in connection with the undertaking, and many more developed as time went on. Brother Osborn wanted to know whether the Voice of Healing would join with him in this project. Would we give him the needed publicity to make it a success?

We made it a matter of much prayer. As Brother Osborn said, there was no doubt that the people would back the program if they knew about it, for it had a strong appeal. Finally, I agreed to co-operate in the project, providing Brother Osborn would work it in close harmony with the various missionary societies. This he did, and for several years the native evangelist crusade worked in co-operation with the several missionary groups. In the July, 1953, issue of the Voice of Healing, the crusade was announced as follows:

"The next step in the project for world-wide revival is the Native Evangelism Plan that has been inaugurated by Brother T. L. Osborn in which the Voice of Healing is participating and which gives it publicity. It is a plan for sending hundreds of native evangelists into the field, thus making the work in foreign lands indigenous. This plan is fully described in the article by Rev. T. L. Osborn, elsewhere in this issue. It is a part of the great project of the Voice of Healing for world-wide revival."

Just as Brother Osborn anticipated, there was a tremendous interest in the crusade. Hundreds of our donors began giving heavily to the native evangelist crusade.

We rejoiced in what God was doing, but it was not long before other missionary-minded individuals wanted us to carry their missionary programs! Brother Osborn helped us out by writing a letter to one in particular. His letter in part was as follows:

"Dear Brother———

"You must consider that Brother Lindsay and TVH (The Voice of Healing) has taken a big step in allowing this Native Crusade to be published monthly. We must realize that this means many thousands of dollars are sent to us for native preachers which would otherwise be sent to TVH for broadcasting and other things, if this Crusade were not being published. Doubtless, Brother Lindsay realizes that thousands of dollars sent to us for native preachers would likely have been sent to TVH. But Bro. Lindsay wants TVH to have a real share in Missions, so he has committed TVH to carry this Crusade, monthly. But we must realize that he cannot keep adding good things to the list. TVH can only do so much. We have to consider that TVH must exist and expand, and it cannot do this if it encourages its readers to give all their money to other GOOD WORKS: TVH must receive help itself, and therefore is certainly limited to what they can present to the public. Every good work they report means so much money given to this good work instead of to TVH." Sincerely yours, T. L. Osborn

And so for several years, the Native Evangelist Crusade grew by leaps and bounds. We believe that the program has accomplished much good, especially in countries where missionaries have put forth a real effort to make the program a success.

Late in the year 1955, Brother Osborn wrote us a letter of appreciation of our help in establishing the Native Church Crusade, part of which is reproduced here:

"We thought that if another page should be carried regularly (if its reader interest warrants it), it might be worth it . . . Whichever way it is handled, it will be more than valuable to Native Evangelism, I am sure, insomuch as the additional photos and reading material will doubtless arouse the interest of many more. I have hesitated to take any such step (of putting out a brochure), since it would involve added expense to Native Evangelism, and I have sought every means to avoid any use of funds for expenses which could possibly be born otherwise, but as a volume of vital information accumulates, I feel it only a wise investment to make at least a limited amount of this thrilling information available to the public.

"As I have often said, TVH has put Native Evangelism before the world to such an extent that it is doubtful if any organization now could stop it. Regardless of how great this institution becomes, TVH will always be credited as the channel through which this revolutionizing Missionary Enterprise was enabled to emerge from its opposers' efforts, to rise as an instrument for Miracle-World-Evangelism in this last harvest age. Thank God for that. The single page is VITAL to the continuance of this Crusade, and if another page might cause unrest by any of the associates, I would not want it mentioned. But if they could assess the values of such a gigantic enterprise, and its almost unbelievable accomplishments, I felt they might like to consider doing what I have suggested.

"I hope I have presented this in a Christ-like way: I assure you these propositions are solely in the interest of spreading more of the Gospel to yet more of the heathen in our generation." Sincerely, T. L. Osborn

We are happy, indeed, that the Voice of Healing could be, as Brother Osborn said, a channel through which this missionary enterprise could be established in this last harvest age.

Brother Osborn has no doubt been one of the outstanding evangelist-missionaries. Although a short time after writing the above, he decided to withdraw the Crusade from its association with the Voice of Healing, we are glad that we had a part in inaugurating this missionary work.

CHAPTER XXXIV
A Visitation from the Lord

During the year 1955, while I was waiting upon the Lord in prayer and fasting, the Lord spoke certain things to me, which I did not fully understand at the moment, but which later became clear. I wrote them down at the time. Among these things of which the Lord spoke was the matter of building churches for the converts, which were multiplying as a result of the deliverance revival.

> "For the church is now sitting for the purifying, and when she shall go into the pot of refining, there will be great persecutions. Therefore, thou must warn my people and thou must influence them to come and hide in me . . . They must not stop at miracles in the great meetings, because when those meetings are ended, many thousands are left stranded without any place of shelter. They must establish places of shelter, and thou must know the men whom thou dost appoint . . . Thou shalt not leave the heathen alone to be devoured by Communism and other things. But thou must prepare shelter for them. And this is the work of the Lord that I will send thee to do."

Several months later, the Lord spoke a second time and said:

> "Now, therefore, count Him faithful Who said unto Abraham, lift up thine eyes and look to the stars. For if thou canst count the stars, then thou canst count the people that I will give unto thee as thou dost go forth. Not unto thee my son for thyself, but for the ministry of thy Lord and for the shelters thou shalt make for them, even the shelters in the southland . . . They who have heard me shall be visited, and shall be sheltered by the projects that thou wilt be shown to do, to make, to give, according to the finances that I will give thee, that they shall increase abundantly. As I have called thee to do, so shall it spring forth out of the ground as it were."

Still again at another time, the Lord spoke concerning the building of shelters:

"For I have called and I have chosen thee that thy God shall be with thee and shall bring thee into the land of possession. That where thou goest there shall not only be a visitation and a short evangelistic effort, but there shall be a permanent place of worship, as thou hast already been shown... Yea, His Spirit moveth into the far away regions of darkness where the shadows of death lurk and destroy both young and old, both infant and old age. He shall reveal Himself to make known where the shelters shall be made, and where the Spirit of God shall hover over."

And then a full year later, the Lord spoke one more time on this subject:

"Build ye, saith the Lord, even build ye bulwarks while the time is before you, around my churches. Build ye bulwarks, build ye castles, build ye the winding stairs. Build ye compartments, build ye so that my children of different degrees of faith shall be able to enter... So therefore, while ye have the time saith God, build ye cities of refuge, build ye shelters of protection. Build, while the land is before you."

In noting the above, the reader will no doubt discern that the Spirit was speaking both literally and symbolically. That the Lord would have us to assist in building permanent shelters for the people that they might have places to worship, and also that we might help build the spiritual house of the Lord, that it might be bulwarked and protected against the storms which are to come.

Some months after the Lord spoke to me in this way, we were in a convention in Fair Park Auditorium in Dallas, Texas. During this convention, a remarkable event took place. Due to the responsibilities of the convention, we had retired at a late hour. It was early in the morning, just about dawn, when I was awakened by what I thought was a telephone intermittently ringing. Since my wife awakes at the slightest sound, and always catches the telephone at the first ring, I by habit let her answer any middle-of-the-night calls.

But here was the strange thing. The phone rang and rang and rang. I was in a state of semi-consciousness, roused from deep slumber, but trying to fall back to sleep again. Yet the phone continued to ring. I was awake enough to notice that my wife stirred when it rang, and I was conscious just enough to wonder why she didn't answer it. Finally, I dropped off to sleep again. When I awoke, I had forgotten about the matter.

A day or two later, after the convention was over, Sister Sarah

Schrader was in our home. This woman has a remarkable gift of prophecy. It was late Sunday afternoon and we were resting for a little while and talking about the things of the Lord. Sister Schrader related how God had spoken to her on one occasion. Then my wife suddenly remembered and began to talk about something that happened to her. She said she had been awakened early in the morning by a phone ringing, sounding as though the operator were putting in a long distance call. She had started to answer it, when to her amazement, the ringing came right from her throat, then her ears, and finally from the top of her head.

Well, she didn't know what to make of this. But the ringing continued for many minutes. She couldn't understand what it all meant. Did it mean she was going to die? She knew it was something supernatural!

As she was telling this to Sister Schrader, she looked around at me and saw the surprised look on my face. I then verified her story, for I had heard the same thing that she had. It was evident that all this was no dream.

The Spirit of the Lord came upon Sister Schrader and she began to tell us in the Spirit what this meant. It was the call of God to a new move on the mission field. That our ministry was to begin to reach out as spokes in a wheel to the whole world, to the sending forth of the gospel, and the building of shelters for the converts. That before long we would be making a trip to set plans in motion for the new work.

And so it came to pass. It was not many months after this that we were on our way to Central and South America, on an exploratory trip with a team consisting of David du Plessis, Don Price, Leon Hall, Clair Hutchins, my wife and I. (Elsewhere, we have described a few of the interesting events of this trip which took us through most of the Latin-American nations.)

It was in San Salvador that the first steps were taken in the development of the new missionary program. Several years before, I had been in San Salvador. At that time attempts had been made to hold open-air meetings, but opposition by the State Church had baffled these efforts.

A few months before our visit to San Salvador, however, Brother Richard Jeffery, one of our brethren, had gone to San Salvador and commenced a campaign in a large open field. God gave him many miracles and soon a large audience was attending the services. The State Church, much aroused by now, used every means to close down the meetings and Brother Jeffery and the missionaries were forced to go to court almost daily. They finally

met with the president of the country. This official, having heard
of the many miracles that had taken place — for the news had
spread even to those in high authority — decided that Brother
Jeffery should be permitted to continue his meetings. And continue he did, twice a day for one hundred days, until the devil's
back was broken! By the time he finished the campaign, instead of
there being one church in San Salvador, with sixty in Sunday
school, there were now several thousand believers and about sixteen congregations!

Paul Finkenbinder related all this to me. He went on to say
that there were two things needed desperately. "First, we need
help on a large evangelistic center. We have gotten an excellent
lot, and we have enough money to start building, but we need
several thousand dollars to put the walls up and the roof on. Could
the Voice of Healing help?" Instantly, we felt that this should be
our first project, and we are happy to say that we were able to
help very substantially with that project.

But Brother Paul had something else on his heart. God had
spoken to him about starting a radio network. Radio time was
comparatively inexpensive, and he wanted to go on the air daily
on many of the Latin-American stations. He had presented his
plan to the missionary board and while they were sympathetic,
they did not see how anything of this nature could be financed.
Consequently, he was stalemated. Could the Voice of Healing
help him get started on the network?

Well, we felt this was God speaking, and so we promised to
give him help. (Pastor H. C. Noah of the Dallas Oak Cliff Assembly of God Church was already helping him on the local San
Salvador station.) So it came about that Brother Finkenbinder
was able to begin his daily network with quite a few stations in
Central America.

Gradually, the network grew as he added station after station.
The missionary board soon realized the valuable work he was
doing, and gave him permission to return to the states and raise
additional funds. This work has gradually grown until at the
present time I understand this Latin-American network includes
over 200 programs a week, on nearly thirty stations.

On our trip to South America, we stopped at many other cities,
which led to important projects that were later developed. We
stopped at Barranquilla, Colombia, and saw the remarkable work
that was being done by the Firths. They had carried on a great
healing ministry among the people, and had nearly completed a
fine church seating a thousand people. They quite surprised us

when they told us that they had previously belonged to a nominal denomination, but had received the light on the full gospel message, after receiving a copy of the Voice of Healing magazine.

The Firths had carried their testimony to the Harry Bartels in Bogota, and now they too had launched out into the deliverance ministry. The two missionary families had joined Full Gospel groups, and God was mightily blessing them, despite the fact that evangelicals of this unhappy nation were going through a most serious persecution that had been fomented and abetted by the State Church. In fact, the flagrancy of its acts which included brutal murder of scores of Protestant worshippers, had aroused the indignation of people all over the world. Protestant churches had been closed down by the scores, and new missionaries were not permitted entrance into the country. Fortunately, the Firths and the Bartels because they had been in the country a long time, were permitted to stay.

We went on to Bogota and met the Bartels. We could feel the spirit of hostility in the city against Protestantism. In fact, on the day we were in the capital, people were waiting momentarily for word of an uprising. Yet despite these things the Bartels were carrying on bravely, and were preparing to purchase property and establish an evangelistic center in this great city. We met one of their nationalist preachers, who had suffered for Christ. Police had forced their way into his church and there before his own congregation, he had been stripped to the waist and severely beaten.

The Bartels took us up on a high mountain that overlooks Bogota and showed us the shrine of the Black Christ. Nearby was a liquor bar where intoxicants were sold to those who completed their penance — which consisted of crawling on their knees up the many steps of the mountainside.

The Bartels told us of many other things that were happening in this land of violence. In Cali, the whole center of the city had been blown up by a dynamite explosion. Yet the Bartels had faith that God would give them a powerful work in Colombia. They asked us if we would be willing to assume the payments on an evangelistic center in Bogota. After having seen the situation first-hand, we could not but feel that we must assume this responsibility. The Voice of Healing took care of the payments until the year 1961, at which time the center was paid out.

At Lima, Peru, we met our friends the William Hunters. They were planning on building an evangelistic center in Callao, a northern suburb of Lima. They did build a beautiful church, and we had the pleasure some time later in helping them finish it.

It is impossible for us to relate our many other experiences on this trip. We stopped in Brazil at Sao Paulo, where subsequently the Voice of Healing built a large portable tabernacle for the Foursquare group. We also visited Rio de Janeiro, a city of contrasts — unexcelled beauty on one hand, and the stark poverty of the slums on the other.

Later, Bob McAlister was to come to this city and do a great work. It has been the privilege of the Voice of Healing to support his daily radio broadcast, which covers this great area of Rio de Janeiro.

When we returned to America, the whole party was solemnly impressed with the grave responsibility that we had to millions of souls that live in the whitened harvest fields of these countries.

Almost immediately, Brother Don Price and Leon Hall began to talk about a trip to Bangkok to build an evangelistic center in that city, and to hold deliverance meetings in the interior of Thailand. The Voice of Healing and Life Tabernacle of Shreveport, joined forces in this joint enterprise. There is not space here to tell of the evangelists' vicissitudes of fortune. The devil fought them on every hand. It seemed impossible that they could even get property on which to build. But God answered their prayers, and through a great miracle the Lord gave them the land, and before they left Thailand, a commodious evangelistic center had been built.

Don and Anna Jeanne Price with her father, Jack Moore, went on to establish their Mission Builders' Program, which has given very substantial sums to the building of Bible schools and churches in foreign lands. They are a wonderful couple and God has used them in a most marvelous way in the promotion of world missions. It was a great joy to us when God permitted them to move to Dallas and join us in the great work of the Voice of Healing.

And so the Voice of Healing went from project to project, the details of which we cannot relate here. The Mombasa center to which we heavily contributed, and which is one of the most valuable pieces of property in that city has at the time of writing, had its first unit completed. Mattson Boze and M. J. Sickler, with several American pastors, have accomplished the remarkable and almost incredible task of training over 650 nationals in evangelism. These men are evangelizing hundreds of thousands of people in Kenya. Last year, according to reports, they baptized around 20,000 people.

The Seoul, Korea, church was one of the largest missionary

projects of modern times. Korea had been saved from Communism by America's intervention and through the spending of a hundred billion dollars in treasure and by the lives of many thousands of its sons. Evangelist Sam Todd had held several campaigns in Korea with extraordinary results. Tens of thousands of people had responded to the altar calls. Both Brother Todd and the Voice of Healing had previously invested heavily in the work in that country.

The Assemblies of God also had a large investment in that land, and they had selected Seoul as a pilot model for their first great global project. But it was a project of such magnitude that it seemed that more help would be needed than their available resources permitted. Brother Todd and the Voice of Healing were invited to join with them in this great effort. The Voice of Healing would raise what it could, and Brother Todd would go on the field and raise money in the churches. Besides the property they already had, it was estimated that $100,000 would be needed.

Altogether, Sam Todd raised some $80,000 in pledges while the Voice of Healing contributed $25,000 directly, including Brother Todd's support on the field. Although several serious problems developed during the construction of the center, eventually these were solved and the Seoul evangelistic tabernacle has become a nerve center for evangelism in that country. During my recent visit in Seoul, I was told by Brother and Sister Earl Mincey, who are operating a fine soldiers' home in the city, that the evangelistic center is proving to be everything and more than it was hoped it would be.

However, in talking with the missionary officials on these matters, it was pointed out, and it made a great impression upon me at the time, that while these large centers are needed and have a usefulness of major importance, yet an even greater need was the providing of churches for the thousands of people in the smaller communities. Moreover, the number of qualified missionaries who could handle a large evangelistic center was strictly limited. In many countries, hundreds of nationals were gathering together small congregations who worshipped in the open air. These congregations were the grass roots of the whole movement. Who would help to provide shelters for them?

CHAPTER XXXV
The Native Church Crusade

It was a rewarding experience to participate in the building of these larger evangelistic centers, which were becoming powerful instruments in promoting the Full Gospel message in the various missionary fields. But I was not satisfied. It seemed wrong that we should put almost all of our effort in a few places, when cries for help were coming to us from so many quarters. This became a matter of much concern and prayer.

I was reminded again of God's call to us to help our brethren in the many fields of the world. For a whole year, God spoke to my heart about the building of churches in the thousands of smaller communities. In fact, I made a special trip to the mission field, where I could personally talk about the Native Church plan with the missionaries. Indeed, it had been pointed out to us time and again that while we were helping with larger centers, we should not forget the great need of the smaller towns and villages. The whole thing was brought home to us so forcibly, that I finally felt that we must provide help for these many congregations that were crying for assistance.

But another thought came to me. If we should receive hundreds of applications, would we be able to obtain the large sums that would be involved? Indeed, I was reminded of the words of Jesus in Luke 14:28:30:

> "For which of you, intending to build a tower, sitteth not
> down first, and counteth the cost, whether he have sufficient
> to finish it? Lest haply, after he hath laid the foundation, and
> is not able to finish it, all that behold it begin to mock him,
> Saying, This man began to build, and was not able to finish."

This brought me to my knees in prayer. If God were really behind the Native Church Crusade, then He would send in the money even as He supplied the widow's oil and meal. He could use either natural means or supernatural means to meet the need. The vision began to unfold. The Lord showed me how we might accomplish this work. He made me to see that every Christian family could sponsor one or more native churches. In the November, 1961, Voice of Healing, I wrote the following:

> "The Native Church is a simple plan by which any American family can sponsor the building of a native church in a foreign missionary field and thus have a vital part in fulfilling Christ's command to evangelize the nations.

> "While it is always good news to hear of new evangelistic efforts on the mission field, the facts are that unless some kind of shelter or church is built to take care of the converts, the work is to a great extent lost, just as it would be lost here in America, unless there is provision made for a place for the people to worship.

> "For years, missionaries have seen the need for trained nationals and have been preparing them. Now, hundreds and perhaps thousands are ready and eager to enter this great crusade. They are ready to depend upon the people to whom they minister, to support them just as evangelists do in America. What they are asking for is assistance to put a roof over the congregations that are formed as a result of their efforts. This is your and my responsibility. It is within the power of the people of America to tremendously accelerate missionary work all over the world through a Native Church Crusade.

> "The main hindrance to world evangelization has not been for the want of devoted missionaries, nor is it the lack for trained nationals, which was a serious problem for many years. The hour has come when we have an eager army of gospel soldiers ready to launch out in faith and to preach the apostolic gospel. And they are doing it! Nor is there a lack of people responding to the message. Any missionary will tell you that almost every place an evangelistic effort is attempted, hundreds and in many cases even thousands will respond. Where then is the lack? It is in the lack of necessary financial assistance that often is not available at the moment the Spirit of God moves in a community.

> "Every missionary will tell you that time and again when a special move of the Spirit occurs in a certain village, that if help could only have been available at the right time, a strong church could have been established. A lot may be secured, building blocks obtained, timber hewn and brought in from the forest, plenty of labor is available, but all this is not enough. There is no money for nails, for hardware, for roofing, for windows and doors, etc. The effort goes just so far, and then comes to a halt. And naturally, people become discouraged just as they do in America, when they have no

place to worship and no prospect of getting one. And so one more congregation is lost to the cause of Christ, that could with a modest but timely amount of help, have become a lighthouse of the gospel.

"Wherever we have gone, missionaries tell us that The Native Church Plan is the answer to the need. Through it, the people of America can supply the needed funds for building these churches. Best of all, the plan is within the reach of almost any American family. *For the cost of a refrigerator, a washer, an electric stove, they can sponsor a native church!*

"Because the cost of building native churches is small, and because the labor, and much of the material, and often even the lot is given by the local people, almost any American family can sponsor a native church! The assistance needed for the average building of this type is about $250. Of course, the value of the completed church is worth much more than this because much of the materials, and nearly all of the labor, are donated. Often it is worth ten or more times the amount of the gift. Occasionally, many more times. *But the gift makes the difference between having a church and not having a church!*

"Of course, the quickest way to get a church built would be to advance the entire sum at once. However, many people are not able to do this. The Native Church Plan enables you to finance a church with payments as low as $20 or $10 per month.

"Some people may wish to borrow the entire amount, or raise the money in some other way. But whether the amount is given in one lump sum, or by the month, you can have the pleasure and the joy of knowing that you have sponsored a church, where the gospel will go forth until Jesus comes.

"The Voice of Healing magazine goes out to thousands of Missionaries and workers in the foreign lands keeping them informed of our activities. In turn, our office keeps in touch with the field. Wherever there is a special visitation of God, we attempt to give help and assistance to conserve the work in that area. In this Native Church Crusade, the missionaries are requested to carefully evaluate their fields and to inform us of their most urgent projects — projects which have reached the stage where with help there is a practical certainty of the project being completed. These applications which come to our office, then receive further evaluation and if accepted, will be assigned to sponsors.

"What a joy and pleasure it will be for a Christian family to know that they have built a church in a missionary field. To know they have done something permanent for the cause of Christ. Most of us have helped build a church at home. Should we not build at least one abroad?

"The Native Church Plan will make possible the building of churches in the majority of the small communities of a country. Of course, it is not intended to meet the needs of a project in the larger cities. These require more help on an ascending scale — from $300.00 on up. While the cost of these is more, the results increase proportionately and we urge those who are able to choose a larger project, to choose the largest one for which they have faith. Churches too are encouraged to sponsor one of these projects. Again, some may wish to build a church or an evangelistic center as a memorial for a departed loved one. What greater memorial could be raised than a gospel tabernacle built in their memory?

"There is still one more wonderful feature to the Native Church Plan. It is a plan that missionaries have developed in recent years, and which they are putting into effect on many fields. It is called the revolving fund plan. It has been proven that people in undeveloped countries would rather have aid than alms. They are quite willing, if given time, to return back the money that has been given them, to a revolving fund that will build more churches in their country. The money does not come back rapidly, it is true, but an actual check of the plan which has been in operation for some years in a certain Central American country, shows that about 12% will come back in one year. (Of course, we leave the handling of this fund to the local missionaries. It does not come back to America.) This means that in a period of eight years, the money can be used twice! Thus your dollar never dies but will be used again and again to build churches until Jesus comes!

"Why not act now while God is impressing you to have a part in this plan of building native churches? Fill out the coupon and mail it to us at once, and a project will be assigned especially to you. And remember the Voice of Healing Magazine and the World Correspondence Course is our gift of appreciation to each sponsor."

We knew that God had spoken to us to go forward in this crusade. The important question now was, had God spoken to the people? We soon knew that God had spoken to the missionaries, for the applications came rolling in! But God did speak to the people. As the applications came pouring in, the people began applying to sponsor a native church. We then set our goal for a church a day. Thank God, when the first year ended, we had assigned over 380 churches! By the end of the second year, we had taken on about 700 churches. The end of this year (1964), we should have assigned nearly a thousand churches, many of them larger ones, which when finished, are worth five or ten thousand dollars.

I am happy indeed to say that my daughter Carole has taken a deep interest in the mission field and during the past year or so has given full time to the Native Church Crusade. She has also done most valuable work on the field in helping establish supervisors in countries where we have large numbers of churches in the process of being built. Gilbert, my oldest son, is now helping us in our printing plant, and Dennis, who is in college, we trust will receive a call from the Lord for some special work for Him.

CHAPTER XXXVI

The Holy Land Crusade

It had long been my ambition to visit the Holy Land. Following the 1952 World Pentecostal Convention, Jack Moore, a number of other ministers, and I made a trip to the land of Israel.

We landed at the Beirut airport, and after passing through the immigration control, were directed to a waiting auto caravan which had previously been arranged for us. Our route lay through the city, and we saw many curious and interesting sights — such as the minarets and other familiar landmarks of a Mohammedan city. We made the tortuous ascent of the adjacent mountains and then dropped down into one of the world's most historic valleys, where great armies have marched and where the famous ruins of Baalbek are located, which required generations to build.

At one of the border stations, we had a little excitement. The officials found something wrong with one of our driver's identification papers. Angry voices arose to a crescendo, and peering cautiously through one of the windows, we saw blows being exchanged.

While all this was going on, a faithful Mohammedan, ignoring the commotion, rolled out his mat and facing Mecca, knelt for a space of ten or fifteen minutes, saying his prayers.

While we were halted at the Jordanian border for visa and custom inspection, the Hashemite king drove up. He jumped out of his Cadillac and with apparent affection, kissed several of the officials.

The thing that most attracted our attention and sympathy was the pitiful and squalid condition of the refugees. The flight of these unfortunate people was occasioned by a miscalculation on the part of the Arab leaders, who were confident they could defeat the Jews and push them into the sea. To their dismay, they found themselves being counter-invaded. Only a truce negotiated by the United Nations enabled them to retain even a part of Palestine. While we believe that it is prophetic that Israel should return to her land, one can only feel sympathy and compassion for these Arabs who have been displaced from their homes.

We came into the City of Jerusalem, arriving late in the day. The following morning, we arose early and went to Gordon's calvary. The tomb of Christ is below Calvary, and on the side of the hill. Around the elevation, a space of fifty yards from the Tomb, is the figure of a skull, which is a remarkable identification of the true site of the crucifixion. (Matt. 27:33)

As we went up the hillside, we followed the path the Saviour trod as He walked that lonely road to Calvary. It is impossible to describe my feelings as I realized that right at that very spot, the Lord Jesus Christ died on the Cross. The very ground below us had received the precious blood of the Son of God, which had been shed for the sins of the human race!

There is no doubt about the location of Gethsemane. The window of our hotel overlooked the Garden which lies at the foot of the Mount of Olives. We drove over to the Garden and walked among the olive trees. These, however, cannot be those that grew in the Garden in the days of Christ, since olive trees live only about 1,200 years.

The climaxing event of our tour was the visit to the Tomb, itself. Awed, we stood at the door of the sepulcher and looked in. It was empty! How many tombs of the great have we visited, but in every instance their bones were still there! Other religious leaders have made their claims, yet their bones lie in their own dust. But the Tomb of Christ is empty! He is not there! He is risen!

We visited Bethlehem, the city that marks the birthplace of Christ. Later, we drove north to Nazareth and saw the city where Jesus spent His boyhood days.

Everywhere, we witnessed the results of the Jew's industry. Deserts blossoming as a rose! Villages springing up. Hundreds of thousands of Jews pouring into the country. The hour of the resurrection of national Israel is surely at hand! I cannot describe the many experiences we had during that memorable visit to the Holy Land. (They are described in my book, *Thunder Over Palestine*.) But even as we prepared to leave that land, I had a feeling that God would open the way for us to do something substantial for Israel. Seven years were to pass, however, before this was to be. Then, God began to deal with me in a special way about the Holy Land Crusade.

* * * *

In the spring of 1959, I felt definitely led to go to Israel. God showed me that the time had drawn near for the dry bones of Ezekiel's vision to arise. But before this could be, they must have the breath of the prophets. They must see the nail-scarred hands of Christ. They must look on the thorn-crowned head of Christ and behold the glory of the Lord. That though their eyes were blinded in the past, they must now perceive that the words of the prophets were God's blueprints to them in the future.

Leaving New York on June 26, I arrived the following day at the Lydda airport. The purpose of this mission to Israel was to set in motion a definite program for reaching the Jews with the Messianic message. Our purpose was to explore the situation in Israel in anticipation of initiating a feasible program to reach God's ancient people with the message of salvation.

My immediate plan was to tour the country, and to make observations of conditions as they existed at the present hour. I had hoped that a photographer might accompany me on the tour to take motion pictures of the scenes which have significance in relation to the fulfillment of prophecy. By a strange providence, whom should I meet in an elevator in the Y.M.C.A., but Evangelist Paul Kopp, who had been touring Asia for several months, holding campaigns in different countries. It was a million-to-one chance that I should meet him just at that time. We chartered a car and driver and drove through the whole country, visiting Dan to the North, and Beersheba to the South, Brother Kopp taking movies as we went.

Our observations in Israel showed that several evangelical denominations had established centers in Israel, but they were not doing much. None of them had more than a dozen or two in attendance. After careful study of the situation, we felt that there was a reason for their efforts being so little rewarded.

So far, most attempts to reach the Jew had been largely through the regular Church approach. We believe that prophetically and dispensationally, this has been a mistake. Traditionally, the Jew has never received the Church message. That door is practically closed, and it is futile to approach him in the same manner as we would the Gentiles. But the door is open to the Messianic message.

Another obvious lack of the Christian Church in reaching the Jew has been the absence of the ministry of the miraculous. How did the Early Church reach the people? Through the ministry of miracles! The ministry must be restored in Israel.

So we laid our plans. We set up an office in Jerusalem. Then we made arrangements to print tens of thousands of thirty-two page booklets, containing four or five strong Messianic articles. These books would be distributed the length and breadth of Israel.

Brother Kopp agreed to return and take oversight of the work. He and his workers went from one part of Israel to the other praying for the sick and giving the people the literature. On the last page of each booklet was an invitation to the reader, if his interest had been aroused, to write to our office in Jerusalem for a New Testament Bible. Since that time, over 11,000 Bibles have been sent out by mail, or given away directly, in answer to inquiries.

Because of the peculiar laws of Israel, new missionaries cannot remain indefinitely in the country. However, the Kaarbys, who have been there for many years are one of the few families who can remain there permanently. In co-operation with a Norwegian missionary society, we helped him establish a chapel, a prayer center, and a reading room in Jerusalem.

God gave us another remarkable young man by the name of Shlomo Hizak. He was the favorite guard of David Ben-Gurion, former prime-minister of Israel. But the Lord got hold of his heart and we believe that he is now the outstanding evangelist of Israel. We have purchased equipment for him, including a car, so that he can go throughout the land preaching the Messianic message and establishing small centers in the towns and villages. Recently, we have added to his staff a young Arab Christian, Fahed Akel, who will help him to reach the Arabs of Palestine.

During the month of March, 1963, we visited Israel again. One of the high points of our visit was a tour we made in a chartered bus that took forty or fifty Jewish and Arab Christians up to the Sea of Galilee, where we baptized several young men in its waters. The happy passengers actually sang all the way. Jew and Arab embraced each other and praised the Lord together! Surely, Christ is the answer to the Jewish-Arab problem. In the evening, we stopped at the village of Kfar Joseph and preached at one of the new centers that has been established. There were nearly one hundred persons present altogether, including those who had come on the bus.

Early in the year 1964, we returned again to set up a small printing and distribution center, so that we can keep in touch each month with the rapidly increasing number of secret believers. An order of 50,000 copies of a new Messianic book was placed. And when these are printed, they will be distributed from city to city and from door to door by our team.

And so the work of Israel goes forward. But we need the prayers of God's people for a real break-through in that land. "Pray for the peace of Jerusalem. They shall prosper that love thee."

*   *   *   *

As most every one knows, the City of Jerusalem is divided in the center by high walls and a no-man's land. The old city of Jerusalem and the temple site with the Mosque of Omar, is in the hands of the Arabs. Israel on the West has built a new city. Actually, a state of war still exists between the two countries. Hostilities are suspended only by the virtue of a truce enforced by the United Nations. The sole passageway between the two cities is by the Mandelbaum Gate. Tourists are permitted to pass through, provided they have no Israel visa in their passports.

In the year 1960, I went to Jordan in the interest of World Friendships, an enterprise developed by Dr. Walter Parr, to send food, tools, equipment and first aid to impoverished countries directly from people to people. Several ships and supplies have been sent overseas through the efforts of Dr. Parr. In 1960, it was on his heart to send a ship to Jordan. I had been asked to serve as president on the board of World Friendships, and in my trip to Jordan I was to meet with the officials regarding the proposed shipment.

Evangelist Sam Todd was with me at the time. We met with the governor, the mayor, and other officials of Jerusalem. They showed extreme interest in the projected plan to send a ship to that country, and called to our attention the dire circumstances of the refugees that filled the camps of their land.

The following day, we drove to Amman to meet with the Prime Minister, Hazza Majah. He was very cordial to us. He took us into his office where he served us coffee, and then discussed the details of the plan. As we left the office, we little realized that the man we met, had only a few more days to live. Even then, Communist-inspired agents from Syria were planning to put a bomb in the very room where we had been sitting! They skillfully concealed it from view, and set its diabolical mechanism to explode when the entire staff of officials would be there in conference.

I was scarcely back in America, when the front pages of the newspapers told how the bomb had exploded, killing eleven persons including the Prime Minister, and injuring forty others. The king escaped by reason of the fact that he had changed his plans about attending the conference. The spirit of Communism is violence. What the Reds cannot obtain by peaceful means, they intend to seize by force. Murder, assassination and treachery are the common tools they employ to achieve their ends.

We might add that the following year the World Friendship's shipment reached Jordan amidst much celebration. On that ship, The Voice of Healing sent a refrigerator and an electric organ to

Mr. Mattar, warden of the Garden Tomb for the Mount of Olives Chapel.

While Sam Todd and I had been in Jerusalem the year before, Mr. Mattar presented a plan to build a chapel on top of the Mount of Olives. It was to be a place of worship where people from all nations, including tourists, pilgrims, notables, and common folk could come to worship. Would The Voice of Healing raise the money for the chapel? After some consideration, we decided that such a chapel would have strategic importance. There were all sorts of shrines of other religions on the Mount of Olives, but there was no evangelical place of worship on the historic mountain. We, therefore, felt that our friends would be interested in helping us raise the funds for this project.

Brother Mattar had secured a site on top of the Mount. This was a remarkable answer to prayer of itself, for almost no property there is available for purchase. On this piece of ground stood the residence of the Turkish official, who was the governor of Jerusalem at the time the city was taken from the Turks by the British.

After the chapel was completed, various evangelical groups would come in and hold services. Famous persons from all over the world would drop in to the chapel to hear the gospel story. Such a moment was the most propitious time to get the message to them. Few people can visit Calvary, the Garden Tomb, Gethsemane and the Mount of Olives, without being greatly impressed.

We felt, however, that in addition to this we wanted to get an active program of evangelism into Jordan. Brother Ayoub Rihany seemed to be the man most actively interested in the evangelization of his country. For that reason he was chosen to supervise our activities in the various cities of Jordan. At the time of writing, we have just finished the building of an evangelistic center in Zerka, a city located near the place where Jacob wrestled with an angel at Peniel. We are also supporting a team which is establishing missions in the various cities of Jordan, including a small church in the suburbs of the City of Bethlehem.

The Holy Land project has been a major undertaking. We are convinced that it has been ordained of God. We are sowing the seed and already we are reaping the first-fruits of the harvest. The hour is at hand when God's promise to pour out His Spirit in the land where the Holy Spirit first fell, will be fulfilled. Jerusalem was the first city to have the gospel preached in it. Strangely enough, it will be among the cities of the earth to be visited again. When God's Spirit falls in copious waves upon the people of Israel, we shall know that the end of the Church Age has come.

CHAPTER XXXVII

Traveling in the Interest of World Missions

When I think of the hundreds of thousands of miles I have traveled in the Lord's work, I marvel at the way God has protected us and kept us from harm. I have found, however, that people the world over are more apt to be kind than otherwise.

Only once can I recall an attempt of violence. That was when I was in Mexico with my family. I was on my way to Central America in the interest of the work in those countries. Since I was making the trip, I thought that I might as well take my family with me as far as Acapulco, where my children might enjoy the beach for a few days.

We arrived very late at night and drove well out of the business district, before we found a place that was satisfactory. My wife asked the prices and we checked in. After we got some of our baggage unloaded, the man in charge came to our apartment and notified us that we would have to pay more. We considered this change of rates as unfair. So we started to pack up to leave. The man said that we had already used a towel and we could not go without paying. We offered him five pesos for the use of his towel but he was not satisfied. Perhaps, I should have paid him the extra amount and stayed there, but I decided that under the circumstances it would be best for us to go to another place.

We picked up our suitcases, and after loading everything into the back of the car, I quietly told my wife to get in and to lock the doors and start up. In the meantime, the desk clerk stood at the back to hold the rear compartment lid open. When my wife was ready, she started the car. He ran to the front, but could not stop her because the car was locked. This gave me a chance to hurriedly close the trunk. Since she didn't want to go off and leave me, she drove very slowly. In the meantime, the motel keeper and his assistant walked along with me beside the moving car. They had an ominous look on their faces.

When we reached the front street, I prepared to get in the car, and that is when they started to attack me, much to my wife's terror, who had little confidence that I was any physical match for these men. (In fact, I too was quite of her opinion.) But I was anticipating this move, and had no intention of entering into a physical contest with them. I suddenly shouted at the top of my voice. The windows of the large motel were only a few feet away. Realizing that many guests would be at the windows in the matter of seconds, my attackers did a rapid vanishing act! There was no doubt in their minds how their adventure would be looked upon by the authorities in Acapulco, a city anxious for tourist trade. Never did men disappear faster than that pair! I got in the car and shut the door much to the relief of my wife, who instantly put her foot down to the floor, on the accelerator. We drove back to the heart of town, and surprisingly, secured excellent accommodations and for less money than at the first stop.

TRAVELING ON THE PAN-AMERICAN HIGHWAY

Speaking of Mexico, brings to mind our trip through that country in a motor car on our way to Central America. This was several years ago, before the Pan-American highway had been completed all the way through.

A friend was driving his car to Guatemala City, and he asked me to go along. I accepted and we reached Mexico City without incident. Leaving the capital we drove on south. The further we went, the more primitive the country became. In some towns, children under seven or eight wore no clothes at all. Yet, civilization was slowly making its way even into that remote area. The people apparently did not have individual radios, but they did have a powerful amplifier in the tower of the local town hall. The large horns blasted forth a volume of sound that could be easily heard for a mile in every direction.

As I have said, the highway at that time did not extend through to the Guatemala border, so it was necessary to have automobiles hauled the last hundred miles on flat cars. As the train was scheduled to leave at five o'clock in the morning, we were hastening to reach the point of embarkation.

In his rather careless driving, the driver completely burned out his main brakes in the mountains. He then used his hand brake, which of course was not designed for steady use. So presently, its linings burned out. Now we were in real trouble. The car was of the type that had a semi-automatic clutch that did not engage the motor at low speeds. We were in the mountains and below us were seven miles of steady downgrade. How could we get down the hill?

Fortunately, the reverse gear still worked. By throwing the car into reverse, we could check the momentum by sliding the wheels, a method that would be grimly disapproved by any car manufacturer. Whatever prevented the gears from stripping, we shall never know. Somehow, the Lord was merciful to us and we managed to get down the long grade. Although we still had no brakes, we found it a welcome relief to be off the mountain, driving over level country.

At three o'clock in the morning, we arrived at our destination. There was only one light in the whole village. I got out of the car and fumbled my way through the darkness into the place where the lone beam of light was shining. It proved to be a saloon. Inside, there was one person and under the feeble glow of the solitary light, he presented what seemed to me a rather sinister appearance. He understood almost no English and I had trouble making him to understand me. I told him I wanted to know where the train depot was as it would soon be time, according to the schedule that had been given to us in Northern Mexico, for the train to pull out.

Perceiving the nature of our inquiry, the man answered my question by making signs for me to follow him. He led us past the depot and to an incline going up to the flat cars. After we had driven up on one of the cars, our guide told us to go to sleep as we had plenty of time. He then laid down on the ramp, apparently to make sure we didn't drive off! He thus established himself as a self-appointed guide for our party.

By means of signs, we indicated to him that it was no time to sleep, that it was almost train time. Whereupon he managed to get us to understand that the published schedule meant nothing. Instead of five o'clock in the morning, the train rarely left before noon! He proved to be right. Evidently, the right hand of the Mexican railroad department did not know what its left hand was doing.

Actually, it was high noon before the train left. A Nicaraguan consul was having his automobile transported on the same flat car as ours. He let us know in no uncertain terms his utter contempt for the dilatory tactics of the Mexican railroad system. However, at length the whistle blew a shrill blast and a diminutive engine, which sent up a dense column of black smoke, started on its leisurely way.

The roadbed south was a steady incline, and the little engine strained heavily against the grade, filling the air with great quantities of smoke and cinders. A few miles out of town, trouble developed. While we were going around a curve, the train parted,

leaving the rear section that we were on to come to a grinding halt, while the forward part went merrily on its way. The Nicaraguan consul fumed in exasperation at what he called a display of utter incompetence. The train crew, of course, soon noticed that their engine was picking up speed too fast. This caused them to investigate, and they discovered that they had lost part of their customers behind. Within a few minutes, they came back into view. Slowly, they backed up until they had re-secured the coupling. They did not seem unduly surprised at the occurrence. It was all in a day's work. Somebody had forgotten to lock the safety. Such things, of course, will happen, Senor. If the train did not reach its destination today, there was always manana.

And so we made our way across the last lap of Southern Mexico. We had opportunity to get acquainted with the train crew, and found them a very congenial lot. Once they prolonged their stop at one place long enough for us to take a picture of the crew arranged in a classic style on the front of the engine. As for schedules, there were none. When the train neared a village — and we stopped at all of them — the engineer would blow the whistle vigorously. The population would stream in from all parts of the town to welcome the important event of the day. The train would then tarry until all business had been completed. Finally, after saluting the village with several blasts, it would leisurely pull out of town.

In one village where we stopped, a funeral procession was passing, the coffin being carried on the heads of the pall-bearers. Approximately fifty people were following in the retinue. We thought we would get a picture of the cortege. When the pall-bearers saw what we were doing, they obligingly came to a halt and waited until we had taken all our pictures. Then the procession resumed its mournful way to the cemetery, that lay a half a mile ahead.

It was nearly midnight, when we at last reached our destination near the borders of Guatemala. On one of the flat cars was a new bus being delivered to Guatemala City and since the brakes of the car in which we had been riding would have to be thoroughly over-hauled, occasioning a two-day delay, I accepted the invitation to ride to Guatemala City in the bus. The combination of an unloaded bus and a "washboard" road made it the most uncomfortable ride I ever experienced. However, at length we reached Guatemala City.

My visit to Southern Mexico, and our survey of the poverty, the primitive conditions, and the need gave me a real burden for these people. I am glad that God has helped us since then, to

something substantial for Mexico. At the time of writing, the Voice of Healing has helped sponsor the building of some hundred and twenty churches in that country.

In order to carry on our world missionary work, it was necessary for us to make a survey of the whole mission field of Latin America. My wife, Don Price, David du Plessis and L. D. Hall went to Central America, meeting with missionaries in the main cities. This was to develop into a rather extensive ministry in the Latin American countries.

While we were in Central America, we decided to fly over to Honduras to meet our old friend, Paul Cooper, whom we had known for many years, and to see how our missionary program could be extended to that country. I shall let my wife tell about the trip as she wrote it for THE VOICE OF HEALING:

* * * *

Because of our desire to visit as many countries while on this trip, to be a blessing to them and also to learn of their needs, we made inquiry to go to Honduras. Since no commercial plane was scheduled into Santa Rosa regularly, Bro. Lindsay chartered a light plane, for perhaps less than what it would have cost us to go commercial. It was a Cessna 70, carrying 4 persons, so Don Price, the pilot, and Brother Lindsay and I went. The pilot was quite confident, assuring us that he had made this trip many times before. The distance is only 125 miles from Guatemala City to Santa Rosa, yet takes 23 hours by car, because of the treacherous roads over the high mountains. The plane climbed to an altitude of 11,000 ft., to avoid the peaks, some of which rose to over 13,000. After we had flown for about an hour, the pilot spotted a village, and informed us this was Santa Rosa. When the townspeople saw us circling, they ran to the "Landing Strip" to clear off the horses. Unfortunately, the horses came running right toward the plane, and as we were about to land, the pilot kept the plane aloft until the horses had had a chance to pass beneath us. When we finally touched the ground, it was so rough that the plane bounced like a jack rabbit. Fortunately for us, it did not tip over. But oh! what a disappointment, when we learned that we were in the wrong town. We took off again, and flew for some time, when the pilot informed us that he was lost. Lost in the high mountains of Honduras! What a feeling!

Soon he spotted another village and decided to make an emergency landing to get his bearings. This time, the cow pasture was worse than the first one, but at least the cows grazed peacefully on either side, and we were able to land between them. Again the

wrong town! Once more, the plane spirals above the high peaks and we see a larger village, and we land. This time it is Santa Rosa, a city of 25,000 population. How relieved we all were, for in answer to prayer, the Lord had given us a safe trip. We were taken to the home of Missionary B. H. La Fon, where we also met our good friends, the Paul Coopers, for whom we held a campaign in Wickenburg, Arizona, some 15 years ago.

* * *

The one thing that my wife left out in her story of the trip, was the description of the take-off from the second airport. We got off to a slow start, as we rumbled along heavily laden with four passengers. The runway was not very long and the numerous rocks kept us from gaining the speed that we needed. Ahead of us was a sheer drop-off, perhaps a thousand feet deep! It looked for a moment as if we were going to pour over the precipice like water over a waterfall! A few feet before we reached the brink, the wings suddenly took hold, and lo we sailed out into the void, safely! My wife never uttered a word. After landing at Santa Rosa, I congratulated her on her nerve, for she had said nothing during that terrible moment of suspense. She stopped me rather shortly and said, "The reason I did not say anything was because I was frozen speechless."

When we got on the ground, we found out that there was a small revolution in progress in Honduras. A one-man army was posted at the airport and as ill-fortune would have it, our pilot had forgotten his ground papers. There was an angry exchange of words in Spanish. We thought, "Is all this trip for nothing?" Then I noticed the bearded guardian of the airport was looking at my camera. I took the initiative, and said, "Would you like me to take your picture?" I had one of those polaroid cameras that had just come on the market. I told him that I would give him his picture in one minute. He looked at me uncomprehendingly. When I gave him his picture a moment later, he was as surprised as a little child. He forgot about the landing papers and smilingly, waved us on our way.

The outcome of our mission in Honduras was that shortly, THE VOICE OF HEALING began the sponsorship of two daily radio programs in Honduras, which we continued to support for five years.

Speaking of revolutions, Paul Cooper told us of an almost historic incident that occurred a few months earlier. He was on a missionary trip in his truck, and came to a river that had been swollen by rain. Since many of these rivers do not have bridges, jeeps and small cars are easily stopped by a freshet. Just as Brother Cooper was about to cross the river, he was approached by some men in a jeep. Seeing his large truck, they requested him to take them across. They were on their way, they said, to Guatemala City on a "special mission." A few days later, Brother Cooper picked up the paper and saw to his great surprise that one of the men that he had escorted across the river, was none other than Colonel Armas Castillo! The Colonel, now considered by the Guatemalans, as their greatest national hero, was on his way to overthrow the Communist regime in Guatemala. He brilliantly succeeded in his undertaking, although he later paid for his heroism with his life.

THE PHILIPPINES

During the summer of 1958, Morris Cerullo and I engaged in a series of tent campaigns that were well attended and quite successful. In January, 1959, we went to Manila. The party included Brother and Sister Cerullo, Lester Sumrall, W. V. Grant, my wife and I, and daughter Carole, and several other brethren associated with The Voice of Healing.

The campaign had been very well planned by Lester Sumrall. He had built the great Bethel Temple at Manila, seating over 2,000. This temple was not only a monument to faith, but it set a new course for the missionary movement. Brother Sumrall's contention was that a strong church was needed as a nerve center in a missionary field — a mother church that could set the pace, train nationals for the ministry, and present a vigorous pattern of apostolic Christianity. He had gone to the Philippines with that vision in mind. However, the many problems that he faced in achieving his vision would have discouraged a less determined man. For months, he labored with a little handful of people in a location totally inadequate for the purpose he had in mind. When he talked about a great revival with many thousands of people attending, and building a church seating thousands, those who heard him thought he was stark mad.

Nevertheless, he secured A. C. Valdez, associated with The Voice of Healing for a campaign in the racetrack. This proved very successful. Likewise, the later meeting with Clifton Erickson reached multiplied thousands. By dint of faith and hard work, Bethel Temple in Manila became a fact.

Now, Brother Sumrall proposed another great campaign in Manila. Plans were carefully prepared to get the very most out of the meetings. Some 50,000 copies of a special edition of the Voice of Healing were sent ahead with a large number of faith books. The magazines were sent for free distribution. Two radio programs a day went out over the most powerful station in the Philippines.

The night services were, of course, given to salvation messages and praying for the sick. Each night thousands responded to Brother Cerullo's altar calls, and many marvelous miracles of healing occurred. Instead of trying to tabulate the names of those who responded to the altar calls at night, a special service was held for them in the mornings. In these meetings they were given free literature, and special instructions on Christian living.

At mid-morning there was a Holy Ghost service, conducted by Evangelist W. V. Grant. During the three-week meeting, it was estimated that about a thousand people received the Holy Ghost. This service was followed in the afternoon by a faith service.

How many souls were saved during the campaign will be a matter for eternity to reveal. On the closing day, in a single baptismal service, twenty-two national pastors baptized 1,000 persons in Manila Bay!

All the funds taken up during the Manila campaign were placed in a bank for the building of the Caloocan church. This beautiful church is now completed and an excellent work is being carried on in this area of North Manila.

CHAPTER XXXVIII
Divine Healing in Our Family

Elsewhere, I have told the story of my healing when I first ventured into the evangelistic ministry, and also of my mother's healing of cancer. Now I want to tell how we took Christ as our Healer, into our home. I feel that my wife, Freda, is able to tell the story best, so I am giving it as she wrote it in CHRIST THE GREAT PHYSICIAN.

*   *   *   *

Every family needs a good physician, for it is doubtful that anyone goes through this life without needing help at one time or another. Let me introduce you to our Family Physician.

Shortly after Brother Lindsay and I were married, twenty six years ago, we went to Billings, Montana, to start a new church. With the work small, and having mostly untrained helpers, I found myself song leader, Sunday School superintendent, young people's president, janitor, etc. Besides this, Brother Lindsay and I were going from house to house daily, passing out handbills and inviting the townspeople to our services.

It was unseasonably rainy. The water seeped into the rough tabernacle, soaking the sawdust and leaving large pools of standing water, before the condition could be corrected. After leading the singing each night, I would come from the platform, many times perspiring, and sit in the crude benches, my feet on the wet sawdust, and with the atmosphere dripping with humidity.

I developed a heavy chest cold with intermittent coughing. My weight dropped to 94 pounds. By this time, Brother Lindsay decided I needed a rest, so he drove me back to Portland, Oregon, to my mother's, leaving me there, while he returned to Billings. Ten days passed, and one morning while attempting to pick up a light footstool, I fell on top of it.

My sister put me back to bed, and then weeping, told me that the whole family was certain that I had T.B., but they had hated to tell me.

THE DREADED TUBERCULOSIS!

T.B. What a horrible word! I, too, was afraid that I had it, but I would not let myself think about it. But now my sister intimated that I was its victim. Could it be true?

At the insistence of my family, my lungs were x-rayed. The result: the best lung was entirely spotted with TB; the other, so full of liquid that it showed up only as a blur. The remedy: one year in bed, either in a sanitarium or wherever I could get constant and good care. Perhaps I would recover. My youth was about the only thing in my favor. What a bleak future for a bride of a few months!

About this time, my husband's parents were greatly stirred. They had lived in Zion City, Illinois, under Dr. Dowie, where they had seen many miracles. So they immediately called their son. Having received the message, he got into his car, drove the 1,000 miles back to Portland, stopping only along the side of the highway to get a few winks of sleep.

Now he stood by my bed. With real faith and determination, he encouraged me in the Lord. He suggested I spend the remainder of the day preparing my heart, and then he would pray for my healing.

I wept and prayed before the Lord confessing any unbelief, and asking God to erase any sin of omission. The Scripture I John 3:21, was quickened to my soul: "If our hearts condemn us not, then have we confidence toward God."

I felt no sense of condemnation. I was now ready for prayer. Brother Lindsay prayed a few minutes with me, and then we began thanking God for answering us. No immediate change was apparent, but I stood on the healing promises. I got up, walked about for a little while, then lay down again. I repeated this several times during the day.

By the third day, we were on our way back to Billings, Montana! Within a month, I had regained most of my strength and was able to resume my duties at the church and in my home. Through the years, by taking a short rest period each afternoon, I have been able to lead a more than active life, with many demands upon my time and strength. How happy I am today, that in Satan's first all-out attack to cut my life short, I turned my case over to our Family Doctor, and I have never had a recurrence of T.B. since.

"Christ hath redeemed us from the curse of the law." (Gal.

3:13) And Deut. 28:22 tells us that a part of this curse is consumption or T.B.

In 1940, our first baby, Carole, was born. She was a chubby, nine pound picture of health. How happy we both were. But on the second day, as I placed my hand under her head, I was startled to feel a large knot, as large as a fifty cent piece and protruding quite badly. I had a feeling that this could be something very serious. But doubt gave way to faith, as we daily thanked the Lord for the answer. Then I forgot about it.

One day, long afterward as I was washing her hair, imagine my joy, when I could find not even a trace of the growth. She has graduated from college and is now working in our Native Church Crusade office. Again, our Family Physician won the case!

When Carole was two, I began to develop a slight itching and burning on my body. We were in evangelistic work and constantly on the go. You know, many times if our affliction is not grave enough to hinder our daily routine, we do not seriously take the matter to the Lord. And so the weeks passed. But by now, I was feeling real discomfort, so much so, that my sleep was interrupted, and many times in my waking moments, I would have to grit my teeth from sheer distress. I told my husband that unless God intervened, I would have to leave the field. A nurse friend of ours said it sounded like cancer to her, and suggested I have an immediate examination.

That night Brother Lindsay announced a healing service and asked those who wished prayer to spend the next two days in fasting. So for those two days, I closeted myself alone with God, then went into the prayer line. No feeling. No apparent change. Only God's promises. But that was enough! During the night, as each attack came upon me, I rebuked the devil in the Name of Jesus. When darkness fled, as the morning rays burst through my window, sweet relief had come and I had the assurance that the victory was won. The Great Physician was present, and I am still healed today!

CROSS-EYES

In 1943, Gilbert, our oldest son, was born. After a few weeks, when his beautiful, large, brown eyes should have normally begun to focus, we noticed that they did not. As we watched him, day after day, we came face to face with the fact that his eyes were hopelessly crossed. At the age of two, the pupil of his one eye would often slide behind the bridge of his nose, so that only the white would show. Many advised treatments or an operation. It was a long battle. I am sure that several thousand times we thanked the Lord for the answer. Today, when we tell strangers about the great victory, it is hard for them to believe it, but we have photographs to prove it. We had made contact with the Divine Optometrist! Ye shall, "through faith and patience inherit the promises." (Heb. 6:12)

THE CAR ACCIDENT

One night as we were returning home from church in our car, I heard the rear door open. Just as I turned my head, I saw Carole, age five, lose her balance as she attempted to close it. Seated in the front and holding Gilbert, I was unable to grab her, as out of the door she fell with a shrill cry, as our car turned a corner.

Slamming on the brakes, my husband rushed to her first. There she lay, whimpering, on the pavement. She had slid along the cement on the side of her face, and it was a mass of blood. Quickly we picked her up, rushing her to our home. By now, she was shaking as though she would go into convulsions. She was bleeding internally and passing blood through her mouth. Needless to say, we mightily called on our God. All night, her father kept a vigil over her. She never suffered any ill effects nor scars, and one week later, as we attended a Fellowship Meeting at the church of Brother Lindsay's sister and brother-in-law, Rev. and Mrs. L. D. Hall, her face had nearly entirely healed, with new baby skin covering the bruises. The Master Surgeon had done a beautiful piece of plastic surgery!

ANGELIC PROTECTION

When Gilbert was four years old, we lived in the picturesque mountain resort of Ashland, Oregon, in the parsonage which was next door to a large gas station and garage that serviced huge, cross-country vans. On this particular day, Gilbert was kneeling on the sidewalk, tying a toy to the rear of his tricycle.

Suddenly, as the station attendant watched, one of those large trucks began backing right in the direction of our child. The man shouted loudly, but the trucker, due to the noise of the motor, failed to hear him and kept right on backing. The attendant threw his hands over his face, feeling certain that the child would be crushed to death. But in that split second, the driver, for some unknown reason, threw on the brakes. The service employee ran to the side of Gilbert, who was complaining that "that old truck tore my stocking." The truck had torn the sock from the child's foot, but left him unharmed! A few more inches, and he could have met death. How relieved we were to have committed our child at the beginning of that day, to Him Whose eye never slumbers nor sleeps.

A DEADLY CARBUNCLE!

Having resigned our church in Ashland, to begin publication of The Voice of Healing, we found ourselves living in the Deep South — in lovely Shreveport, Louisiana.

As the children were in school, we felt it best for me to stay with them during the school year. My husband often went on speaking engagements. On this particular trip, he had gone to Baltimore, sitting up most of the night in a drafty airport waiting-room. The next night he was up again until almost dawn to help a fellow-minister. But he noticed a soreness in his neck, which became steadily more painful in the next several days.

By the time he was to return home, his neck was giving him serious trouble! Stopping off at Memphis, Tennessee, he went quickly to a doctor's office for an examination. The doctor diagnosed it as a carbuncle at the top of the spine, and urged him to go to the hospital at once for an operation. Brother Lindsay told him that it was necessary for him to complete his trip to Shreveport. Only with the promise that he would see a doctor immediately, did the M.D. reluctantly release him. My husband assured him without delay, upon his arrival home, he would get in touch with his *Family Doctor*.

Arriving home from the office, I found him lying on the sofa, his face drawn in pain. Yet, I did not get the full impact of his condition at once. We prayed, but for several days the back of his neck increased swelling, while the carbuncle took on a reddish, ominous, dark hue. Friends dropped in. Some intimated that it had gone into blood poisoning. Another very dear friend called a wonderful Christian doctor, who advised an operation at once, due to the danger of spinal meningitis setting in, because of the location of the carbuncle.

The first few days at home, he urged me to bring from the office a medical book so that he could read the information under the word "carbuncle." I read it at the office and this is what it said: "A very painful and dangerous infection . . . often in the nape of the neck . . . causing great exhaustion from the poisoning . . . death often follows." I decided right then and there that he did not need that kind of encouragement, so neglected to bring it each night.

But now, he rarely talked to anyone, keeping his face to the wall most of the time. Should he go to the hospital? He chose to stay at home. The doctor suggested I put hot packs on his neck to give some relief. This I did, desperately clinging to God. Finally, after what seemed an eternity of blackness, the light began to shine through. The witness was born in our hearts and we knew God had heard. Within a few hours, the carbuncle took on multiple heads, all of which seemed to break at once, while a tea-cup of pus ran from them. Four days later, he was in the House of the Lord, magnifying the Great Deliverer!

"YOUR BOY'S RIGHT EYE IS BLIND"

In 1952, The Voice of Healing Offices were moved to Dallas, the commercial center of the South — an ideal location for evangelists and missionaries passing through. We settled in our house, put the children in school, and became busily involved with our Lord's work. Then after dinner one night, I received a telephone call from the school nurse concerning our youngest child Dennis, now eight. She said that she had been observing Dennis' right eye for a period of six weeks, which on first examination appeared to be nearly blind. Since children that age sometimes feign blindness, especially if they see someone in the class with a new pair of glasses getting a lot of attention, she told me that she waited for several weeks, and then checked him again. Pretending to have forgotten which the bad eye was, she said to him, "Now, let's check the good eye first," as she covered the left eye. Immediately he called her attention to the fact that the left eye was the good eye. She said she looked at his record with a pretended rebuke, "I have the card right before me. You are wrong." Again he remonstrated. So convinced of his truthfulness, she once more made a thorough check.

She said that beyond a shadow of a doubt, the child was nearly blind in the right eye. Had he been hit by a ball, or received a hard fall? We were at loss! She urged us to have his eyes x-rayed, for it could be something serious. Immediately I was reminded of a friend who shortly before had lost the sight of one eye. Tumors! They removed the one eye, and hoped the other would not be affected. Could this be the case of my child, with maybe total blindness awaiting him?

We tested the eye and found that it was blind as the nurse had said. I quickly ran to my husband. He quietly said that we would trust God. He wanted to spend a few days waiting on God before praying. Before he was ready, one Sunday night, the children and

I attended a revival at a Full Gospel church, held by one of our deliverance evangelists. A prayer line was formed. I caught my little boy's attention as he sat on the front row. He appeared to be about half asleep as I nodded for him to get in the line. He shook his head several times, "No." As I prayed silently, I saw him get up slowly and make his way to the rear of the church, as by now the line had become very long. Only one tiny girl was behind him.

By the time the evangelist prayed for all those people, he was very weary. When he came to our boy, he quickly said, "God, heal this little boy," and passed him on. Being quite human, I was disappointed. I thought, "The evangelist didn't even ask what was wrong with him, and what a short prayer!" However, as we drove home, I felt a rebuke for having felt the way I did, so determined not to make a negative statement. As we stepped inside the house, I asked Dennis, "Did the Lord heal you?" To which he replied as if surprised that I would ask such a superfluous question, "Yes." I took him into the bedroom, away from the rest of the family, locked the door and pointed to a large number on the calendar, having covered his good eye. Without any difficulty he read the figures. Next I picked up my Bible. He read it perfectly. Then I tried him on a very small type testament. He could read very little.

In the presence of the family, we went through the same tests. We praised God for what He had done. Turning to Dennis I said, "Now tomorrow morning before you go to school, we shall let you read out of the small testament." His vision was some improved by the next morning. The second morning, he missed only a few words, and on the third, praise God, he could see every letter clearly!

By this time, Dennis had been transferred to a new school, built about four blocks from our home. Knowing that the new nurse would have all the old records, I made an appointment with her to have Dennis' eyes checked. This she did, saying he had 20-20 vision! But when she pulled out his card, she was not a little non-plused. "What's happened here?" she exclaimed. I then testified to his healing, but she flatly refused to believe, saying "Those things don't just happen. It must have been a temporary blindness that corrected itself." How sad that some today will not give glory to God.

But then I called the first nurse, and told her that Dennis' test showed he now had 20-20 vision! I told her how he was healed.

With gratitude for my calling her, she said, "Isn't that wonderful! I believe every word of it!"

THE MUMPS!

Several years ago, we sold our home so that we would have funds to build The Voice of Healing Printing Plant, that we might economically print millions of deliverance books and magazines. (God has since made this come to pass.) We therefore moved our family into a downstairs apartment at the office. Moving is always a big job, especially with three children. Wearily, I climbed into bed at the close of that Memorial Day, and fell into a sound sleep. The next morning, I awoke feeling quite rested, and praising God for the sweet peace that came as a result of having done what we felt He wanted us to do.

I had been awake only a few minutes when Gilbert came into the room, his face badly swollen. When I asked him what the trouble was, he said, "It might be the mumps. I've been playing across the street with Butch, and you know, he's had them for two weeks."

No, I didn't know that Butch had the mumps! What a development! Here, the editor's family, living in the quarters of The Voice of Healing, and down with the mumps! Satan just would not win with this sort of strategy. An indignation came over us as my husband and I prayed. Within a few hours, the swelling had gone down, his fever left, he ate normally and played all day, while we sang the praises of God. Our Specialist in Child's Diseases had brought the cure!

Several weeks passed, and Brother Lindsay was again out of the city. One day I noticed that my jaws were giving me trouble as I chewed. The discomfort increased as time passed. On Sunday night, I returned from church to find I had a bad headache. Thinking I could sleep it off, I went right to bed. After a few hours, I awoke with a raging fever. My neck was very sore and I knew that I had picked up Gilbert's mump germs. All alone, I got on my knees in bed, and served notice on the devil that he had lost the first battle, and that according to God's word, he was about to lose the second! Again and again, I quoted the promises of God out loud, while the children slept soundly on, in the next room. Finally, I fell asleep, and when I awoke, I was wringing wet with perspiration. The fever had vanished and I was well! Our Family Physician, who is never too tired, never too busy, nor out of His office, made the call in the middle of the night, and I was healed!

"HE THAT DWELLETH IN THE SECRET PLACE"

When Gilbert was fifteen years old, he was returning home one afternoon, from high school. With him was a group of boys, all of them running for a bus, which had stopped for them on busy Jefferson Street. Gilbert was in the lead, and failed to see a car that was coming very rapidly. All in the second lane of traffic had already stopped for the boys, but the man in the third lane said that he actually did not see the boys.

At that moment, when Gilbert saw that he was going to be hit, he said that he gave a desperate leap. The car miraculously missed him, but caught the trumpet that he was carrying, and hurled it clear across that wide intersection. Strangely enough, when he picked up his horn, neither it nor the case was in any wise damaged. When he told us about it, we reminded him that he had been dedicated to the Lord as a child, and also recalled the night that he received his trumpet, when our whole family knelt in prayer and dedicated it to the Lord. How wonderful and true the words of the Psalmist, "For he shall give his angels charge over thee, to keep thee in all thy ways. They shall bear thee up in their hands . . . "

How do others live without Him? I wonder. Many don't. They go to premature graves. Even some useful Christians are cut short through lack of knowledge of God's healing power. I feel it would be criminal to know the message of Divine Healing and not share it with a dying world.

In the twenty-six years of our marriage, not including the time when our three children were born, we have spent perhaps a total of fifty dollars for doctor bills, such as for examinations and shots when we were going into a foreign country, etc. But by the preceding pages, you can see that Satan has not left us unchallenged. What a different story from the conversation I heard a few weeks ago in a crowded super-market.

Said one man to another, "You know, most of my check for the past year has gone to the doctor." To which the other replied, "That's my complaint. My family has had nothing but doctor and hospital bills all year, until I feel like turning my whole check over to the doctor each week, no questions asked. He gets it anyway. You might say, 'I'm just working to support the doctor'."

True, doctors perform many wonderful services, and with much of the world having little knowledge of God's promises of healing, they do a vital work. But how much better it has been for us personally, to have invested our resources in the spreading of the

Gospel and the salvation of souls, thus laying up treasures in heaven, and being spared many times the pain of operations and long treatments, and the cost of thousands of dollars, by having as our personal Physician, Doctor Jesus! We can say from experience, "Who forgiveth all thine iniquities, who healeth all thy diseases!" (Psalms 103:3)

* * * *

I do not think that I need to add to my wife's testimony, except to say that it is all true. Divine healing works! I shall, however, summarize a few of the lessons that we learned from these experiences we have had. While it is true that we have had some severe tests, nevertheless, with few exceptions, we have enjoyed uninterrupted health. We can truthfully say that sickness has had a very minor role in our lives. And when it has come, we have found that invariably Christ, the Great Physician, was there to deliver us. Our chief interest in recording these things is to help others to likewise enjoy the great benefits of Divine health. It is really much easier to receive and maintain the blessing of health than it is to be constantly seeking healing from this or that affliction after it has become intrenched. From our experiences, related in my wife's account, I shall briefly note a few of the important lessons we learned.

1. In the case when my wife was struck down with TB, it was apparent that she had gone beyond her strength. Many Christians do just that. Under the burden of the work, many pastors and pastors' wives overdo, fail to take proper rest, and as a result have a breakdown. That was the case of Epaphroditus. (Read Phil. 2:25-30) We rejoiced in my wife's great deliverance, which came with spectacular swiftness, considering the seriousness of her condition. But we realized that she must take care of her body. From then on each afternoon, she set aside a short period in which she completely relaxed. The result has been that she has been able to do much more, and do it well, than she had during the time when she took no time out for rest.

2. In the case of the cancer symptoms, there was no apparent change in the symptoms after my wife was prayed for. Had she not been instructed, she could have said as do countless others, "Well, I didn't get healed this time, but I'll try again." Had she confessed such unbelief, she would not have received deliverance. But by reckoning God's word was true, that the work was done, and by confessing faith instead of unbelief, her healing came and the symptoms never reappeared.

3. In the case of the crossed eyes, we had to stand on the

promise a long time, but finally the answer came. Gilbert's eyes have experienced a most wonderful miracle.

4. As regards to the accidents or near-accidents that happened to our children, we make this comment. No Christian parent should let a day pass but what he puts his family into the hands of the Lord. "The angel of the Lord encampeth round about them that fear him, and delivereth them." (Psalms 34:7) We cannot be on the alert twenty-four hours a day, but we can put our family into the keeping of Him "whose eye never slumbers nor sleeps."

5. In the case of the healing of Dennis' blind eye, a very important truth is brought out. Jesus said, "They shall lay hands on the sick and they shall recover." Yet the average person will not believe, if only this simple command is carried out. They want to relate in full detail all about their symptoms, both real and imagined. After that, they want a nice long prayer made. If the evangelist does not do it in just that way, they are disappointed, and may make no effort to believe. Dennis, however, believed that when the evangelist touched him, he would be healed. And that is exactly what took place.

CHAPTER XXXIX
Mother's Passing

In another chapter, I tell the story of my mother's marvelous healing of cancer, while I was holding meetings in the south. She had other testings, but her faith in God always prevailed. Mother had a rather frail body, often subject to infirmities. Without her strong faith, she would no doubt have been gone many years before, but her love of life and will to live was strong. When the enemy came with the symptoms of some disease, she would resist it, refuse to accept it, and invariably would have deliverance.

She also was of an adventurous spirit, far more than father — a quality no doubt she imparted to some extent to me. Even after she was well past the seventy mark, she had father cross the continent several times in a car, visiting relatives or attending one of our large union meetings. During the summer of 1951, father and mother visited Zion City with me, and then spent several months with us at our home then in Shreveport, Louisiana.

The following year, however, at the age of 77, mother experienced her severest testing, when she had a stroke that affected the brain. It was during the year 1952. I had made plans to attend the Pentecostal World Conference in London, where I was scheduled to speak, after which I intended to fulfill a long ambition to visit the Holy Land. Just a day or two before I was to leave, I received the distressing intelligence that my mother had suddenly suffered a severe stroke which had affected her mind. So serious was the attack that she was unable to recognize anyone. A stroke affecting the brain is always grave, but in the case of a person at her age of 77, the result is usually fatal. Perhaps it was time for her to go, but if so, I certainly wanted to be near at hand. In Palestine, I would be out of all contact with home for several weeks. What should I do?

This situation placed me in a most awkward dilemma. Was it God's will that I cancel my plans for going to London and the Holy Land? I prayed, but it seemed difficult to arrive at a conclusion. However, my relatives felt that I ought to go, and so therefore, with some misgivings, I took the plane for England.

Faith is an act, and it was a step of faith to make this decision.

Arriving in London, I was restless in my spirit and spent considerable time in prayer in my room in the Baker Street Hotel. The seriousness of the attack, added to the fact of my mother's advanced age, made me realize that nothing less than an unusual miracle could cause her to recover. The whole situation weighed upon me heavily. I continued in prayer, but finally, sadly admitted to myself that I was getting nowhere.

As I knelt in my room, depressed and baffled by the circumstances, something seemed to say, "If this mountain is too great for you to move, why don't you let the Holy Spirit move it?" The force of these words impressed me greatly. I continued to kneel, but I did no praying. For perhaps half an hour I remained motionless, not saying a word. Then something began to happen. There was a moving of the Spirit. I began to pray in the unknown tongue, but it was not I that was praying, but the Spirit within me. Then prayer began to roll in a torrent. The Spirit of God was rebuking death! It was abolishing sickness! There was not the slightest doubt that things were happening now. How long I continued in prayer, I do not know. But suddenly, I found myself on my feet and on my way back to the convention hall. All my anxiety had gone, and there was no doubt in my mind that God had taken care of the situation. From London I went on to the Holy Land, and then several weeks later returned to Paris where my wife's niece was studying, in preparation to going to Africa as a missionary. She handed me a letter. It was from my mother. I opened it and saw written, the praises of God for her complete deliverance! I was not surprised. I knew that a miracle took place that day while I was in that room in London. Where I failed, the Spirit of God had brought the answer.

The lesson I learned from this is that there is always a way out. That we are not to be overwhelmed by even the most adverse symptoms nor circumstances. The devil was present, of course, to tell me that the case was hopeless. Was not mother 77 years of age? Was it not time for her to go? Had she not lived out her days? Beside, this was a stroke of the brain which was ordinarily fatal to those of advanced age. The answer to all this was that while it was true that God has a time for us all to fulfill our days in this world, yet He does not work against Himself. I was to go to London to address Full Gospel ministers from all over the world, and in a way I would represent the deliverance revival. In fact, I was told that that was one of the purposes in my speaking. Then when all preparations were made, was it the will of God that I should cancel my plans, lose my ticket (I had a tourist club ticket that was too late to cancel), forego my plans to see the Holy Land, so that I could attend my mother's funeral? I have long learned that our God is a reasonable God, and surely this was not His way of doing things. I felt certain God wanted me to make the trip, and therefore it was His will that mother should be healed, regardless of her age or the severity of the stroke.

But it is also true that there is an hour when we all, whether saints or sinners, must receive the call that our days are completed on this earth, and that we have finished our course.

I have no patience with that ridiculous notion called "the immortality of the flesh." True, God will even "renew our youth." He will give us extra days if we need them to fulfill our work. Moreover, when Jesus comes, if we are alive we shall be translated like Enoch and not see death. (I Thess. 4:13-17) But this is something quite different from the teaching of the "immortality of the flesh." There have been many expounders of this fiction, who have led astray gullible followers. Yet the error was always self-defeating, for the deluded leader sooner or later had to die. But beyond all this, who with common sense would want to live forever in this mortal body, constantly subject to infirmities? We look rather to be clothed upon with one like unto His glorified body!

Nearly four more years passed. Our whole family gathered at our parents' home to celebrate their golden wedding anniversary. Mother's strength was no longer what it had been. We all had a feeling, and she did too, that God would soon call her home.

And now, because I feel that it will give help to others who meet the same problem, I must record the following incident that marked her passing a few months later. For many and complex are the circumstances that enter into living and dying. Even at the time of passing, things may happen that may not be in the will of God. During the Christmas season, in the same year, we received a letter from dad that mother, after eating Christmas dinner, had become ill and had to go to bed. She went into a sort of a coma. When she awoke, she had lost the power of speech. The following day she showed no improvement, and it was then that her children all received word that the end was probably near.

In a day or two, we were all at my sister Fern's home in Porterville, California, where mother and dad had been staying for a few weeks. Mother recognized us all, but we were puzzled by one thing. She had not only lost the power of clear speech, but more than that she seemed to be bound by something. We felt the time of her going was at hand. Several days went by and her condition appeared to be unchanged. Absolutely helpless, it appeared that she might linger a long time in that condition. This would be distressing indeed, for under these circumstances it would be much better if she could go to be with her Lord.

In accordance with state laws that when death seems imminent a physician must be called, we summoned a good Christian doctor to the house. After examining mother, he conceded that she might linger on many days.

Naturally, we wanted our loved one with us as long as possible, but we all knew that this unfortunate physical condition was very distressing to mother. I felt that if it was not her time to go, then she should be healed. But if it was her time, then she should be loosed from this bondage.

At two o'clock Sunday morning, on New Year's day, I awoke and heard mother praying. I got up and went into her room. The Spirit of God came upon me, and I rebuked the binding spirit in the Name of Jesus. Then something happened. I knew God had come on the scene. For two wonderful hours mother and I had a long-to-be-remembered prayer meeting together. I knew and she knew, that it was the last one we would ever have on earth. She held my hand tightly, as she continued to pray and praise God. It seemed as if all the energy of her soul had been summoned in this last glorious prayer meeting.

At length, I retired and secured a few hours of sleep. Morning came and she was still gently praying. We all knew now it was only a matter of moments. Then as we watched, the lips still moved, but the voice ceased to be audible. A great peace had come upon her countenance. We could see that her spirit was now intent on another world. Then, suddenly, we saw a smile come upon her face. Her face lighted up for a brief instant, and her hands were lifted upward as if welcoming someone. Then they quickly dropped, and she was still. Angels had come to meet her, and we knew that she was in the presence of the Lord.

Here was another lesson. Divine deliverance may be needed even at the end of the way. How many of God's saints have experienced months and even years in painful physical bondage, wanting to go to be with the Lord, and something seemed to bind them to make their last days distressing and unspeakably miserable. The Bible tells us that the devil has the power of death (Heb. 2:14), and we need Divine power and Divine deliverance even at the last step of the way.

Father lived for several more years. So dependent was he upon mother that he could never fully adjust himself to the new situation. In his last year, he declined rapidly. In September, 1961, I was in Central America in the interest of the Native Church Crusade. The tour would require at least two or three weeks. After completing our survey in Panama, I prepared to go on to Trinidad, as my ticket indicated. That day, however, I received a strong and almost overwhelming impression that I should return at once to the states. All day the feeling grew stronger. Do what I could, I was unable to shake it off. Finally, I called the airline, cancelled my Caribbean tour and ordered instead, reservations that would return me to Texas. Arriving in Houston, I called my wife, and immediately she told me in excited tones that my father, almost 89 years of age, had passed away on the day I flew into Panama. She had been calling all over Central America, but each time had just missed me. The family was resigned to having the memorial services on the following day without me. Certainly, the Spirit of God had definitely led me to return, though I had not been given the reason. It is comforting that God is considerate of our purely personal matters, apart from the great over-all responsibilities of His Kingdom.

How much I owe to my godly parents can never be estimated. How petty and trivial are gold and silver, if that is all that parents have to leave their children. How much greater in comparison is the heritage of faith that all, whether rich or poor may leave, if they so choose.

CHAPTER XL

The Ministry of Evangelism

The ministry of the evangelist is one of the most important in the Church. Without it, the Church would have remained an insignificant Jewish sect. The evangelist is in the vanguard, announcing the good tidings of the gospel. Yet he also warns of judgment to come. As the messenger of God, he stands between the living and the dead.

The evangelist takes the gospel out of the academic sphere and applies it to the individual in terms of life and death and human experience. He reminds men that they are but one heart-beat from eternity; that beyond this world there is an after-life, and one moment after death he faces the solemn alternative of entering the abode of the righteous, or the regions of eternal night. His message to the sinner is briefly: "Except ye repent ye shall all likewise perish." (Luke 13:3) The skillful evangelist appeals to the mind, but even more strongly to the heart and the conscience.

The office of the evangelist is one of the most demanding of ministries. Unless he is a man of prayer, he will surely fall. All his gifts and talents will not make him a success.

The evangelist who holds a meeting in a local church is more or less at the mercy of the pastor, who gives him for his services what pleases him, which in some cases is precious little. On the other hand, many pastors are more than fair in their dealings.

An evangelist who fails to show up when the advertising is all out, comes under adverse criticism, and rightly so; yet a pastor may also at the last moment cancel a scheduled revival, and it never occurs to him that his action will seriously inconvenience the speaker, who ordinarily cannot make substitutes in his schedule at short notice.

A couple of decades ago the office of an evangelist was regarded as the humblest part of the ministerial spectrum. If he had a family with him, he probably had to live in a trailer to cut down expenses. During the days of the Depression, an important asset for an evangelist was to have one or two relatives who would send him their tithes.

These circumstances put the evangelist under the temptation of trying to conjure up new sensations, that would give him an advantage in the pulpit over competitors. No matter how great a saint he was, if he could not draw a crowd, his services were in little demand.

Thus, the evangelist was more or less under pressure to develop a "gimmick." For example, he had good possibilities if he were an ex-convict. If he had outraged the law in some way, had headed a prison break, or if he had escaped the hangman's noose, it gave him something special to tell his audience. Advance advertising was particularly effective if it could show an ex-convict in prison stripes, perhaps accompanied by ball and chain. We should all be thankful indeed for these great miracles of grace, but the effective preaching of the gospel should not be dependent on a person having an exceptionally sinful life before conversion.

A few resorted to methods that could not be recommended at all. They employed such things as legerdemain and magic. While a little sleight-of-hand might be appropriate for a Sunday School audience of small children, it is difficult to reconcile such methods with the sacredness of the pulpit.

Certain specialized methods of evangelism have a real value, although they are by no means a substitute for the preaching of the Word. Good spirited singing by consecrated singers certainly reaches many hearts. Music can exert a powerful appeal if followed by a sound gospel message. Illustrated sermons came into special favor at one time. They can, on occasion, have good results. They can, however, be overdone. One noted evangelist who had unusual results in the healing ministry, turned to the use of illustrated sermons. But when dependance was placed so strongly on the illustrated sermon, the healings gradually diminished. Other speakers have employed huge charts. These have proved especially valuable for the teaching of prophecy. But their usefulness is limited. Slides and motion pictures of the right kind have an educational value, especially for portraying the missionary field. Nevertheless, none of these methods is a substitute for God-anointed preaching, and the manifestation of the Gifts of the Spirit.

It had always been my view that evangelism should be accompanied by a ministry of the supernatural. Jesus gave us the Great Commission, which carries the responsibility of the evangelization of the world. But He deliberately defined it as a ministry to be followed by certain miraculous signs. (Mark 16:15-18) This had always been clear to me from the time of my conversion. I had first seen these things happen in the ministry of John G. Lake. I, myself, prayed for the sick in the meetings, and had fair results, but never in these early years did I feel that I had been able to fully enter into that ministry. Nonetheless, I continued to pray and seek God for the moving of His Hand.

God has His times and seasons, and shortly after the late war, He began to move in a special way. Dr. Charles S. Price saw the revival coming, and spoke of it often. Dr. Price, however, felt that he himself would not live to see this special visitation. Strangely enough, the principals of the great healing revivals of the early part of this century were taken from the scene, all at about the same time. Shortly after this, came the visitation that has had such a powerful impact upon America as well as on the missionary field.

As soon as I became involved in this revival, it was impressed upon me that the apostolic ministry was for more than just a few outstanding evangelists. For that reason, the pages of The Voice of Healing were used to encourage and promote a widespread revival of the sign-gift ministry. During the Fifties, this ministry verily stirred the nation. Although revivals have their ebb and flow, and for a while somewhat diminished, the tide has now risen again and resurgence of this ministry will reach beyond all that has gone before. However, first there had to be a cleansing within the Church — the chaff had to be separated from the wheat.

Apostolic evangelism is that which is attended with a definite manifestation of one or more of the gifts of the Spirit. Now it has happened that with gifts of healing and working of miracles, the manifestation of the word of knowledge and discerning of spirits began to appear and evangelism moved from a state of relative passivity, to a ministry in which churches vied one with another for its services.

Herein was a danger. Many individuals are so constituted that they cannot stand prosperity, if it comes too much and too soon. A man's ministry may develop so rapidly that he becomes much in demand. He may for that reason by-pass the normal training period that a minister requires. He may be able to command large offerings, and thus discover that money has a certain kind of power. He is then apt to rely upon the power of money, rather than on the prayer life that enabled him to bless the people in the first place. King Uzziah is an apt lesson of the disintegrating effect of too much prosperity. (II Chron. 26:15-16)

Nevertheless, we reject the view advanced by some, that evangelists as a whole are less ethical than other ministers. Taken collectively, they both average out about the same. We consider it unfortunate that some have felt themselves called upon to run an expose of the failings of evangelists.

I have never seen a person who resorts to the indiscriminate attacking of personalities, who has prospered in the end. Strangely enough, such persons have often been found guilty of the very evils they denounce. I remember some years ago two men who set up an office in a large city of America, dedicated to publishing scandal and uncovering the moral delinquencies of prominent figures in the religious world. One of the participants in the notoriety was a preacher that had been converted from a life of crime. His preaching for several years was distinguished by powerful results. He should therefore, have been very humble and given himself a real soul-searching, before setting himself up as a judge of the faults of others. As it invariably happens in the case of those who resort to publishing a scandal sheet, sooner or later they print something that is grossly untrue. They then become a subject for a libel suit, and that was exactly what happened in this case. The libeled parties, smarting under the attacks, sued and were awarded a verdict of $5,000 damages. Since the erstwhile publishers could not raise the money, they were remanded to the custody of the warden of the county jail. My brother-in-law and I visited the pair. Apparently, they had not learned their lesson for they were still complacent and cocky. They compared themselves to Paul and Silas, and considered themselves as martyrs for the cause of Christ.

I am of course referring to public attacks on personalities, or special groups of persons. We would quite fail in our duty if we did not warn the ministry as a whole against the dangers that beset it. It is a matter of history that the indulgence of the clergy in extravagant living has led to its corruption and degeneration. Those whose chief objective is to achieve material prosperity, and who employ any method so they can live extravagantly, bring the ministry into disrepute.

Ministers as a whole, are subject to three special temptations — money, moral temptations, and popularity.

The Scriptures are not without ample warnings along these lines. Paul said, "the love of money is a root of all evil." (I Tim. 6:10) We have the case of Balaam who was a true prophet, for his prophecies rank among some of the most beautiful in the Scriptures, as for example, his prophecy of Christ — "A star shall arise

out of Jacob." Yet Balak's promise of a reward caused Balaam to
ignore God's warning to have nothing to do with him. After receiving a clear prohibition, Balaam sought to get the Lord to
change His mind. The result was that Balaam was permitted to
pursue his head-long course, which ended in disaster. Balaam
began as a man of God, but became a hireling prophet, and finally
died a soothsayer. (Josh. 13:22)

Judas Iscariot must have had some good qualities, for he was
chosen as the treasurer of the apostolic party. It is significant that
even on the eve of the betrayal, there was nothing to distinguish
Judas from the rest of the disciples. Artists picture him as a sinister character, but it is probable that he was a very personable
fellow. Apparently none of the disciples had the least idea that he
was to become a traitor. (Jn. 13:21-28).

We are told that Judas shared the apostolic ministry, and therefore must have performed miracles of healing as did the rest of
the disciples (Matt. 10:1) Yet, greed got a hold of him and apparently this resulted in a veritable personality change. The love
of money brought him to utter ruin.

The desire for popularity is another area of danger for the man
of God. This was the case of Saul who started out well. At the
beginning, he was a humble man. (I Sam. 16-17), but his exaltation to the Kingship caused him to become proud, and pride was
his ruination. Although he had committed a serious sin of dis-
obedience, he still wanted Samuel to honor him before the people.

There is a minister whom we know, who was once greatly used
of God. Then he fell into sin, that brought him into conflict with
the law. Since the sin was committed in public, there was only one
thing for him to do, that was acknowledge it. God would have
blessed him for his honesty. Instead, for the sake of retaining the
confidence of the people, he preferred to publicly deny the court
records. We need not dwell on the sad story that followed.

Finally, the third great temptation concerns the minister's relation with the opposite sex. It should always be remembered that
temptation is not sin; it is the yielding to it that is sin. How many
men of God have fallen in that way. The Scriptures enjoin a man
to "touch not a woman." If they will remember that one injunc-
tion, they will be safe. For a minister to go into a hotel room or
some private place with a member of the opposite sex, is like
handling dynamite with the fuse lit. Rather play with forked
lightning, instead.

I know of another man who was held in the very highest esteem.

He was considered a man of honor and judgment. Yet, he fell so low as to regularly consort with lewd women, while at the same time carrying on his work in the ministry. Finally, despite his cleverness in covering his tracks, his double life was uncovered, and he was caught in a motel with his paramour. I was witness of the scene where he came before several ministers, to make his confession. He appeared to me as one who had just come back from the regions of the damned. The poor fellow tried to make a comeback, but it was ineffectual. He had given himself over too completely to the forces of evil. His ministry was gone forever.

The great majority of pastors and evangelists are true men of God. They sacrifice and labor and give themselves for the cause of Christ. But there is a certain proportion who fall by the wayside, just as they did in Bible times. We should pray for our brethren, that God will enable them to to stand in the midst of temptation. But if any do fall, we must not allow this to become a stumbling block.

The contention that evangelists as a whole are more unstable than other ministers, is a false premise. All evangelists and ministers are subject to temptation. An evangelist, however, is under the pitiless spotlight of the public eye. Any mistakes or moral deviations are revealed before a much larger audience than that of an indiscreet pastor. Moreover, an effective evangelist is by the nature of the case, usually a high strung person and apt to be more vulnerable to temptation than the average pastor. His habits are more or less irregular. He may be away from home much of the time; his financial affairs are subject to unpredictable fluctuations.

In other words, the God-anointed evangelist is in the front-line trenches and subject every moment to the open fire of the enemy. Pot shots are taken at him from all directions. He surely needs the prayers of God's people. For if the office of evangelism were to cease from the Church, the loss would be irreparable. It is largely through this ministry-gift that the gospel has been spread to the ends of the earth.

If the weakness of some evangelists is emotional instability, so the tendency of the clergy in general has been to ecclesiasticism, the development of a form of religion and the freezing of it into a static condition. An office in the Church can be made a professional thing, a means of making a living. A man caught in the toils of its vicious circle is to be pitied. God called the minister to be a guardian of the souls of men. How sad if he becomes a mere ecclesiastic, who is nothing more than a paid functionary.

The fact that there are hirelings in the ministry, means we must learn to separate the chaff from the wheat. Too often a man blindly follows a discredited leader until at last he discovers that his idol has feet of clay. Then because he has no root in himself, he falls away, disillusioned, another backslider, a spiritual derelict on the seas of time.

There are some things that are warning signals which should put us on the alert. I am going to list a few of them, although in no particular order. I do not refer to any one phase of the ministry. These evils can develop in the most unexpected places. They can be associated with the most legitimate and Scriptural practices, yet twisted and prostituted out of their divinely intended function. Consider the matter of sending out prayer cloths.

The use of the prayer cloth is indeed a Scriptural one. (Acts 19:11-12) How many people have applied them to their bodies and have received a blessed and wonderful deliverance. Yet when a man says that the prayer cloth turned to red color supernaturally (as one minister claimed) and thereby has much greater virtue, he is doing two things. First, he is telling an untruth, and second he is playing on the superstitions of his followers.

Sensational publicity stunts are a miserable substitute for the gospel. One minister tore the shirt off his back and ripped it up, declaring it had some extra-special virtue which called for a special offering. On another occasion, a preacher suddenly shouted that he saw an angel walk upon some tent shavings, whereby he had them gathered up in a wash tub and mailed out in small quantities to people for an extra-special offering.

I have seen some use a crowd picture that was not his own, to create an impression that his ministry was drawing vast audiences. One free-lancer used a capacity crowd photograph of an audience in Prince Albert Hall, London, which was not his congregation. Such tactics are of course nothing but pure dishonesty. Representing another man's audience to be his own, is a pious fraud and the man himself by so doing becomes a religious mountebank.

Perhaps the most serious scheme to raise money is one promoted by a certain religious adventurer who promises the people that God has given him the gift to make them wealthy, if only they will give him a good offering. Such assertions approach to the crime of blasphemy.

A letter was forwarded to my desk some time ago from a woman who received it from a preacher in the East. The letter requested her to keep it secret and not let anyone know about its contents.

She was to come to a "closed meeting," at a certain hall where a "great revelation" would be made known to her and others who were equally favored. Incidentally, she was to bring along at least three dollars!

We have to be constantly alert to avoid anything which would be contrary to good ethics. We are never certain how some person will take a most innocent statement. A few years ago, a newspaper in Canada blasted The Voice of Healing because we carried the story of a remarkable healing of a lady by the name of Florence Nightingale. The newspaper pointed out that Florence Nightingale was already dead! I admit I was astonished. It never occurred to me that anyone would confuse the person healed, with an historical character born ten years after George Washington died! The deliberate twisting of a fact to fight the ministry of healing is wicked and mischievous. The healing of Florence Nightingale of England, as the result of Brother Branham's ministry, is a remarkable one and true. I was present when he prayed for her, when she was only skin and bones. Months later she was a normal, healthy woman. We carried the "before" and "after" pictures in a later issue of the magazine.

There is another problem that we often meet, in the publishing of photographs of crowds. The great tendency is to over-estimate their size. Police officers are no exception, and when they tell the evangelist that twenty-five thousand people are present, they are merely saying what 99 percent of the audience also believes. For example, in the great New York open-air meeting of Billy Graham whose reputation is beyond reproach, the police estimated the crowds to be a certain number, and it was so reported in the Billy Graham publications. However, Life Magazine took pictures of the crowd and had the photographs blown up so their employees could count the people one by one. They came up with a number of about one-third that of the published report! Such mistakes may be said to be an error of judgment rather than of the heart. Nevertheless, such things continually remind us that many eyes are watching us, and we must be on the alert at all times not to be found deliberately guilty of the sin of exaggeration.

In the case of miracles of healing, we have to recognize the fact that some people who are healed, get sick again. Lazarus got sick and died. Jesus raised him from the dead. But apparently he died again. At least nobody has seen Lazarus around for a long time!

Some spiritual moves have been blessed of God, and then suddenly have faded away because of the presumptuous and erratic conduct of certain of the leaders. One such move occurred some years ago in America. We shall not identify it, for some very devoted Christians were associated with it. At first we rejoiced in this outpouring of the Spirit. But very soon we saw something develop that alarmed us. Some of the leaders were claiming that they were the "Powerhouse" and all other churches were "dried up." They said that the people should come to them to get recharged. When we saw such bold pretentions, we realized that the usefulness of such leaders could not last long.

A further development occurred that wrote "Ichabod" to this movement. Certain self-appointed prophets brought out a new "Revelation," which in substance declared that Pentecostal people had made a great mistake in preaching against worldliness. That God was not interested in such petty things. That we were living in the dispensation of grace, and we were more or less at liberty to do as we pleased. But it was not liberty they were preaching, but *license!* In other words, if a man's conscience did not hurt him, he was free to indulge in most anything. All this went under the name of grace. It wasn't grace at all; — it was disgrace! If as they claimed, they saw a "new light" it was not the light from heaven, but the glow from the bottomless pit! Not a few wrecked their ministry over this satanic delusion.

Sometimes we are asked why we do not publicize the meetings of evangelists as we did in times past. There are a number of reasons for this. For one thing, many of the evangelists have settled down and become pastors. Only those blessed by the strongest physique are able to continue in this demanding ministry indefinitely. Others have established offices and publications of their own. While the policy of The Voice of Healing will always be to emphasize evangelism, the scope of its ministry has broadened to include all the gift ministries of the Church. The Voice of Healing seeks to encourage cooperation and unity between all members of the Body of Christ. God's people have a great task to accomplish before Jesus returns — the evangelization of the nations, even as Jesus said, "When this gospel of the kingdom is preached in all the world as a witness to all nations, then shall the end come." (Matt. 24:14).

We believe with all our heart that the greatest manifestation of God's Power is yet to come. May He grant that all of us will give ourselves to prayer as never before that we may have a part in and participate in this last great outpouring of the Spirit.

CHAPTER XLI
Life for Death

"Verily, verily, I say unto you, He that heareth my word, and believeth on him that sent me, hath everlasting life, and shall not come into condemnation; but is passed from death unto life." (John 5:24)

It is a thrilling thing to receive life for death. There is no greater drama than this. Some years ago when we were preaching in a city in Arizona, news reached us, at the close of a Sunday morning service, of a tragedy that had occurred nearby. Four lads driving at a high rate of speed, had overturned in an open car and two were dying. We were called to the hospital where they were taken, and we shall never forget the scene. One of the boys for whom no hope was held, was the son of a godly mother, a member of the church where we were preaching. She had real faith in God, and we are glad to say that as the result of the prayer of faith, this son miraculously recovered, and later gave his heart to God. But the other lad came from an ungodly home and the mother had little interest in the things of God and rarely, if ever, went to church. We had no Scriptural reason to expect a miracle in his case.

It was heart-rending to witness the death-agonies of this young man, who a few hours before, was carefree and full of life with never a thought of eternity. But now death had called, and there was no refusing its call.

But it was around the bedside of this young man that a strange drama unfolded in the next moments. While we stood watching the sad scene, a nurse ushered a woman into the room. The lady, we learned, had been informed that her son was dying, and as she entered the ward and glanced with fearful eyes at the blood-streaked face that seemed familiar to her, she gave one pitiful cry, was about to fall when strong arms caught her and escorted her away. For a long moment no one spoke. At such a time no one feels like speaking. Then a young lady who was present in the ward found her voice, and excitedly broke the silence, saying, "This is all a mistake! That boy is not that woman's son. Her son is in another room and only slightly injured!"

Suddenly, we comprehended the situation. The stricken lad had been covered with blood, and to a certain extent unrecognizable and the mother having been told that he was her son, in her shocked state of mind had accepted the statement, believing it was true. We then said to the nurse, "Let us not delay; let us go to the mother at once and inform her of the mistake!" The nurse was confused, but finally realizing her error, went with us to the reception room. There we saw the poor mother sitting in a daze. The full impact of the tragedy had burst upon her, and she was as one in a trance. We tried to talk to her and explain the mistake. But she had already abandoned herself to despair, and it seeemd she feared to entertain a hope that might only be dashed to earth again. Besides, she was sure she had recognized the dying lad as her son.

At length we prevailed upon the woman to go with us, and we took her to the ward where her boy was. As she entered the room, she stopped short, her eyes opening wide. Then suddenly, a great light broke, and she accepted the incredibly good news. Tears ran unchecked down her face while she sobbed with joy and relief. Rushing to the boy, she grasped him to her breast, as if still slightly fearful that what she was seeing was only a dream.

The drama of that scene was beyond description, and indelibly registered itself upon the memories of all who witnessed it. Yet there is another drama that is greater — that of a soul finding Christ.

There is a beautiful Scripture in Daniel that reads, "And they that be wise shall shine as the brightness of the firmament; and they that turn many to righteousness as the stars forever and ever." Most persons are strongly moved when they see a human life in danger, but not so moved when a soul is about to perish, which is the greater tragedy. Once while travelling through the Panhandle of Texas, a young man and I were caught in a severe storm. A tremendous cloudburst deluged the entire countryside. The car we were driving lost traction and we were forced to come to a halt on the side of the road.

A truck with dual wheels, which helped it to hold the road, passed us. But when it reached a point one hundred yards ahead, suddenly before our startled gaze we saw it turn over on the side. Water had undermined the road! A man climbed out of the side of the overturned cab and jumped down to the ground. To our amazement, he vanished into the earth! While we were trying to fathom the mystery, his companion climbed out of the truck and began to cry for help at the top of his voice.

Hearing the cry of distress, I rushed up to the truck to see what had happened. No explanation was necessary for I saw that the man after he leaped had gone right through the road leaving an opening which resembled a crudely shaped man-hole. We stood there looking at the opening in the road in dismay for we knew that the way that the water was rushing underneath, there was no chance of anyone escaping it, once he was swept into the current. Suddenly as we continued to look in frozen horror at the murky stream, we saw something deep in the water that resembled fingers! The man by some superhuman effort had managed to hold on grimly to the lower edge of the hole! But already two or three minutes had elapsed and the raging torrent would certainly in a few more seconds dislodge his grip, and end any possibility of a rescue. Reaching down, the two of us got a good grip on his arm and managed to pull him out against the force of the raging current.

We could well understand the emotion that stirred the man as he felt helping hands grasp him, and he could feel himself being drawn from the treacherous water to safety. It took a few moments for him to shake out the water that had gotten into his lungs, but when he finally was himself, what words of thanks flowed from his lips, and how appreciative he was of those who had saved his life! He pointed toward a small town which could be seen in the distance and said, "There is a wife and several little children over there who will see their daddy tonight, instead of waiting for one who would never return alive." We parted firm friends, though perhaps never to meet again in this life.

It was a bad evening. We were soaked to the skin, and spent a most disagreeable night, cold and uncomfortable, but strangely buoyed, and without regret that we had to spend the night on the road. For a man's life had been saved.

If saving a man from physical death brings joy, what pleasure is it to win a soul from eternal death, by bringing to Him the One who gives life eternal.

And yet the greatest thrill of all awaits us in the near future — the glorious experience of the rapture when Christ comes for His people! What a day that will be! The day of which Christ spoke, "If I go away I will come again and receive you unto myself." The dead in Christ shall rise first, and we that are living shall be changed. What a day, when the graves shall be opened and those who have died in the faith shall come forth! When corruption will be swallowed up in incorruption, when mortality shall be swallowed up in immortality! Yes, it will be an experience never to be forgotten as long as eternity lasts. We shall see Him face to face and be satisfied.

> "It will be worth it all when we see Jesus.
> Life's trials will seem so small when we see Christ.
> One glimpse of his dear face, all sorrow will erase.
> So bravely run the the race till we see Christ."

*   *   *   *   *

And now as I bring this story to a close, there is one more thing that I wish to say. I believe that a new move is about to begin in the Church of Jesus Christ to bring God's people together into one, a move preliminary to the Second Coming of Christ. Jesus prayed just before He gave His life on the Cross, saying, "That they all might be one, as Thou Father art in me, and I in thee, that they also might be one in us; that the world might believe that thou hast sent me." (Jn. 17:21) It is essential that the Body of Christ become one in Spirit, to fulfill that prayer of Jesus. This does not mean that there will not continue to be different churches and groups, nor that God's people should not be loyal in a special way, to those with whom they are working. But the hour of the competitive spirit, the petty rivalries and the seeking of preeminence is over. We must find a way by which we may recognize all members of the Body of Christ. We must find a means by which the ministry-gifts that God has set in the church may be used for the benefit and blessing of the whole. We must move past the place whereby the men are held together by petty ecclesiastical rules rather than by the Golden Rule. We always have denominations and groups, but we dare not allow this to divide the Body of Christ or to build fences that separate God's people from each other.

Prophecy indicates that the Church of Jesus Christ will gravitate into two distinct divisions in the end-time: The Philadelphia or the faithful Church, and the Laodicean, the lukewarm Church. God is pouring His Spirit today upon the old historic churches. Let us therefore who have enjoyed the great Pentecostal blessing beware that we do not become complacent and rest on our laurels, lest the warning of Jesus find fulfillment in us. "The first shall be last, and the last shall be first." And above all, let each one of us make our full consecration to fulfill our part in Christ's great Commission — the evangelization of the world. Then will Jesus our

Lord return to the earth again and take us to be with Him. As He has said, "And this gospel of the kingdom shall be preached for a witness in all nations, and then shall the end come." (Matt. 24:14)